VIGILANTES BEYOND BORDERS

Vigilantes beyond Borders

NGOs as Enforcers of International Law

Mette Eilstrup-Sangiovanni and
J. C. Sharman

PRINCETON UNIVERSITY PRESS

PRINCETON AND OXFORD

Published by Princeton University Press
41 William Street, Princeton, New Jersey 08540
99 Banbury Road, Oxford OX2 6JX

press.princeton.edu

ISBN (cloth) 978-0-691-229324
ISBN (pbk) 978-0-691-232232
ISBN (e-book) 978-0-691-232249

British Library Cataloging-in-Publication Data is available

Editorial: Hannah Paul and Josh Drake
Production Editorial: Brigitte Pelner
Jacket Designer: Layla Mac Rory
Production: Erin Suydam
Publicity: Kate Hensley (US) and Charlotte Coyne (UK)

Jacket Image: The *Nisshin Maru* blasts the *Bob Barker* with water cannons and rams it into the *Sun Laurel*. Photo by Eliza Muirhead / Sea Shepherd

This book has been composed in Adobe Text and Gotham

10 9 8 7 6 5 4 3 2 1

CONTENTS

'Laws without enforcement are merely good advice'.
—ABRAHAM LINCOLN

'Governments are not enforcing the laws, so we have to'.
—PAUL WATSON, ENVIRONMENTAL ACTIVIST

The well-known statement, widely attributed to President Abraham Lincoln, that law in the absence of enforcement amounts to little more than 'good advice' appears in the email signature of one of the many transnational activists we interviewed for this book. The second quote is directly from an activist. These statements—and countless similar ones by NGO representatives we spoke to—demonstrate that these groups view themselves as suppliers of a vital function without which international laws protecting human rights and the environment and guarding against corruption often remain simply a dead letter: enforcement. Some may object that, as nonstate actors, these groups lack legal authority and thus their actions do not amount to law enforcement. We disagree. Insofar as organized transnational groups provide surveillance, investigate, gather evidence, interdict, and arrest and prosecute criminal offences, they perform every step of the enforcement chain—often playing the role of both police and prosecutor. They do so with similar objectives as public law enforcers, and using similar means, but with less regard for national borders. Their private status means that their enforcement often amounts to transnational 'vigilantism'—that is, unsolicited autonomous actions by private parties to compel compliance with public law—but it is nevertheless enforcement.

In focusing on transnational enforcement, we call attention to a fast-growing but widely overlooked phenomenon in global governance. Observers of global politics have long focused on the role of nongovernmental organizations in promoting new norms, raising political awareness, lobbying governments for political change, and providing services like humanitarian relief, but rarely have they looked beyond these roles to transnational enforcement.

In addition to bringing to light a largely unnoticed aspect of global politics, this book seeks to challenge and expand current accounts of global governance as being (ironically) too state centric. While the mounting influence of nonstate actors on processes of norm creation, rule-making, implementation, and monitoring has drawn much debate, law enforcement remains—in both popular and scholarly imagination—firmly associated with the state. By highlighting the growing pluralization and privatization of international enforcement, we wish to broaden existing notions of transnational authority to reflect that states and nonstate actors are joint guardians and underwriters of the international rule of law.

To what extent, and in what sense, are the transnational enforcers we focus on acting as 'vigilantes'? Although much decentralized, transnational enforcement unfolds within and through the institutions of the legal system, some is 'extra-judicial' in the sense that it occurs without the permission or use of the judicial system—hence the label 'vigilante'. Some may view this term as negatively laden. That is not how we intend it. Vigilantes may be bad or they may be good; were they real, comic book superheroes like Batman, Wonder Woman, and Superman would be vigilantes. A vigilante, according to the *Oxford English Dictionary*, is a person 'who undertakes law enforcement in their community without legal authority, typically because legal agencies are thought to be inadequate'. On this understanding, a vigilante is somebody who seeks to enforce the law absent state enforcement but *not* somebody who uses arbitrary rules which they themselves define to hold others to account. Vigilantes are self-appointed enforcers of *public law*, and therein differ from criminal gangs and 'frontier justice' groups who enforce their own private rules.

In writing this book we received help and advice from many friends and colleagues. Eyal Benvenisti generously hosted us at an authors' workshop at Cambridge University's Lauterpacht Center for International Law. Kim Bouwer, Rochelle Dreyfus, Jennifer Hadden, Nina Hall, Giovanni Mantilla, Ezequiel Gonzalez-Ocantos, Surabhi Ranganathan, Joanna Setzer, Len Seabrooke, Kristian Teleki, and participants at seminars at Copenhagen Business School, the Department of Social and Political Science and the Robert Schuman Centre for Advanced Studies at the European University Institute, Nuffield College Oxford, and Sidney Sussex College all provided valuable feedback on different versions of this work and helpful suggestions on relevant material and cases.

We are very grateful to Clara Korsgren for her initiative, ingenuity, and tireless research assistance in gathering and verifying information about transnational enforcement groups. We also thank Teale Phelps Bondaroff, former PhD student in the Department of Politics and International Studies at Cambridge University and co-founder of OCEANSASIA, whose enthusing first-hand reports from his voyage 'Sailing with the Sea Shepherds' was instrumental in fuelling our interest in transnational vigilante enforcement. Interviews and informal conversations with those in NGOs were a crucial source of information and inspiration for this book, and we are very grateful for the time and invaluable insights provided by all those who spoke with us. Three anonymous reviewers commissioned by Princeton University Press took a great deal of time to engage with the text and our ideas and provided many thoughtful suggestions. We also thank Hannah Paul and Josh Drake at Princeton University Press for shepherding us through the publication process. Finally, we would like to acknowledge financial support from the Department of Politics and International Studies at Cambridge University.

VIGILANTES BEYOND BORDERS

Introduction

In April 2015, three crew members from the *Bob Barker*, a ship operated by the environmental group Sea Shepherd Conservation Society, clambered aboard a sinking vessel, the *Thunder*, to collect proof of its illegal fishing. As the ship sank, activists hastily grabbed crucial evidence (including the captain's logbooks, a computer, mobile phones, charts, and a decomposing 200-pound toothfish) which they handed over to Interpol.[1] The sinking of the *Thunder*—a renegade trawler on Interpol's most-wanted list since 2013—ended a 110-day-long pursuit, during which environmental activists chased the outlaw fishing boat for more than 10,000 nautical miles before prompting its captain to scuttle his ship.[2] Once the *Thunder* began to sink, its crew were rescued by Sea Shepherd activists and escorted to shore, where they were met by local police. Based on evidence submitted by Sea Shepherd, the captain and senior crew members were tried and convicted on charges tied to illegal fishing.

In October 2017 Teodorin Obiang, son and heir apparent to the president of the oil-rich West African republic of Equatorial Guinea, was convicted of multiple corruption and money-laundering offences by a French court. Obiang had used the proceeds of his corruption to go on a massive spending spree, including a $120 million Paris mansion, a $120 million yacht, a $38 million private jet, $20 million at Yves Saint Laurent's estate auction, $5 million on watches, and $1.8 million worth of Michael Jackson memorabilia,

1. See Urbina 2015; Hune 2015.
2. Milman 2015.

1

including a $275,000 white crystal-studded glove from the 'Bad' tour—wildly exceeding his $80,000 official annual salary.[3] A group of NGOs in France, Spain, and the United States first followed the money trail to amass proof of Obiang's looting, and then successfully prosecuted him for corruption and embezzlement in a French court, leading to the confiscation of the mansion and a fleet of luxury cars. They did so in the teeth of opposition from the French and Equatorial Guinean governments, both of which repeatedly tried to sabotage the case.

These examples are far from unique. Whether it is environmental activists intervening to halt illegal fishing or confiscate poached wildlife, anti-corruption campaigners tracing dirty money, or human rights groups prosecuting torturers, nongovernmental organizations (NGOs) are increasingly taking justice into their own hands in compelling compliance with international law. In doing so, they are not lobbying, seeking to persuade or shame targeted actors to abide by international rules; they are intervening directly—often as what controversially might be called vigilantes.[4] Working from such examples, this book focuses on the growing, but so far neglected, role of NGOs as independent enforcers of international law.

Over the last few decades, more and more NGOs have moved beyond a focus on educating, socializing, and pressuring states to act to instead take direct action aimed at enforcing international laws. Although some of the tools used by these groups—patrolling and surveillance to document criminal conduct, gathering and supplying evidence to police and public prosecutors, and filing cases before national and international courts—may seem familiar, the significance and combined effects of these actions cannot be meaningfully understood as just some passive process of monitoring. When NGOs independently identify, investigate, and pursue suspected criminal actors, bring unsolicited proof of wrong-doing to state police and public prosecutors, and then, if public agents decline to act, pursue criminals through private prosecutions, they are not acting merely as passive monitors or as hired guns for states. When the same NGOs bring legal cases against governments for breach of international human rights and environmental obligations these NGOs cannot meaningfully be seen to act as deputies or delegates of governments. Rather, they are assuming the role of autonomous enforcers of justice, perhaps even vigilantes.

---

3. United States of America vs. One White Crystal-Covered Bad Tour Glove, U.S. Department of Justice In Rem prosecution, Central District of California, 13 October 2011; Sharman 2017: 4.

4. For a discussion of how we define and use the term 'vigilante', see the book's preface.

At the heart of this book is a proposition that international enforcement by NGOs can be understood within a broader concept of transnational authority which treats states and nonstate actors as co-authors and joint suppliers of global governance. Although much has been written about global governance, observers have been largely blind to the widening pluralization and privatization of international law enforcement. This is due to an overly formalistic conception of law enforcement which holds that actions aimed to compel compliance with the law only qualify as law enforcement if carried out by state authorities, thus ruling out nonstate enforcement by definitional fiat. This narrow perspective limits our understanding and misses the growing reach and importance of transnational enforcement. Consider an analogy.

Imagine that we insist, on formal grounds, that firefighting is officially done only by firefighters. Therefore, when people who are not employed by the fire brigade don a helmet and put out a fire in a burning house, they are not really *firefighting*. Without official credentials, they are doing something that is functionally the same as firefighting, with the same results, but that nevertheless does not count as such. To our mind, this approach is unduly formalistic and restrictive, as it prevents us from recognizing firefighting as a *practice* rather than merely a formal concept. As we seek to demonstrate in this book, as a matter of fact, or practice, actors other than states are increasingly enforcing international laws. Our goal is to explain what drives this phenomenon and to consider its consequences for world politics.

As we discuss in chapter 1, we view enforcement as compelling compliance with international law by helping to hold transgressors to account. This includes a spectrum of activities from surveillance, investigation, and evidence gathering to litigation, prosecution, and interdiction. In focusing on the role of nonstate actors in international law enforcement, our narrative both challenges and expands existing accounts of the pluralization of global politics. Since the 1970s, scholars working from a variety of perspectives have emphasized the growing multiplicity of global actors and voices as human rights activists, environmentalists, religious societies, scientific bodies, banks, and international corporations have taken on political roles once reserved for state representatives.[5] A large literature has discussed how NGOs pressure and socialize governments into making and enforcing

---

5. Keohane and Nye 1977; Rosenau and Czempiel 1992; Barnett and Duvall 2005; Avant, Finnemore, and Sell 2010.

international rules.[6] Others have considered how NGOs assist states in implementing rules as contracted agents of governments or as intermediary actors 'orchestrated' by international organizations.[7] Still other work has focused on the rise of transnational regulation in the form of voluntary standards and codes of conduct, created and implemented by private actors.[8] Yet there has been little attention to NGOs working in an enforcement role. To the extent that NGOs are recognized as participants in monitoring, investigating, and prosecuting international crime, their role is mostly portrayed as contracted monitors acting at the direction of others or as neutral suppliers of information.[9] This portrayal, we argue, either misses or mischaracterizes a large spectrum of NGO activities.

Questions and Answers

Our analysis is devoted to answering two main questions. First, why have we seen the recent rise of independent nonstate enforcement at the international level? Second, why do some NGOs embrace enforcement, while others stick with more traditional strategies of advocacy or delivering services for governments? To answer these questions, this book explores how and under what conditions transnational enforcement has developed across three domains of global politics: human rights, environmental protection, and the fight against corruption.

In the longer historical view, private law enforcement has been the rule rather than the exception. Britain was the first country to develop a professional police force in 1829. Here and in other countries, except for crimes directly against the state (e.g., treason or failure to pay taxes), criminal and civil justice alike were previously handled either on a do-it-yourself basis or by for-profit actors like bounty hunters. In this sense, having a range of enforcers of domestic law apart from state agencies is not new. Likewise transnational law enforcement is not entirely a recent phenomenon. During the nineteenth century, international courts for the suppression of the

6. Risse-Kappen 1995; Meyer et al. 1997; Keck and Sikkink 1998; Finnemore and Sikkink 1998; Price 1998; Florini 2000; Hafner-Burton 2008; Neumann and Sending 2010; Carpenter 2011; Peterson, Murdie, and Asal 2018.

7. Abbott and Snidal 2010; Abbott et al. 2015; Hale and Roger 2014; Tallberg 2015.

8. Biersteker and Hall 2002; Cutler 2002; Pattberg 2005; Lake 2010.

9. McCubbins and Schwartz 1984 developed the concept of 'fire brigade monitoring' as opposed to 'police patrols' to explain the prevalence of third-party monitoring as a means of congressional oversight.

slave trade heard cases against slave-trading vessels—some brought by private groups[10]—and claims commissions adjudicated private litigant disputes arising out of war.[11] However, the number and scope of such cases were limited. As we illustrate in the chapters to follow, within each of the three policy domains analyzed in this book, nonstate enforcement has grown in magnitude, variety, and sophistication and has become increasingly cross-boundary in scope. As such, transnational enforcement is a novel phenomenon that demands further attention.

In explaining the recent growth in private international law enforcement, we present an argument which focuses on changing demand and supply conditions wrought by legal and technological innovation, as well as by inter-organizational dynamics. Starting with demand, the number and scope of international treaties and agreements have grown exponentially in recent decades. From human rights to endangered species, from election monitoring to money laundering, and from arms control to financial accounting standards, most policy issues are today subject to multiple transborder agreements.[12] However, enforcement has tended to lag behind; international agreements to safeguard the environment, protect human rights, and combat cross-border corruption often amount to little more than a dead letter. The continuing expansion of international law, along with states' limited capacity (and inclination) to police and enforce international agreements, has produced what we call an 'enforcement gap'.[13] In turn, this gap has created new demand for nonstate enforcers to step into the breach.

Alongside growing demand triggered by a widening enforcement gap, we point to supply-side factors which have enabled enforcement by transnational actors. In order to contribute to international enforcement, NGOs must have access to effective tools for surveillance, investigation, and, ultimately, intervention. Here technological advances have greatly enhanced the ability of nonstate actors to contribute to enforcement through independent monitoring and investigation. In particular, the diffusion of massive computing power, the availability of satellite imagery, drones, Geographic Information Systems, digital sensors, and vast data leaks from Wikileaks to the Panama Papers have produced a step change in the armoury available to transnational enforcers. NGOs now have access to sophisticated data-gathering and data-analysis techniques which were once the exclusive

10. Martinez 2008.
11. Steinitz 2019.
12. Alter and Meunier 2009.
13. See also Nurse 2013.

preserve of state militaries and intelligence agencies. As a result, we see these groups uncovering mass graves, surveilling wildlife poachers, and forensically following trails of dirty money.

A second supply-side factor relates to changes in law. Not only are there more laws governing global issues, but avenues of access for nonstate actors to the international judicial system have also multiplied and widened. The past few decades have witnessed a substantial increase in international dispute settlement institutions: human rights courts, administrative tribunals, arbitrational tribunals, and internationalized criminal courts, among others.[14] At the same time, many national constitutions and regional treaties have widened participation rights for NGOs, granting rights to intervene on behalf of third parties or the general 'public interest'. The multiplication of legal frameworks and judicial bodies has led many legal scholars to express concern about 'fragmentation' of international law. Critics worry about forum-shopping by litigants, rivalry among judiciaries with overlapping jurisdiction, and conflicting application of law which threatens to undermine the coherence of the international legal system.[15] Yet for many NGOs these developments have also had an empowering effect in making the international judicial system more open to strategic litigation and allowing activists to select legal venues hospitable to their claims. As a result, it is increasingly common to see NGOs engage in parallel litigation whereby they bring the same case(s) to different courts and base their claims on both national and international law across different substantive domains—for example, human rights and environmental law.

Organizational Competition and the NGO Scramble

Beyond changing demand and supply factors stimulated by broad legal and technological changes, our third postulated driver of transnational enforcement focuses on relationships among NGOs themselves.[16] One of the most remarkable recent trends in global politics is the explosive growth in international NGOs. Bush and Hadden put the number of legally constituted international NGOs at around sixty thousand in 2012—a fivefold increase from the 1980s.[17] In fact, these are only the larger groups which are suf-

14. Alter 2011a.

15. Guilluame 2001; Benvenisti and Downs 2007; Alter and Meunier 2009.

16. Cooley and Ron (2002) coined the term 'NGO scramble' to capture increasingly competitive relations among a growing NGO population.

17. Bush and Hadden 2019.

ficiently established to be recorded in official databases. The actual total is therefore probably closer to six figures. This staggering population growth has intensified competition for scarce resources, such as public funding and political and media attention. The NGO representatives we interviewed for this book repeatedly spoke of having to seek out or create their own particular niche to differentiate themselves from competitors. The result has been increasing strategic and tactical innovation, differentiation, and experimentation with new ideas, along with heightened receptiveness to the need for organizational learning and adaptation.

In a competitive environment which encourages differentiation, why do some NGOs embrace enforcement while others stick to more traditional approaches such as lobbying governments to pass new legislation or assisting state-led policy implementation? In explaining this pattern, we point to intrinsic characteristics of NGOs which can make it less costly for some to engage in enforcement, and to patterns of learning. As 'instrumentally principled' actors, that is, actors driven by competitive market incentives as well as by principled commitment to particular causes,[18] NGOs tend to favour strategies that enhance organizational growth and survival. Yet NGOs cannot endlessly re-invent themselves. Strategic flexibility is often tightly circumscribed by prior organizational legacies and pre-existing resources. We find that groups that have invested heavily in gaining privileged access to policy-makers, or in building strong ties to corporate actors, are often reluctant to adopt confrontational or risky strategies like enforcement. In contrast, groups are more likely to engage in enforcement if they lack secure access to policy-makers and/or define themselves as outsiders in opposition to 'mainstream' advocacy groups.

An important determinant of NGO strategy is money. Over the past three to four decades, major NGOs such as Amnesty International, Greenpeace, Transparency International, and World Vision have vastly increased their financial resources and, as a result, public profiles.[19] Starting from humble beginnings, such NGOs today have multimillion-dollar budgets, sprawling global bureaucracies, and extensive ties to state and corporate actors which sometimes limit what they are willing to say or do publicly and lead them to favour moderate strategies so as not to alienate supporters.[20] The increasing concentration of financial resources, lobbying power, and media attention

18. Cooley and Ron 2002; Bob 2005; Mitchell and Schmitz 2014.
19. Thrall, Stecula, and Sweet 2014.
20. Stroup and Wong 2017; Zelko 2013: 316.

among a small cluster of large, mainstream global advocacy organizations has reduced the resource space in which other NGOs can operate. In turn, this trend has created incentives to adopt more aggressive strategies, such as enforcement, which are often cheaper to execute and less dependent on political access and media exposure. Depicted by some as 'second best',[21] in contrast we regard such choices as evidence of the growing pluralization of actors and strategies in international law enforcement.

In summary, the emergence of new global issues, impacts of technology, innovations in law, and a proliferation of nonstate actors have combined to produce a novel context for transnational activism. Together these structural changes have created wider opportunities, greater capacity, and stronger organizational incentives for NGOs to autonomously enforce international law. Whereas NGOs have long engaged in private and public interest litigation and other forms of enforcement at the domestic level, the private enforcement we focus on in this book is increasingly *transnational* in scope. Not only are the laws in question international, but increasingly so are the NGOs involved in monitoring and enforcement. By their nature, the problems to be addressed more commonly have a strong cross-border dimension, from global climate change and illegal fishing on the high seas to complex corruption schemes that snake through multiple jurisdictions.

Implications for World Politics

If transnational enforcement is increasingly practiced by nonstate actors, what are the implications for the international legal order? The question of ensuring compliance with international law constitutes a proverbial holy grail for those studying international law and politics. How can international rules be enforced in the absence of a world state or supranational police force? Nonstate enforcement may present a partial answer. Since human rights violations, corruption, or mass environmental degradation often involve crimes committed by state officials, or with government complicity, the state often has a conflict of interest when it comes to prosecuting such offences.[22] Rather than the law enforcers, governments are too often the law-breakers. NGO vigilantes can help to secure justice where governments are conflicted or directly culpable. Yet it is important to emphasize that the relationship between state and nonstate enforcers is not necessarily antagonistic.

---

21. Grant 2001; Stroup and Wong 2017.
22. Michel and Sikkink 2013.

Transnational enforcement can often provide a welcome supplement to state actions, bringing additional resources to an under-resourced system. Sometimes, states simply lack the capacity or technical knowledge to rigorously enforce rules set out in international treaties.[23] Our interviews with those in public law enforcement bodies and NGOs often revealed a subtle game of tacit cooperation between state and nonstate enforcers, as each sought to hold law-breakers accountable. NGO enforcement can thus help to secure global public goods in areas where governments are hostile, weak, absent, or merely indifferent.

Whether it supplements or substitutes for state-led enforcement, transnational enforcement challenges governments' (purported) monopoly on law enforcement. This in turn raises thorny questions about the legitimacy and accountability of NGO enforcers. NGO enforcers often present themselves as selfless crusaders advancing the global public good. But given the concerns evoked by the phrase 'vigilante justice', and the methods of questionable legality adopted by some NGOs in the name of law enforcement, what are the downsides of transnational enforcement? In reflecting on this question, one consideration is whether (and under what circumstances) vigilante justice can be regarded as morally acceptable and legitimate. A second set of questions turns on effectiveness: NGOs may supply a public good but, by doing so, may tempt governments to put even less effort into enforcement, reasoning that NGOs will pick up the slack. More questions follow: If transnational vigilantism presents a warranted addition to state-led enforcement, what mechanisms can ensure due process and guard against self-interested application of law by unrepresentative 'special interest' groups? We address these questions in the final chapter but, perhaps unsurprisingly, do not provide conclusive answers. Our goal is more modest and logically prior: to document and explain the recent rise of private enforcement. Until we recognize nonstate enforcement for what it is, it is impossible to evaluate these practices in either political or moral terms.

This book argues that international law enforcement can no longer be conceived merely in terms of governmental control and self-policing by sovereign states. International law enforcement now involves a plurality of different actors. In some respects this development is not new. What we are witnessing represents in part a return to an earlier historical model in which states neither exercised nor claimed a monopoly on law enforcement. Yet this (re)turn has not been reflected in scholarship. Few scholars today

---

23. Chayes and Chayes 1993.

dispute that political, legal, and technological changes have fundamentally transformed relationships between governments and nongovernmental actors and limited the scope of state autonomy and control. Nevertheless, these developments have failed to shift the presumption that international law enforcement is a state monopoly. Our theories and concepts have failed to keep up with the pace of change in the way world politics works.

Some of the enforcement practices we discuss in this book are new; some are older. It is easy to fall into the trap of regarding one or the other as predominant; nonstate enforcement is either an unprecedented novel phenomenon or 'nothing new under the sun'. We reject this simplistic either/or stance. Surveillance and investigation, for example, have long been used by transnational activists and written about by scholars, especially in the area of human rights. However, the nature and significance of these activities have often been mischaracterized as advocacy designed only to shame law-breakers by highlighting the plight of victims. We argue for the possibility that such autonomous monitoring, investigation, and prosecution by NGOs may comprise a strategy to hold law-breakers directly to account, and hence is better understood as enforcement than advocacy. Too often, we have been looking at NGO enforcement without recognizing it as such. The growing frequency, scope, and sophistication of NGO investigation and prosecution infuse new meaning into seemingly familiar processes and actions, producing a system of nonstate international enforcement in parallel to the state-based system.

The Shape of the Book

What do we mean by enforcement? What explains the growing role of NGOs in enforcement? Chapter 1 is devoted to laying out our answers to these questions. The first task is to explain how we define NGO enforcement and distinguish it from advocacy or service delivery. The second part of the chapter identifies the conditions under which transnational enforcement is likely to unfold. We set out our explanation for the rise of transnational vigilantism by elaborating the main drivers of this trend: (1) a growing misalignment between the reach and depth of international legal agreements on the one hand, and lagging and inadequate state enforcement efforts on the other hand (the 'enforcement gap'); (2) growing opportunities for private actors to engage in international enforcement thanks to advances in law and technology; and (3) growing competition among NGOs which stimulates strategic innovation and specialization, including a turn to autonomous enforcement.

The third part of the chapter considers why some NGOs are more likely to embrace enforcement than others.

Having laid out the frame of our argument, in the following three chapters we then apply it to the fields of human rights, environmental protection, and the fight against corruption. In addition to their inherent importance, we focus on these areas for three main reasons. First, they each demonstrate a strong upward trend in NGO enforcement. Second, while all three domains offer fertile conditions for nonstate enforcement, these conditions also vary, which allows us to explore how different contexts shape NGO action. Third, the different timing of the emergence of vigilante enforcement across the three domains allows us to scrutinize how ideas and practices spread across different issue areas of global politics. In many ways, the pioneering NGOs in enforcing international law were human rights groups in Latin America. When governments sought to draw a veil over the past, these groups gathered evidence and privately prosecuted those individuals guilty of torture and disappearances, basing their work on international human rights law. Environmental and later anti-corruption groups learned from these experiences and, as relevant laws and technologies became available, applied, extended, and innovated enforcement strategies in their domains. In some cases, the same NGOs pursued enforcement strategies across more than one of these areas.

In addition to exploring differences in autonomous transnational enforcement across the domains of human rights, environment, and corruption, each chapter reveals that only some NGOs within each domain have embraced vigilante enforcement, while others have stuck with more conventional advocacy and service delivery roles. Early adopters of vigilante strategies have often been small and relatively resource-poor groups striving to find a niche in a densely populated world of competing transnational groups. Over time, however, the growing visibility of NGO enforcement has in some cases created pressure for other groups to adopt enforcement strategies so as to not lose out to their peers. In backing up our claims, we draw on a wide range of primary documents, court records, and numerous interviews conducted by both authors over the last decade, supplemented by secondary sources.

Finally, in the conclusion we integrate and extend our arguments and findings and look to the future. We start by drawing out lessons and patterns from a comparison of NGO enforcement across different policy areas. Next, we consider the wider implications of vigilante justice for the international legal order. The global NGO community has important resources to bring to international law enforcement, especially in weak jurisdictions where governments may lack capacity to enforce laws that transcend international boundaries. Yet these positive effects may be cancelled out by negative influences on state incentives if the contributions of NGOs invite governments to shirk their duty by reducing efforts to enforce international law. At the same time, transnational vigilante enforcement raises thorny questions about legitimacy, due process, and accountability. Although our goal is to offer a new understanding of law enforcement beyond the state rather than advocate for or against vigilante enforcement on normative grounds, it is impossible to avoid the vexed moral aspects of these questions.

1

Vigilantes and Global Governance

What explains the growing incidence of transnational law enforcement by NGOs? What are the implications of such enforcement for the state-led international legal order? These questions take on growing importance as the magnitude of global problems and the number of global rules and regulations designed to address them steadily multiply. Given a fast-expanding system of international law, how can international rules be enforced in the absence of a world state or a supranational police force, and what role can and do nonstate actors play?

Enforcement of international law is traditionally considered the preserve of states. Governments may enlist the help of other actors in monitoring and enforcing law, but ultimately the notion of sovereign statehood implies that the state enjoys a monopoly on the legitimate use of force—including criminal prosecution and punishment.[1] Yet over the past few decades, nonstate actors have assumed a growing, and increasingly *independent*, role in enforcing international law. Their activities range from monitoring and investigating unlawful action to litigation, blockades, and seizing or destroying illegal equipment. For example, environmental NGOs have directly intervened to halt illegal logging or block unauthorized fishing vessels, while human rights and anti-corruption organizations increasingly investigate and prosecute abuses across borders. Sometimes, NGOs choose to cooperate with official law enforcement agencies, but often they compensate for a lack of state enforcement or engage in enforcement despite state opposition.

1. Weber 1968; Michel 2018: 5.

In exploring the enforcement role of NGOs, this chapter both challenges and expands existing accounts of the pluralization of global politics. Over the last thirty years the idea of global governance has gained currency, understood broadly as complex patterns of cooperation among states, inter-governmental organizations, firms, and a host of other nonstate actors aimed at responding to problems transcending national borders. States have increasingly delegated tasks of policy-making and implementation to inter-governmental organizations and corporations.[2] Public-private partnerships have proliferated.[3] NGOs have also become increasingly involved in implementing international rules as contracted agents of states or as intermediaries 'orchestrated' by clubs of states.[4] Yet despite growing attention to forms of international authority and governance beyond the state, transnational enforcement has so far been neglected. Enforcement is generally seen to lie outside the purview of global governance, belonging to the traditional world of inter-state politics.

There are several reasons for this blind spot. Drawing on a traditional notion of the state holding a monopoly on legitimate coercion, observers of international politics have tended to rely narrowly on a formal legal conception that limits enforcement to actions by states. Effectively, because states are the locus of legitimate political authority—that is, the right to issue commands with which other actors have an obligation to comply—states are therefore presumed to hold a monopoly on the legitimate use of coercion to ensure obedience with those commands. By insisting that actions to compel compliance with the law only count as enforcement if undertaken by state authorities, scholars have thus ruled out nonstate enforcement by definition.

As we show in the chapters to follow, NGOs in practice frequently seek to discipline wayward states and private actors in accordance with international law. Giving up the formal definition of law enforcement as enforcement by states and opening our eyes to actual practice is an important step in understanding the international legal order as it is: a pluralistic order consisting of multiple sources of rule-making and implementation, in which NGOs play an important role in law enforcement alongside states.

Although the concept of transnational enforcement may be new, there are long-standing examples of such practices. In some cases NGOs have

---

2. Hawkins et al. 2006; Green 2013; Green and Colgan 2013.
3. Raymond and DeNardis 2015; Westerwinter 2021.
4. Abbott and Snidal 2010; Abbott et al. 2015; Hale and Roger 2014; Tallberg 2015.

fulfilled a crucial role in independently monitoring, policing, investigating, and prosecuting violations of international law for decades. Too often, however, we have been looking at NGO enforcement without recognizing it as such. A formalistic, state-centric understanding has prevented us from taking into account widespread practices of decentralized law enforcement by NGOs, thereby making a tautology of the assumption that states have a monopoly on international enforcement.

While transnational enforcement is not unprecedented, we suggest it is growing. The past few decades have seen a strategic shift by many NGOs beyond lobbying and service delivery to taking enforcement of international law into their own hands. Since the turn of the twenty-first century there has also been a proliferation of transnational NGOs whose primary goal is to enforce international rules. Understanding why is a major aim of this book.

Our analysis begins with a general discussion of transnational enforcement that serves to answer basic questions about the concept, including whether the sorts of actions that we discuss here really qualify as law enforcement. The following section offers a brief review of the extensive literature on global governance and transnational advocacy to show how NGOs acting in an enforcement role have gone largely unnoticed. The next section surveys different types of transnational enforcement and discusses the general mechanisms that are responsible for the growth in transnational enforcement. As foreshadowed in the introduction, we focus on three broad drivers of transnational enforcement: a widening enforcement gap as the growth of international law has outpaced state enforcement capacities and efforts; advances in law and technology which facilitate NGOs enforcement; and growing competition among NGOs. Nevertheless, as already discussed, far from all NGOs embrace enforcement. The discussion of drivers thus prepares the way for an exploration of distinctive group characteristics that make some NGOs more prone to engage in enforcement than others. The final section offers preliminary reflections on the benefits and pitfalls of transnational enforcement, previewing the longer discussion in the concluding chapter of the book.

What Are NGOs? What Is Enforcement?

If this book is about nongovernmental organizations, what exactly are they? According to the United Nations, 'a non-governmental organization (NGO) is a not-for-profit, voluntary citizens' group, which is organized on a local, national, or international level to address issues in support of the public good'.[5] We follow existing understandings in insisting that voluntary groups must have a legal status and some element of institutional infrastructure to qualify as NGOs.[6] This distinguishes NGOs from broader social movements or fleeting grassroots initiatives which may lack both.

Beyond these basic criteria (NGOs are legally constituted, non-profit, and based on voluntary participation), NGOs differ tremendously. Some are sleek conglomerates with offices and paid staff all over the world; others are tiny collectives staffed entirely by volunteers. Some have extensive policy portfolios spanning multiple domains of global policy; others focus on a single, narrowly defined issue. Thus a central premise of this book is that we cannot speak of NGOs as if they were a homogeneous crowd. Rather, a basis for understanding changes in NGO roles and strategies is to focus on differentiation and competition within the NGO community itself. So far, scholarship on transnational advocacy has focused predominantly on a small segment of larger and richer NGOs with a high-profile media presence and global span. As we discuss later in the chapter, these organizations often face different opportunities and constraints than most other international NGOs. Once we broaden our view beyond these 'usual suspects' to focus on some of the tens of thousands of NGOs working globally to advance specific causes on smaller budgets and with limited political access or media coverage, we see that the activities, strategies, and goals of NGOs are highly varied. In turn, this wider perspective has important implications for how we understand the relationship between states and nonstate actors.

If enforcement is the central focus of our study, what do we mean by this? What counts as transnational enforcement and what is excluded? In this section we lay out our definition of transnational enforcement and answer some potential objections: Is what we are talking about really enforcement? It is really transnational? Is it new?

The term 'enforcement' is often used rather loosely in international politics to describe broad efforts to expose and document failures of compliance or to encourage obedience to international law by shaming transgressors.[7] For example, one overview of international enforcement mechanisms highlights 'issuing of findings' which increase audience costs of non-compliance,[8] while others define international enforcement as

---

5. http://www.ngo.bham.ac.uk/definingfurther.htm.
6. Stroup and Wong 2017: 139; Bush and Hadden 2019.
7. Yang 2006.
8. Abbott and Snidal 1998.

'mobilization of peer pressure' to induce state compliance.[9] We use a more restrictive definition of enforcement as action aimed at *compelling* (rather than merely encouraging or facilitating) compliance with the law. Among lawyers and policing experts, such action is generally understood to include detection, investigation, arrest, indictment, prosecution, conviction, and punishment of those who break the law.[10] In modern societies, these activities are typically carried out by police or other official enforcement agencies. Yet nothing in this conception of law enforcement limits enforcement to states; historically, nonstate enforcement has been at least as common as state-supplied enforcement. Not all enforcement by nonstate actors is outside official judicial institutions or processes; indeed much of the material to follow focuses on civil and criminal lawsuits by NGOs. However, all transnational enforcement is self-directed and autonomous, lacking direct authorization or solicitation by states.

We see law enforcement as extending across a spectrum, which we elaborate further in a later section. The softer or more indirect end of this spectrum covers activities like monitoring, surveillance, evidence gathering, and investigation. Harder or more direct techniques include civil or criminal legal action, and in extreme cases physical intervention to halt illegal activities, seize evidence, or temporarily detain offenders. Some NGOs specialize in just one of these activities, while others engage in activities across the enforcement spectrum. As a category of international actor, NGOs increasingly contribute to *all* steps of the enforcement chain, independently of states. In practical terms, NGO enforcers often choose to collaborate with governments, and work within state-controlled structures, as when they bring cases to court or submit unsolicited evidence to police. Yet in other cases transnational enforcers bypass official authorities altogether and act in a vigilante capacity.[11]

What is being enforced? For us the answer is law, specifically international laws and their domestic legal emanations, but not more informal norms or shared values. The focus on formal rules provides the clearest test of our argument about transnational actors taking on functions conventionally reserved for states. Violating norms does not lead to formal sanctions, whereas breaking laws does (or at least should). The idea that nonstate actors seek to enforce informal norms or values is not surprising, as this is seldom

---

9. Bradley and Kelly 2008.

10. Akella and Canon 2004: 4–5; Yang 2006: 1134–35; Interpol 2019.

11. By vigilante we understand someone who assumes the responsibility of investigating and/or punishing crimes because formal mechanisms of law enforcement are thought to be inadequate. Brenner 2007.

seen as the state's core responsibility. Many scholars have produced excellent accounts of how NGOs promote such norms and apply moral pressure on those who violate them.[12] In contrast, the kind of enforcement action we are interested in typically ends with law-breakers being held to account in the court of law, not just the court of public opinion. At the same time, actions that some NGOs defend as law enforcement may themselves be of dubious legality, a dilemma we take up in the concluding chapter.

It is also important to emphasize that while enforcement is one means to the end of compliance, enforcement and compliance are not the same thing. Not all enforcement actions succeed in bringing about compliance. Nor is enforcement the only way to improve the effectiveness of international laws. Information provision, lobbying, and 'naming and shaming' all play important roles. To the extent that actors lack the capacity to follow a rule, by itself punishing them for breaking this rule will not help, whereas capacity building may.

Central to our understanding of transnational enforcement is that it is *autonomous* from states; it is this autonomous aspect of NGO enforcement that makes it truly significant. After all, nonstate actors assisting state authorities in the enforcement of rules at both the domestic and international level is relatively commonplace. For example, there has been a widely publicized recent resurgence of for-profit private security actors, ranging from security guards at shopping malls, to auxiliary troops in combat zones provided by firms like Blackwater in Iraq,[13] to private armed guards protecting against piracy on the high seas.[14] These companies are fundamentally distinct from the NGO enforcers that are the subject of this book. The most obvious difference is that they are for-profit firms. More important, however, is that private military and security companies are contracted agents delivering specified services to states or other actors. They are paid to deliver a service; there is none of the autonomous initiative and action that distinguish the NGO enforcers featured in the chapters to come.

What about NGOs supplying evidence of wrong-doing to states and inter-governmental organizations? The majority of international agreements governing human rights, the environment, and corruption rely on national self-reporting, creating obvious incentives to withhold information on progress and compliance. Furthermore, many states simply lack

12. Finnemore and Sikkink 1998; Keck and Sikkink 1998; Price 1998; Carpenter 2007, 2011; Neuman and Sending 2010.
13. Singer 2003; Avant 2005; Krahmann 2010; Abrahamsen and Williams 2011.
14. Liss 2011.

the tools and resources to adequately gather the relevant information.[15] As independent actors, NGOs are often well positioned to collect sensitive data and provide independent assessments of states' compliance. Such efforts can be broadly conceived as a 'service' to states, enabling them to assess the effectiveness of international laws and to sanction delinquent parties. At the same time, it is clear that not all states welcome this 'service'. As one NGO representative highlighted: 'We work in dictatorships. No governments want it [enforcement]. They don't want to be supervised. We are not service providers to governments; we are here to correct a systemic failure [of non-compliance]'.[16]

In this context, NGOs have some advantages compared to public enforcers. While the doctrine of sovereignty makes it relatively easy to oppose monitoring and investigation by other states or inter-governmental organizations, the informal status of NGOs means their monitoring activities are less readily blocked.[17] NGOs are often among the first to witness crime scenes or obtain first-hand evidence from local populations.[18] To the extent that it serves to expose and provide actionable evidence of wrongful state behaviour, NGO monitoring can thus be said to constitute transnational enforcement, but only insofar as it remains independent, being neither formally solicited nor paid for by states.

Yet this crucial distinction raises a question. How autonomous must transnational enforcers be to be considered an independent source of law enforcement? It could be argued that because NGOs are acting to enforce international laws created by states, and ultimately depend on state authorities to issue judgements or put law-breakers behind bars for criminal breaches, they are in effect acting as servants of states rather than autonomous enforcers. We take a different view. The fact that states draft and commit to international laws does not mean they are always keen to abide by or enforce these laws. For example, autocratic governments routinely sign on to international human rights agreements without any intention of abiding by them.[19] Even democratic governments may want to pick and choose in following their international legal obligations, especially as these obligations are almost always open to a range of interpretations.[20] In such cases,

---

15. Chayes and Chayes 1993; Raustiala 1997.
16. EAGLE interview 2020.
17. Raustiala 1997: 729.
18. Heinze 2019.
19. Hathaway 2007; Vreeland 2008; Nielsen and Simmons 2015.
20. Hurd 2018; Putnam 2020.

NGOs may act to hold governments to account for failures of compliance. An illustrative example might be the tiny NGO Plan B blocking the British government's decision to expand Heathrow Airport in February 2020, on the grounds that it contravened the UK's commitments under the Paris Accord on Climate Change.

Even when NGOs' actions coincide with governments' preferences in enforcing international law, this does not mean that NGOs are acting at the behest of governments. Two parties' interests and actions can coincide, and they can align their actions on this basis, without either controlling the other. When an NGO independently investigates and gathers evidence of law-breaking and then passes this evidence to police, or when a group of environmental activists take it upon themselves to seize a renegade fishing trawler on Interpol's 'most-wanted' list, this amounts to neither advocacy nor service delivery, as the NGO has not been contracted, directed, or indirectly 'orchestrated' to fulfil this role. Rather, it comprises a direct, autonomous effort to combat international crime that may or may not coincide with what governments want.

Ultimately, it could be said that even vigilante enforcement depends on the state. After all, it is the state, rather than the vigilante, that creates the rules that the latter claims to defend. It is also the state that maintains the court system through which NGO litigators file suits, either criminal or civil.[21] Yet to say that all NGOs taking action through courts are doing so at the behest of or under control of governments makes little sense—not least because many of these cases filed by NGOs are mounted against governments for breach of particular international legal obligations.

Is It Really Enforcement? Is It Transnational? Is It New?

In this section we seek to pre-empt some possible objections to the definition of transnational enforcement we have just offered and, in doing so, further clarify our argument. The first of these potential criticisms might suggest that the idea of transnational enforcement of international law is based on a definitional sleight of hand which improperly stretches the understanding of enforcement. Do, for example, surveillance, investigation, and evidence gathering really count as law enforcement? Looking at the epitome of law enforcement, the police, it seems clear that such activities do qualify. Detectives and investigating magistrates are classic law enforcers; these roles

---

21. Hale 2015; Kahler 2020.

embody core policing functions. To say that investigation only counts as enforcement when done by the police is to adopt an untenably formalistic perspective, as we have criticized already. It is equivalent to saying that governance is only governance when it is carried out by governments, a stance that has been rightly rejected by those writing about global governance and private corporate governance. Once again, the idea of a state monopoly on law enforcement should be a proposition to be tested against evidence, not a tautology or an article of faith.

Perhaps it might be said that because NGOs are only involved in some aspects of the law enforcement process (for example, monitoring, investigation, and prosecution) but leave judging to state officials they are not true enforcers. Yet the agencies that epitomize state-led law enforcement are also limited to certain aspects of the enforcement process. Police investigate and arrest, prosecutors prosecute, and judges convict, but no one party is formally empowered to be judge, jury, and executioner all in one. In addition, one might argue that it is not only what enforcement actors *do* but also what they *aim* to achieve that defines enforcement. When NGOs gather evidence for enforcement purposes they do so as police would: with the explicit goal of convicting and punishing particular offenders through formal sanctions (e.g., civil litigation or criminal prosecution), whether or not NGOs themselves oversee the process of applying those sanctions (as police may hand over to public prosecutors, or governments may engage private law firms). Importantly, this pursuit of direct legal sanctions against law-breakers is fundamentally different from 'naming and shaming' campaigns where NGOs may publicize evidence of criminal behaviour (or harms arising from it) to raise awareness or to pressure states to 'do their job' in ensuring adequate law enforcement.

Moving on to litigation by NGOs, some might argue that this is better viewed as a means to encourage or facilitate compliance rather than a form of enforcement. Yet this would be a category error: losing a court case imposes a financial cost, a punishment, and involves a legal compulsion to observe a law. For example, when an NGO obtains an injunction against a government to prevent it from sequestering ancestral lands, destroying evidence of human rights abuses, or authorising environmentally damaging infrastructure, this is not a suggestion, encouragement, or facilitation from the judge: it's a binding court order.

What about classifying *civil* litigation as enforcement? Does doing so stretch the concept of international law enforcement? Although primarily used as a system for resolving disputes among private parties, civil law is also routinely used by state agencies as an enforcement tool. Indeed, for bodies like the U.S. Securities and Exchange Commission civil suits are the most common means of punishing transgressors,[22] while police forces increasingly resort to civil law to try to confiscate criminals' ill-gotten assets.[23] Tort cases against major energy companies are often brought by regional or local governments in anticipation of the costs to them of dealing with negative climate impacts.[24] In a range of areas from economic sanctions to competition law to disability access, governments legislate for public rules to be enforced via civil suits between private parties.[25] As Michel notes, the right to private criminal prosecution poses an interesting paradox to traditional notions of sovereign state power.[26] It is a prerogative increasingly employed first by human rights NGOs and now by their environmental and anti-corruption peers as well.

A further objection might relate to the distinction between domestic law enforcement, on the one hand, and international or transnational enforcement, on the other. As noted, the enforcement problem is qualitatively different in international politics than domestically, and this book is concerned with the former. Many cases discussed in the following chapters fall straightforwardly under the rubric of 'international law enforcement', as when an international NGO like the Sea Shepherd Conservation Society headquartered in the United States uses a ship registered in the Netherlands to block the Japanese whaling fleet from violating an international ban on commercial whaling in the Southern Ocean. But does it really count as international enforcement when, for example, a British-based NGO like Plan B takes the UK government to court to stop the expansion of London's major airport? We argue that it does, because the law upon which this specific challenge hinged (the Paris Accord on Climate Change) is international, as is the problem addressed by the dispute (global climate change).

As we illustrate in later sections and chapters, in the age of globalization some legal actions are brought before international tribunals, but a much larger number of international and transnational legal disputes come before domestic courts.[27] It is a commonplace that international law is gener-

22. https://www.sec.gov/Article/whatwedo.htm.

23. Fenner-Zinkernagel, Monteith, and Gomes Pereira 2013.

24. Bouwer 2020.

25. Ayres and Braithwaite 1991; Burbank, Farhang, and Kritzer 2013; Fine 2017; Buxbaum 2019.

26. Michel 2018: 5.

27. Roberts 2011; Efrat and Newman 2020; Saiger 2020.

ally implemented and enforced through domestic legislation and domestic courts. Domestic courts often act as the last line of defence to hold states accountable for compliance with international obligations. This is true particularly in the domain of human rights law, but the same principle applies in other areas as well.[28] The label 'transnational' is indicative of broader efforts in the study of politics to capture political processes that are hard to categorize as purely domestic or purely inter-state, such as domestic courts asserting jurisdiction over the foreign subsidiaries of multinational companies, or NGOs organizing and working across national borders.

To be clear, we do not claim that all or even most of what NGOs do amounts to enforcement. That would simply be an empty relabelling exercise. For example, not all surveillance and monitoring activities amount to enforcement. But if the aim of surveillance is to gather explicit evidence with which to hold particular actors accountable for breaching specific rules, then for us this is part of the enforcement process. This is different from, say, an environmental NGO monitoring air pollution or fish stocks and then simply publishing the results in order to 'raise awareness' or shame wrongdoers, which is not enforcement. Often, NGOs may assist governments or corporations in implementing targets or honouring legal commitments that these actors are willing but unable to implement by themselves. Insofar as such activities do not aim to either deter or punish transgressions they do not amount to enforcement.

A final objection might be that the concept of transnational enforcement is old wine in new bottles, that NGOs have long used investigation and litigation to advance their causes, and hence there is little novelty here. In response, we argue that transnational enforcement is novel, both as a concept and partially as a behaviour. Certainly, it is true, as we have already discussed, that many mechanisms of enforcement such as evidence gathering, investigation, and litigation have been used by NGOs for decades. However, as we show in subsequent chapters, recent years have seen a step change in the scale and sophistication of NGO enforcement across many policy areas. Furthermore, and perhaps more importantly, observers have generally failed to recognize previous instances of transnational enforcement for what they are; autonomous action with the explicit aim of punishing and deterring those transgressing international law. As a result, there has been a corresponding failure to appreciate the significance of the rise of transnational

28. Quintanilla and Whytock 2012; Michel and Sikkink 2013; Gonzalez-Ocantos 2014; Dancy and Michel 2016; Gallagher 2017; Michel 2018; Efrat and Newman 2020.

enforcement for international politics more broadly. Our intellectual focus and concepts have failed to keep up with a changing global context, thus obscuring important change.

Transnational Actors in Global Governance

Even efforts to break new ground in exploring previously neglected aspects of world politics are crucially reliant on a foundation of previous work. Below we elaborate these foundations to explain how we build upon them and to further clarify what is new about the argument of this book.

Since the term was coined in the early 1990s,[29] the concept of global governance has been used to describe a wide range of governance activities 'beyond the state'. Scholars have recognized a growing role for inter-governmental organizations, NGOs, and corporations in setting agendas, providing information, building expertise, promulgating informal rules and standards, and assisting states in drafting, implementing, and monitoring international laws. Yet, by and large, states are still viewed as the sole source of law enforcement.

Focusing on international NGOs, the first generation of scholarship on transnational advocacy illustrated how NGOs promote new norms and cooperate across borders to bring attention to global problems.[30] In their role as 'norm entrepreneurs', transnational advocates were seen to educate, persuade, lobby, and challenge states to accept new norms and then translate these into policies and law. NGOs were also understood to play a central role in pressing for norm compliance. According to the popular 'boomerang model' of transnational advocacy, local NGOs can seek redress from the actions (or inactions) of home governments by appealing to peer organizations in other countries to recruit their own governments (or international organizations) to apply external pressure on non-compliant states.[31] Transnational advocates may also encourage compliance by publicizing violations of legal norms and naming and shaming transgressors.[32] Yet in all these capacities, NGOs' contributions to law enforcement remain indirect, focused on challenging states to take action rather than on taking direct action themselves.

29. Rosenau and Czempiel 1992.
30. Keck and Sikkink 1998; Finnemore and Sikkink 1998; Risse, Ropp, and Sikkink 1999; Khagram, Riker, and Sikkink 2002; Price 2003.
31. Keck and Sikkink 1998; Florini 2000; Yanacopulos 2005.
32. Sikkink 2002: 39; Price 2003; Hafner-Burton 2008; Murdie and Davis 2012a.

In addition to focusing on NGOs as advocates, scholars have portrayed NGOs as providers of various services to states and inter-governmental organizations.[33] Whereas NGOs in an advocacy role lobby and mobilize concern, service delivery NGOs contribute directly to implementing public policies by assuming operational functions like health-care provision, education, or election monitoring.[34] Many NGOs are contracted or funded by states to act as first responders to humanitarian emergencies. Other service functions delegated by states to NGOs may include information provision, analysis, or technical support aimed to increase states' compliance capacity. For example, states and inter-governmental organizations often rely on NGOs to monitor compliance with environmental treaties.[35] Crucially, however, in providing commissioned services to states, NGOs, like contracted for-profit companies, act on invitation by and according to the instructions of state authorities (and subject to state funding) rather than autonomously.

Delegation and Orchestration

Related to the notion of NGOs as service deliverers is the idea of states directly or indirectly delegating political authority to nonstate actors. Most states today participate in dense networks of international cooperation that requires them to delegate authority to other actors to make or implement decisions.[36] Delegation implies 'that third parties have been *granted authority* to implement, interpret, and apply the rules; to resolve disputes; and (possibly) to make further rules'.[37] So far, literature on delegation has mostly focused on delegation to inter-governmental organizations,[38] but scholars recognize that states may also grant conditional authority to private bodies to make and implement rules.[39] For example, the European Commission has mandated that EU member states must follow the standards of the International Accounting Standard Board, an independent, privately funded body that sets international financial reporting standards.[40]

---

33. Breitmeier and Rittberger 1997; Mitchell and Schmitz 2014.
34. Breitmeier and Rittberger 2000: 142–47; Cooley and Ron 2002; Betsill 2014: 196.
35. Dai 2002: 405; Tallberg 2015; Green and Colgan 2013.
36. Bradley and Kelley 2008.
37. Abbott et al. 2000: 401.
38. Hawkins et al. 2006; Bradley and Kelley 2008.
39. Green 2013.
40. Bradley and Kelley 2008: 9; Mattli and Büthe 2005; Muegge and Perry 2014.

Delegated authority may sometimes appear to cast private actors in an enforcement role. An example would be the Secretariat of the Convention on International Trade in Endangered Species enlisting an NGO network (TRAFFIC)[41] as a formal collaborator in tracking illegal wildlife trade.[42] Since such delegation involves an explicit grant of authority to monitor compliance with commitments on behalf of states, NGOs assuming such a role effectively act as contracted agents or deputies of states or inter-governmental organizations rather than autonomous enforcers. Importantly, when delegating authority to nonstate actors to implement or monitor poli-cies, states tend to limit discretion and autonomy through formal oversight mechanisms.[43] Finally, whereas states may delegate generic monitoring functions to international organizations and NGOs, governments have been found to rarely delegate explicit enforcement functions.[44]

What of delegation of rule-making authority? In a globalized world, NGOs and private corporations promulgate the vast majority of standards and codes of conduct, from certification of fair-trade coffee and dolphin-free tuna to ethical guidelines for production and trade in diamonds, apparel, and forest products.[45] In doing so, they become both authors and implementers of global rules in their own right. But do they thereby also become autonomous enforcers in the way we intend? We don't think so. While they may be effective, standards and codes of conduct promulgated by private actors lack the status of law.[46] As voluntary, non-binding rules they are subject to enforcement only by moral suasion and naming and shaming (or in the case of certification schemes by exclusion), which is not what interests us here.

Moving on from direct delegation, what of the idea that seemingly autonomous actions by NGOs can be indirectly shaped and controlled by states and clubs of states? Abbott and Snidal describe how inter-governmental organizations 'orchestrate' private actors like businesses and NGOs as intermediaries to tackle problems which states lack capacity to

---

41. A decision by the Parties to the Convention on Biological Diversity and the CITES Con-vention has entrusted TRAFFIC (a joint initiative by the World Wildlife Fund and the Interna-tional Union for Conservation of Nature) to undertake certain inspections within the territory of Treaty Parties in cooperation with the Secretariat of CITES.

42. Tallberg 2015.

43. Green and Colgan 2013; Green 2013.

44. Green and Colgan 2013.

45. Büthe 2010; Green 2013.

46. Lake 2010: 590.

address by themselves.[47] Tallberg explores how inter-governmental organizations recruit NGOs as allies in improving state compliance.[48] This kind of orchestration may involve enlisting NGOs as watchdogs, even when states have been reluctant to offer private actors a formal role in enforcement, or providing funding or training for NGO litigants.[49] In contrast to traditional modes of governance by delegation, orchestration is indirect, since inter-governmental organizations work through NGO intermediaries over which they lack direct control.[50] This might seem to correspond to our notion of transnational enforcement. Yet the examples said to epitomize orchestration—for example, TRAFFIC (itself an alliance of states and NGOs within a hybrid body) monitoring wildlife trade or NGOs being coordinated by the Bureau of the Ramsar Convention on Wetlands to supply compliance information[51]—strike us more as examples of delegated monitoring than orchestrated enforcement. Insofar as governments or inter-governmental organizations may occasionally provide training or no-strings financial assistance to potential private litigants,[52] this could be conceived as a form of orchestrated transnational enforcement. Yet it is important to highlight that on our understanding NGO enforcement involves genuinely autonomous actions aimed to substitute for and/or trigger state enforcement. As we shall see in the coming chapters, although some enforcement actions by NGOs are welcomed by states, in many cases, transnational enforcement involves wresting control from states that seek to evade or violate legal commitments.

To sum up, the conventional wisdom on NGOs sees them fulfilling multiple roles: they raise issues, promote norms, lobby governments, gather and disseminate information, build expertise, and deliver contracted services, sometimes including monitoring and capacity building. When fulfilling these roles, NGOs contribute to creating and implementing international law, but they do not thereby provide autonomous enforcement. Finnemore and Sikkink summarize received wisdom when arguing that transnational actors are 'rarely able to "coerce" agreement to a norm—they must persuade'.[53] Others concur, noting that '[transnational] activists rely more heavily on methods

---

47. Abbott and Snidal 2010.
48. Tallberg 2015.
49. Ibid.
50. Hale and Roger 2014; Hale 2020.
51. https://www.wwt.org.uk/our-work/projects/world-wetland-network/#. These examples are cited in Tallberg 2015.
52. Tallberg 2015.
53. Finnemore and Sikkink 1998: 900.

employing persuasion, socialization, moral pressure and information provision, rather than coercive methods'.[54] Genuinely autonomous enforcement beyond the state, then, has yet to find its proper place in the discussion of global governance.

A Typology of Transnational Enforcement

The types of transnational activism we have identified so far—advocacy, service delivery, and enforcement—are not mutually exclusive. Many NGOs combine greater or lesser measures of each. Nevertheless, there is an important analytical distinction between the former roles and the latter which has so far gone largely unrecognized.

Thus far, we have focused on distinguishing transnational enforcement from other types of transnational activism. Here we briefly distinguish different types of transnational enforcement activity. These fall on a spectrum from 'soft' to 'hard', corresponding to different stages of the law enforcement chain. Some NGOs focus mainly on a single stage, whereas others work across the enforcement spectrum.

Activities that fall towards the soft, investigative end of the enforcement spectrum may involve surveillance, patrolling, guarding, evidence gathering, investigating, and giving testimony in court. As we have previously noted, many of these tactics have long been practiced by NGOs, especially in the areas of human rights and the environment. However, their nature and significance have often been mischaracterized as exclusively forms of advocacy designed to shame law-breakers or highlight the plight of victims by 'bearing witness'. We seek to recast these established NGO practices as potentially being instances of enforcement. After all, historically the two core tasks of public policing have been patrolling and criminal investigation.[55] Autonomous monitoring and investigation by NGOs are often part of a strategy to hold violators directly to account (e.g., by building a legal case through carefully documented evidence), and hence is better thought of as enforcement rather than advocacy.

The harder end of the enforcement spectrum involves actions designed to block, prosecute, and punish non-compliant behaviour. These may range from direct interventions or 'citizen's arrests', whereby activists interfere to prevent or halt a criminal action, to preserving evidence or holding suspects

54. Khagram, Riker, and Sikkink 2002: 11; Betsill and Corell 2008; Stroup and Wong 2017: 9.
55. Bayley and Shearing 2001.

until public police arrive in an explicitly vigilante manner. More commonly, they may involve criminal or civil litigation before national and international courts, thus unfolding within formal, legal processes. However, even 'softer' enforcement activities such as autonomous investigation and evidence gathering may be seen to comprise vigilantism insofar as they are autonomous actions by private citizens aimed to compensate for inadequate public enforcement.

Some NGOs specialize mainly in gathering evidence of crimes which they hand over to police or building case files for prosecutors, while others prefer more direct intervention. Insofar as NGOs identify targets, initiate investigations, and control the process of gathering and processing evidence and bringing suspects before law enforcement offices, both types of activities amount to autonomous enforcement. Most of the groups we spoke to that specialize in gathering and passing intelligence to police, or building evidential case files for public prosecutors, stressed the importance of their work being free of financial support or supervision by authorities. As the director of one self-styled 'NGO Intelligence Agency' put it: 'We are a law enforcement NGO. We don't apologize for that. Our activities are not supervised. We run the show. We insist it's fully independent'.[56]

The Effects of Transnational Enforcement

Transnational enforcement has both direct and indirect effects. A direct effect is to reduce immediate harm from criminal activity by, say, protecting people's human rights or vulnerable habitats, or tracing and recovering embezzled funds. Environmental cases that win in court may contribute directly to reducing environmental harm by legally prohibiting the construction of high-emitting infrastructure or other damaging activities.[57] Many activists we spoke to also stressed the objective of changing the cost-benefit calculation of dirty corporations, corrupt officials, human rights abusers, and smugglers by raising the spectre of retribution. NGO enforcers often focus on targeting the worst offenders or supplying enforcement in weak jurisdictions in order to maximize direct effect.[58]

Successful interdiction or court victories are not the only measures of success for NGO enforcers. According to activists, legal cases are important

56. EAGLE interview 2020; also Black Fish interview 2015.
57. Bouwer and Setzer 2020.
58. Hsu 2008; Humby 2018; Bouwer and Setzer 2020.

tools to push environmental issues into a central position in legal and political discourse.[59] Environmental litigation can set a baseline for state action and put pressure on governments to achieve more.[60] Likewise, human rights NGOs that litigate in favour of victims often engage in a form of 'cause-lawyering' with the goal of provoking social change.[61] Enforcement by NGOs may also serve to call attention to inconsistencies between political discourse and action. For example, litigation brought to establish the incompatibility of specific public policies with international law highlights gaps between publicly stated commitments and government policy. The prosecution of Vice-President Obiang of Equatorial Guinea for corruption (referenced in the introduction and detailed in chapter 4) highlighted the role of Western countries playing host to wealth looted from the developing world. As such, some transnational enforcement actions may be said to entail an element of advocacy via awareness-raising and shaming. Yet, unlike naming and shaming campaigns, NGO enforcement results in direct sanctions against non-compliant actors.

As with other forms of law enforcement, the indirect effects of transnational enforcement may be as important as its direct impacts. Human rights lawyers point out how private prosecution by NGOs serves to strengthen the rule of law 'from below'.[62] Transnational enforcement confronts a state enforcement system that is failing to do its job and exposes either lack of will or lack of capacity, thereby putting pressure on states to improve their enforcement efforts. By bringing law-breakers to justice, NGOs may deter future offences both by changing the cost calculations of individual would-be offenders and by establishing legal precedent. For example, in bringing legal cases against oil and gas companies, environmental and human rights groups are mirroring strategies earlier adopted in the fight against big tobacco, where the growing prospect of compensation claims led both companies and governments to change their conduct.[63] At a broader level, NGO enforcement can be seen to shape and reinforce legal norms in practice. Frequent non-compliance with treaties or laws undermines the establishment of a 'compliance pull' and encourages states to take international law less seriously or disregard it altogether.[64] Repeated violations, if unchallenged,

59. Peel and Osofsky 2018.
60. Mission 2020.
61. Dancy and Michel 2016.
62. Ibid.; Michel 2018: 5–10.
63. Patrick 2019.
64. Franck 1990: 24; Franck 2006: 91; Cogan 2006.

may thus create a status quo that makes it more difficult to challenge the further proliferation of similar practices.[65]

Whether confronting unwilling state prosecutors or compensating for inadequate state capacity, NGO enforcement is ultimately supportive of state objectives through the enactment of international law. Unlike radical or 'eco-terrorist' groups, enforcement NGOs do not see their actions as challenging or contravening the state-sponsored legal order but rather portray themselves as self-appointed guardians of the law. Vigilante transnational enforcement involves the identification of a gap or weakness in state enforcement and the substitution of a private means to address this gap.

The Drivers of Vigilante Enforcement

What accounts for the growth in transnational enforcement? We point to three structural factors which increase both the demand for and NGOs' ability to supply international law enforcement. First, the last few decades have seen a rapid growth in international treaties, conventions, and standards governing all aspects of global politics. However, enforcement has tended to lag behind with the result that international agreements protecting the environment and human rights or combatting cross-border corruption often amount to little more than empty promises. The growing gap between proliferating international agreements and states' limited ability (and inclination) to police them has led to increasing pressure for nonstate enforcers to step into the breach.

Aside from increased demand, we also point to permissive factors which strengthen the ability of NGOs to contribute to law international enforcement. One such factor is changes to procedural laws in many jurisdictions which widen NGOs' access to courts. The second is technological innovations which enhance the ability of nonstate actors to contribute to international enforcement through independent surveillance and investigation.

A third structural factor which encourages transnational enforcement is a rapid growth in the number of NGOs operating globally. Growing institutional density has increased competition for scarce resources such as political attention and funding, prompting NGOs to search for ways to differentiate themselves and their strategies from peers and thereby stimulating strategic innovation and 'niche seeking'. Together these structural

65. Huelss 2017.

changes have created wider opportunity, greater capacity, and stronger organizational incentives for NGOs to engage in transnational enforcement. We here review each in turn.

THE PROLIFERATION OF INTERNATIONAL LAW AND THE ENFORCEMENT GAP

The past few decades have seen a rapid proliferation of international treaties and agreements outlawing specific international and transnational activities, from human rights abuses to money laundering, from killing of endangered species to trafficking in weapons, people, and drugs.[66] Along with other areas of global governance, the three domains covered in this book—human rights, environmental protection, and anti-corruption—have each been subject to significant legalization.

Since the Universal Declaration of Human Rights in 1948 there has been a steady expansion of international human rights law, leading to both a broadening of substantive rights and an increase in mechanisms to protect these rights and to assist states in carrying out their responsibilities.[67] Legalization of environmental governance has been equally dramatic. Since the Stockholm Declaration on the Human Environment in 1972, world leaders have signed more than one thousand multilateral environmental agreements and an even larger number of bilateral accords, amounting to a thirty-eight-fold increase in international environmental laws.[68] The last few decades have also seen the extension of international rule of law into new areas such as foreign bribery, money laundering, transnational organized crime, and the financing of terrorism. Corruption and anti-corruption have gone from taboo topics to central and increasingly legalized aspects of the 'good governance' agenda.[69]

Yet despite a proliferation of legal frameworks, law enforcement officials around the world have reported a significant increase in the range and scope of international criminal activity since the early 1990s.[70] Human rights scholars have found that international human rights treaties often make little

66. McCormick 2010; Pauwelyn, Wessel, and Wouters 2014; Mitchell 2017; Simmons, Lloyd, and Stewart 2018: 249.

67. HYPERLINK "https://www.ohchr.org/documents/publications/factsheet30rev1.pdf" https://www.ohchr.org/documents/publications/factsheet30rev1.pdf.

68. International Environmental Agreements Database 2020; United Nations Environmental Programme 2019; Mitchell et al. 2020.

69. Eigen 2013; Gutterman 2014; Sharman 2017.

70. United Nations Office on Drugs and Crime 2010.

difference to state conduct.[71] Statistical indicators of human rights protection likewise show poor progress.[72] Government enforcement of environmental laws has also fallen short. The first global assessment of environmental rule of law released by the UN Environmental Protection Agency (2019) finds that while environmental laws have become commonplace around the globe, too often they exist mostly on paper because government implementation and enforcement is irregular, incomplete, and ineffective. Despite the dramatic increase in legislation, meaningful progress has been made towards meeting only four of the ninety most important environmental goals and objectives spelled out in international legal frameworks.[73] Twenty years after it came into force, a majority of signatories to the most important anti-bribery convention have never undertaken a single enforcement action.[74] The UN estimates that less than 1 percent of all the criminal money crossing borders is confiscated by authorities.[75]

There are several causes of poor enforcement of international laws. Verification and enforcement provisions of many treaties remain weak. The majority of international agreements rely on national self-reporting, meaning that state parties are entrusted to report on their own progress and compliance (or lack thereof). The same is true at the domestic level, where national reporting and ranking systems often require companies and other target actors to self-report monitoring and compliance data. A second problem is jurisdictional limitations. While globalization has allowed law-breakers to operate virtually without regard to borders, governments and law enforcement agencies remain constrained by national boundaries and resulting jurisdictional restrictions and sovereignty concerns. Resource limitations present a further barrier. Police and judicial systems in many countries are ill-prepared to combat crime and ensure compliance because they lack adequate resources, personnel, or technical capacity.[76]

But a major barrier to enforcement remains lack of will. According to the United Nations Environment Programme, governments often lack political will to implement environmental laws due to the potential impact on livelihoods, lands, properties, and profits.[77] Environmental and corruption

---

71. Neumeyer 2005; Hathaway 2007; Vreeland 2008; Lupu 2013.
72. https://www.ohchr.org/.
73. United Nations Environment Programme 2019: 3.
74. Organization for Economic Cooperation and Development 2018: 5.
75. United Nations Office on Drugs and Crime 2011: 7.
76. Chayes and Chayes 1993.
77. United Nations Environment Programme 2019.

offences are often 'victimless' in the sense that none of the parties impacted have a direct and immediate personal interest in bringing the matter to the attention of the police. Consequently, offences are only registered and followed up when police take the time and effort to actively investigate. Some enforcement agencies lack the capacity, or the mandate, to do this;[78] many lack the desire. When it comes to human rights abuses and corruption, government officials are often themselves directly culpable, giving rise to obvious conflicts of interest. Finally, corruption often incentivizes enforcement officials to turn a blind eye to law-breaking. As one of our interviewees put it:

> The problem is not capacity building. Those two words epitomize the problem. When a capacity building hammer is all you have then everything looks like a capacity problem. The problem I saw was law that was never enforced. Law that is not enforced even a single time is a symptom of a larger systemic failure. . . . If you have laws that have *zero* enforcement, then you cannot explain that with . . . lack of capacity. You need to look at systemic corruption. Zero enforcement shows something is really wrong and it's not even specific to our problem [wildlife crime]. It reveals the nakedness of the international system and the so-called international community. Corruption is hiding behind a blanket of lacking capacity.[79]

In short, enforcement in many policy areas often falls far short of the commitments and expectations set by a sprawling body of international law, whether due to lacking capacity, will, or even direct incentives to abet crime, thereby creating a gap for NGOs to fill.

WIDER ACCESS TO COURTS

Not only are there more laws governing different areas of global politics, but avenues of access to the legal system for nonstate actors have multiplied, thanks to changes in procedural laws and to a proliferation of international judicial bodies. Since the turn of the century there has been a sharp increase in the number of international courts, tribunals, and dispute settlement mechanisms.[80] More laws, more courts and tribunals, and a growing willingness in many jurisdictions to grant standing to private actors, including NGOs, to bring suits on behalf of public interests have made the legal system

---

78. United Nations Office on Drugs and Crime 2010.
79. EAGLE interview 2020.
80. Mackenzie et al. 2010; Alter 2011a, 2014.

a friendlier place for private litigants.[81] Taken together, these developments have enabled NGOs to move beyond 'naming and shaming' to pursue direct enforcement through private civil and criminal litigation.

Starting with judicial bodies, the post–Cold War era has seen an exponential growth in new international courts and tribunals—ranging from permanent inter-state tribunals with global reach like the International Tribunal for the Law of the Sea and the International Criminal Court to ad hoc criminal tribunals, regional human rights courts like the African Court on Human and Peoples' Rights, and regional economic tribunals.[82] Whereas in 1985 there were six permanent international courts, by 2010 twenty-six such courts existed which were being invoked by litigants to render binding rulings in cases where states or international institutions are the defendants, and more than one hundred quasi-legal and ad hoc systems that assess compliance with various international laws.[83] These bodies have jurisdiction to hear cases involving human rights issues or war crimes or, in many cases, have a general jurisdiction that allows them to adjudicate any case litigants choose to bring. A similar development has unfolded at the domestic level. In the environmental area alone, over 350 specialized courts and tribunals have been established in over fifty countries for resolving environmental disputes.[84] Thus, along with 'treaty fatigue' some government leaders have expressed concern over 'tribunal fatigue'.[85]

Not only are there more international courts, but they are also used with greater frequency by diverse actors. While international courts used to rule only in disputes between states (e.g., the International Court of Justice), newer courts differ in that they tend to have compulsory jurisdiction and provide access for nonstate actors, including private litigants and international prosecutors, to initiate litigation. They are therefore far more likely to be ruling in cases where states are reluctant participants.[86] According to Alter, by the end of 2008, international courts had issued over twenty-four thousand binding legal rulings where an international organization or state actor was the defendant. Nearly 90 percent of these rulings were issued since the end of the Cold War. Since 2010, an explosion in climate litigation

---

81. Boisson de Chazournes 2004: 622; Peters 2009; Ulfstein 2009; Mackenzie et al. 2010; Tallberg 2015.
82. Alford 2000: 160; Boisson de Chazournes 2004; Ulfstein 2009: 127; Alter 2011a.
83. Alter 2011b.
84. Preston 2016; Pring and Pring 2016.
85. Alford 2000: 160.
86. Alter 2011b.

has caused a further increase in litigation against governments.[87] While the majority of cases are brought before national courts, twenty-seven such cases were reviewed by international courts, most of them brought by non-state actors.[88]

An expanding international judiciary has gone hand in hand with a broadening of the notion of jurisdiction in the international legal order.[89] This has resulted mainly from the extension of international law into areas previously covered only by states' domestic laws, for example, criminal justice including new areas such as anti-corruption and terrorism. At the same time, both regional and domestic courts are increasingly accepting jurisdiction for cases involving international elements or foreign actions by multinational corporations domiciled in their jurisdiction.[90] An expanding notion of jurisdiction has been particularly evident with regard to universal jurisdiction provisions. This principle allows domestic courts to hear criminal and civil cases regardless of the location of a crime or the citizenship of the offender or victim. Traditionally, states have often resisted applying universal jurisdiction because it is seen to encroach on the sovereignty of other states.[91] However, this appears to be changing. While some have argued that universal jurisdiction is in decline, many others document a 'quiet expansion' in both the number and geographical scope of universal jurisdiction cases.[92]

A third significant transformation in the international judicial system has been its gradual opening to nonstate actors, including NGOs.[93] Whereas international courts have traditionally been limited to inter-state disputes, many international courts now allow NGOs to file court actions in defence of collective or 'general interests' (*actio popularis*). International treaties provide for direct private access to bodies such as the European Court of Justice, the European Court of Human Rights, the Andean Tribunal of Justice, and the East African Court of Justice.[94] In the realm of human rights

---

87. Peel and Osofsky 2018; Grantham Research Institute on Climate Change and the Environment 2020; Sabin Center for Climate Change Law 2021.

88. http://blogs2.law.columbia.edu/climate-change-litigation/non-us-jurisdiction/. Of 27 climate cases before International Courts 11 were Non-compliance Procedure Cases before the UNFCCC. Of the remaining 16 all but 3 were brought by NGOs or individuals aided by NGOs.

89. Boisson de Chazournes 2004.

90. Gwynn 2018; Boyle 2018.

91. Peters 2009.

92. Langer and Eason 2019: 782; see also Han 2017; Quintanilla and Whytock 2012; Center for Constitutional Rights 2019.

93. Boisson de Chazournes 2004: 622; Mackenzie et al. 2010.

94. Alter, Helfer, and Saldias 2012; Tallberg 2015.

some speak of a 'justice cascade' fuelled by changes in procedural law which have expanded private prosecution rights at both domestic and international levels.[95] In a European context, the 1998 Aarhus Convention[96] constituted a watershed by granting NGOs rights to challenge environmental policies on public interest grounds. So-called 'open-standing' provisions which allow any private person to seek remedy for violations of environmental legislation now exist in many countries around the world.[97]

Growing numbers of international courts and tribunals have led many to worry about conflicts arising from overlap of jurisdictional scope, inconsistent rulings, 'forum-shopping', and parallel litigation which threaten to undermine the integrity and coherence of international law.[98] As noted in the preceding chapter, however, NGOs have often benefitted from legal 'fragmentation'. Fragmentation has meant that a given legal dispute may be brought before more than one international dispute settlement mechanism, either simultaneously or sequentially, creating new opportunities for vigilante enforcement. At the same time, a proliferation of treaties affords NGOs a wider choice of overlapping frameworks on which to base legal claims. Many groups we spoke to described a careful process of 'legal framing' or 'convention shopping' whereby activists strategically consider whether presenting an offence as an environmental violation, as a human rights transgression, or as organized crime holds greater promise.[99] The expansion of universal jurisdiction rules in some countries also widens opportunities for legal 'venue-shopping' by NGOs, creating scope to look for hospitable courts, especially in human rights cases. In short, venue-shopping is not restricted to powerful states that use such practices to 'loosen legal obligation'[100] but also practiced by NGO enforcers with the opposite effect.

To be sure, legal developments are not only in one direction. The United States Supreme Court has reeled in the ability of private entities to bring extra-territorial civil claims in areas such as human rights. Some European countries, like Spain and Belgium, have also rolled back universality laws due to perceived overreach by courts and activists. However, many other

95. Sikkink 2011; Langer 2011; Michel and Sikkink 2013; Dancy and Michel 2016; Gallagher 2017; Michel 2018.

96. The United Nations Economic Commission for Europe Convention on Access to Information, Public Participation in Decision-making and Access to Justice in Environmental Matters.

97. International Bar Association London 2020.

98. Boisson de Chazournes 2004; Benvenisti and Downs 2007; Drezner 2009; Ulfstein 2009: 137; Alter and Meunier 2009; Alter and Raustiala 2018.

99. Mission 2020; EarthLeague International interview 2020.

100. Benvenisti and Downs 2007; Drezner 2009.

countries have continued to endorse universal jurisdiction, and new states have stepped in to fill the gap—including Argentina and the five Nordic countries.[101] Meanwhile, access for private actors to regional and domestic courts continues to expand in many parts of the world.

ADVANCES IN TECHNOLOGY

Alongside legal factors, a second driver of nonstate enforcement has been innovations in communication, surveillance, and data-gathering technologies which allow NGOs to conduct monitoring and investigation more effectively and cheaply than ever before. Growing sophistication and declining costs of cellular internet-connected devices capable of audio, photo, and video recording allow activists to document, verify, and archive abuses of international law and to submit court-ready evidence to investigators and prosecutors across borders with growing ease.[102] Some interviewees identify a break point in the diffusion of smartphones and social media around 2010 as a crucial fillip to nonstate investigators.[103] Widespread availability of information technologies like Global Positioning Systems (GPS) and Geographic Information Systems and new surveillance tools like drones have also enabled more NGOs to contribute directly to law enforcement. For example, NGOs have used drones to detect oil spills and reveal illegal fishing, find previously hidden mass graves, and film and broadcast the opulent mansions and super-yachts of corrupt politicians.

Meanwhile, greater access to satellite images permits NGOs to collect information on suspect activities that previously could only be learned from government sources. Many large-scale environmental problems like deforestation or desertification can only be reliably seen from space.[104] Satellites allow for the surveillance of labour camps in closed areas like North Korea, Tibet, or Xinjiang, or the perpetrators of genocide in Sudan.[105] Once the preserve of technologically advanced states, the growing availability of commercial satellite imagery and other types of remote sensing has giving rise to a new form of 'satellite-based transnational activism'.[106] NGOs also increasingly use GPS trackers to monitor the location and status of their staff in

101. Langer and Eason 2019: 796.
102. Langer and Eason 2019: 794.
103. eyeWitness interview 2020; Bellingcat interview 2020.
104. Baker and Williamson 2006.
105. Parks 2009; Herscher 2014.
106. Aday and Livingston 2016; Witjes and Olbrich 2017; Rothe and Shim 2018.

the field to keep them safe from threats such as kidnapping. At a time when harassment or even killings of anti-corruption, environmental, and human rights activists are on the rise in many countries, technology thus provides NGOs with new possibilities to investigate crimes from a safe distance.

Not only does the growing availability of commercial remote-sensing tools allow NGOs to gather direct evidence of law-breaking, but the revolution in information and communication technologies also provides wider access to secondary information and greater capacities to process that information. For example, in recent years, a number of new official databases on international crimes and court cases have been established which NGOs can freely access. Data and imagery processing that once required computer mainframes can now be run on personal computers, making this data intelligible to a growing range of users.[107] Together such innovations in technology mean that NGOs now have unprecedented capacity to obtain, analyze, interpret, and transmit evidence enabling effective law enforcement. Many NGOs have responded to such technological opportunities by providing training for victims or activists on how to capture and store evidence in ways that increase the likelihood that it will be useful to prosecution efforts.[108]

To digital detective groups and nonstate 'intelligence agencies', like Bellingcat and WildLeaks, who rely on the analysis of crowd-sourced data or 'open source intelligence' in tracking human rights, environmental, and corruption offences, finding evidentiary needles in the haystack of free online information has become key. For example, investigators analyze social media to 'map networks of relationships among suspects, invaluable for tribunals that want to prosecute the highest level responsible'.[109] The success of tech-enabled enforcement NGOs is indicated by the fact that they now out-pace not only traditional investigative journalists but also state law enforcement and intelligence agencies when it comes to establishing the culpability of those responsible for war crimes and terrorism[110] or corruption and illegal trafficking.[111] A number of NGOs also specialize in designing sophisticated technological solutions to specific monitoring problems. Some provide massive open source databases of corporate ownership. Others track and project the movement of ships at sea. Yet others create three-dimensional

---

107. Baker and Williamson 2006.

108. Langer and Eason 2019; www.eyewitnessproject.org; Koenig 2017; eyeWitness interview 2020.

109. Higgins 2021: 182.

110. Bellingcat interview 2020.

111. EarthLeague International interview 2020.

architectural reconstructions and virtual-reality settings based on the integration of satellite and social media imagery—all with the purpose of evidencing and prosecuting law-breaking.

Technology is no silver bullet. Many activists emphasize that for them the real challenge remains how to connect with actors on the ground and build relationships of trust that enable fact-finding.[112] Technology-enabled enforcement tools do not extend everywhere. Mobile phone access and even access to electricity remain limited in many parts of the world.[113] As the name suggests, the NGO Women on Web (WOW) depends heavily on the internet. One of the main challenges facing the group is limited internet access—due to poor infrastructure in the areas where WOW works and because governments in many countries try to censor its website and close down access. Yet, fittingly, the group has devised a technological fix: to circumvent censorship WOW has developed an app that can be downloaded to a smartphone through which women can access its services from anywhere in the world and also download a manual in sixteen languages on how to evade censorship using simple steps such as changing the IPN address.[114] As this and other examples in this book illustrate, although it clearly doesn't solve all problems—and may create new challenges of its own—technology offers a range of new, cost-effective tools for developing transnational enforcement strategies.

A CROWDED MARKETPLACE: STRATEGIC DIFFERENTIATION

As we have already noted, one of the most remarkable trends in post-war politics has been the explosive growth in international NGOs. Whereas the number of inter-governmental organizations has grown on average 3 percent yearly since 1990, NGOs have expanded at a rate of nearly 10 percent annually.[115] The NGO population grew especially fast during the 1980s and 1990s—more than quadrupling from 12,000 in 1980 to some 50,000 by 2000[116] and reaching 60,000 by 2012.[117] While NGO numbers have expanded

112. Ibid.; EAGLE interview 2020; Environmental Justice Foundation interview 2020.

113. Conservation Drones interview 2020.

114. Women on Waves interviews 2020.

115. Abbott, Green, and Keohane 2016.

116. Barnett, Raustiala, and Pevehouse 2020. For a comparable figure the *Yearbook of International Organizations* listed 51,509 NGOs in 2005 of which some 7,400 were international in scope. See Bloodgood 2011.

117. Bush and Hadden 2019: 1134.

across all policy areas, proliferation has been particularly pronounced in human rights and the environment.[118]

As the global NGO population has grown, competition for resources and attention has intensified. Cooley and Ron's account of the 'NGO scramble' was among the first to focus on how growing institutional density and resource competition affect NGO strategies.[119] Initially, an expanding NGO peer group was seen to create convergence and sameness.[120] Either groups responded to political opportunity structures or 'market pressures' by rationally adopting the same optimal strategy, or learning and socialization effects inculcated common perceptions of appropriate behaviour and institutional form through mimicry. In contrast, later analyses have focused on how resource scarcity and organizational crowding may spur NGOs to adapt by seeking to strategically differentiate themselves from competitors through developing new tactics and seeking out 'niche functions'.[121] Some studies have found that in dense NGOs populations, collaborating with other NGOs entails an elevated risk of organizational termination due to resource deprivation,[122] disincentivizing inter-NGO cooperation. Such models may provide a useful template for understanding how competitive pressures may motivate some NGOs to embrace enforcement.

Along with explaining the overall increase in transnational enforcement, attention to competitive dynamics also helps to answer our second question: Why have only some NGOs embraced enforcement strategies, while many others have stuck with advocacy and service delivery? The drivers of transnational enforcement identified earlier in this chapter are mainly structural and contextual: broad changes in technology and law which facilitate NGOs' efforts to investigate and prosecute violations of international law together with a growing organizational population. But while these changes may seem to confront all NGOs equally, their effects are mediated by organizational profiles and resource endowments: simply put, to survive in a competitive environment, NGOs face pressure to adapt to environmental pressures and seize upon new legal and technological opportunities. How they do so, however, is likely to be shaped by prior organizational interests and access to resources.

118. Sikkink 2002: 41.
119. Cooley and Ron 2002; also Sell and Prakash 2004; Bloodgood and Clough 2017.
120. Keck and Sikkink 1998; DiMaggio and Powell 1983; Wang and Soule 2012: 1677.
121. Eilstrup-Sangiovanni 2019; Bush and Hadden 2019.
122. Bloodgood and Clough 2017.

Among the resources for which NGOs must compete, media attention is often said to be in particularly short supply.[123] Literature on transnational advocacy has focused strongly on the ability of NGOs to use the media to garner public attention, to introduce new issues into public arenas, and thereby to set the agenda for policy-makers.[124] Yet not all NGOs find it easy to access mainstream media. Four international NGOs—Oxfam, Friends of the Earth, the World Wildlife Foundation, and Rotary International—have been found to account for about 50 percent of mentions in international media.[125] Other crucial resources such as public and private funding and access to political decision makers and international negotiation fora are also highly unevenly distributed. Leading 'brand-name' NGOs have wider access to global policy-makers and international bureaucrats, and they are more likely to cooperate with and receive funding from corporate actors than their smaller peers.[126]

In the introduction we distinguished enforcement from advocacy and service delivery. These labels refer to distinct forms of activism but not necessarily distinct activist groups. Most NGOs engage in some form of advocacy in the process of doing their work—whether through public education or via their effectiveness in promoting particular views on a topic.[127] Yet given a competitive environment we also expect an element of strategic and tactical specialization. An important insight from organizational ecology studies is that growing institutional density imposes resource constraints on a sector and pushes individual organizations to adopt either 'generalist' or 'niche' strategies to survive.[128] This strategic choice is not random but depends on underlying organizational factors. 'Niche' strategies such as public protest or enforcement can be politically costly in terms of limiting access to political decision makers and mainstream media[129] and by weakening an organization's appeal to public audiences.[130] For NGOs that have invested heavily in gaining political access or cultivating a public image as trusted sources of scientific knowledge, vigilantism may thus be damaging to their broader agenda. Instead, such groups tend to adopt 'softer' strategies which

123. Thrall, Stecula, and Sweet 2014. This point was a recurring theme in our interviews with NGOs.

124. Bob 2005; Ron, Ramos, and Rodgers 2005; Carpenter 2007; Stroup and Wong 2017.

125. Stroup and Wong 2017: 45; see also Thrall, Stecula, and Sweet 2014.

126. Hoffman 2009; Stroup and Wong 2017.

127. Stroup and Wong 2017.

128. Hannan and Freeman 1977; Carroll and Hannan 2000; Baum and Shipilov 2006.

129. Binderkrantz 2005: 699; Dür and Mateo 2013.

130. Stroup and Wong 2017.

are compatible with maintaining political access and public appeal.[131] It is also important that 'inside tactics', whereby NGOs rely on privileged information and expertise to lobby governments and international organizations, tend to be more resource demanding than 'outside tactics', involving protests and boycotts or other forms of confrontational action.[132] It takes significant resources to engage in successful policy framing or to reduce policy uncertainty through the provision of scientific expertise.[133] This is especially true at the transnational level, where mobilization in great numbers and over many years tends to be very expensive.[134] For resource-poor groups, such strategies may be simply off the table.

Strategy is shaped not only by material resources but also by organizational histories and identities. For example, while moderate outside strategies such as public education or media campaigns are generally compatible with political lobbying, more confrontational outside actions tends to limit political access.[135] Confrontational tactics may also restrict opportunities for coalition-building, as partners may fear negative implications of being associated with 'extremist' groups.[136] Such dynamics may in turn reinforce tactical specialization.[137] For NGOs with high public profiles and long-standing histories of cooperating closely with governments and other public authorities, the reputational costs of confrontational strategies may be just too high. For example, government-funded NGOs tend to focus more on political lobbying[138] and to be more moderate in their political demands than independently funded groups, which are freer to use confrontational tactics or pursue radical agendas.[139] For established NGOs litigation might curtail their lobbying power.[140]

But while generous government funding, hard-won political access, and high media profiles may make some NGOs reluctant to embrace enforcement, for others enforcement may present an alternative means and strategy for survival. Enforcement does not depend on capturing large 'hospitable'

---

131. Ibid.; Thrall, Stecula, and Sweet 2014.
132. Tarrow and Della Porta 2005: 45; Betsill and Corell 2008: 39; Dür and Mateo 2013; Hadden 2015; Binderkrantz et al. 2015: 100.
133. Krause 2014.
134. Tarrow and Della Porta 2005; Zürn 2014: 62; Eilstrup-Sangiovanni 2019.
135. Binderkrantz 2005.
136. Bloodgood and Clough 2017.
137. Eilstrup-Sangiovanni 2019.
138. Binderkrantz et al. 2015.
139. Zelko 2013: 316; Stroup and Wong 2017.
140. Peters 2009.

global audiences.[141] The targets (individual law-breakers and select enforcement authorities) constitute a relatively narrow audience that can be effectively targeted without appealing to general public opinion. Indeed, rather than seeking publicity, many NGOs engaged in investigation and prosecution of international crimes depend on their activities going unnoticed by the public.[142] For this reason, enforcement may appeal particularly to smaller NGOs that lack privileged access to policy-makers, large memberships, or strong media profiles.

Enforcement may also appeal to less well-established and/or relatively resource-poor NGOs for a different reason. Donors generally target their funding to NGOs with a demonstrated ability to achieve tangible results. Thus, to attract funding, NGOs have incentives to focus their efforts on achieving visible outcomes that are easily attributable to them.[143] Court victories or successful missions to uncover and prosecute specific international crimes may deliver such results faster and more recognizably than years of behind-the-scenes political lobbying. At the same time, enforcement may also help such groups establish legitimacy by differentiating and defining themselves in opposition to mainstream groups.[144]

Finally, law enforcement may serve to level the playing field between relatively resource-poor NGOs and more powerful state or corporate targets. Legal norms have a high degree of procedural legitimacy compared to other types of international norms.[145] Rather than entering the often long and costly battle to persuade global audiences of the rightfulness of particular substantive norms or principles which may cut against entrenched economic interests or invite competing moral claims, an appeal to 'legality' can establish a more direct claim to having legitimate cause.[146] As such, by invoking the law even marginal NGOs can make their voices heard. At the same time, by highlighting the illegality of the activities they intervene against, NGOs can make it politically costly for states to sanction them.[147] As Omar Todd of the Sea Shepherd Conservation Society stresses when asked whether his organization's direct interventions to enforce international fisheries

141. Keck and Sikkink 1998; Sell and Prakash 2004.

142. Burgis-Kasthala 2019; Environmental Justice Foundation interview 2020; Earth League International interview 2020.

143. Gent et al. 2015.

144. Stroup and Wong 2017.

145. Franck 1990; Finnemore 2000.

146. Eilstrup-Sangiovanni and Bondaroff 2014.

147. Ibid.

regulations are legal and welcomed by governments: 'The Sea Shepherd Conservation Society has been around for more than forty years so of course what we do is legal—otherwise we wouldn't still be registered'.[148] In legal terms, there can be little doubt that the SSCS has often broken some laws in the name of enforcing others.[149] When it comes to the Sea Shepherd's pursuit and arrest of the *Thunder*, for example, maritime lawyers are largely in agreement that confiscating its fishing gear was illegal. 'But no one would prosecute this because it pales in comparison to what the *Thunder* was doing', said Kristina Gjerde, an expert on high seas policy based at the International Union for Conservation of Nature. 'Sea Shepherd knows this'.[150] The 'shielding' effect of adopting an enforcement role may be particularly attractive to smaller, poorly established groups that operate on a financial shoestring and/or lack powerful political allies.

Conclusion

Law enforcement is traditionally seen as the preserve of states. While NGOs have long been known to assist states in implementing and monitoring international laws, and to challenge states to formulate additional laws, their role in enforcement has been viewed as indirect, pressuring or facilitating states in doing their job as law enforcers. In the following chapters we show how NGOs are increasingly challenging this traditional view of the natural division of labour between states and nonstate actors by taking law enforcement into their own hands. Unlike advocacy or service delivery, transnational enforcement does not strive to solve global problems by advocating for new treaties, nor does it operate by putting pressure on states or intergovernmental organizations to increase their enforcement efforts. Instead, NGO enforcers seek to strengthen environmental and human rights protection or anti-corruption laws by holding law-breakers directly accountable. In doing so, they act not as hired hands of governments but on their own initiative—often with states as their targets.

We have pointed to several drivers of transnational enforcement, along with reasons to expect some NGOs to embrace enforcement more eagerly than others. Our discussion so far gives rise to a general expectation that transnational enforcement will be more likely in areas where there is a

---

148. Sea Shepherd Conservation Society interview 2019.
149. Khatchadourian 2007; White 2013.
150. Urbina 2015.

conspicuous gap between the letter of the law and behaviour; where technologies and legal infrastructures are available that permit nonstate actors to take effective action against transgressors; and where competition for resources creates pressures for outsider and late-comer NGOs to look for alternatives to the conventional approaches of advocacy and service delivery. In the next three chapters we illustrate how these dynamics have played out first in the realm of international human rights protection, next in the environmental domain, and lastly in regard to international efforts to stem corruption.

We focus on these three areas for two main reasons. First, human rights and the environment are perhaps the most common areas of NGO activity (along with humanitarian and development work). Most readers interested in understanding new dynamics of transnational activism will want to know about implications for these two domains. Corruption, on the other hand, is a relatively new focus for NGOs and therefore provides interesting contrasts with the other two areas in bringing to light a neglected domain of NGO activity.

Second, as already discussed, human rights and environmental politics have seen a remarkable growth in both the number of transnational activist groups and international law-making. These domains thus allow us to illustrate how expanding legalization combined with new technology and growing numbers of NGOs fuel enforcement action (our central supply and demand factors). This second set of criteria may seem to raise a question about whether our ecological argument about growing population density encouraging strategic niche-seeking fails to apply to the anti-corruption sector, where NGO population density is lower. Importantly, ecological population density is not a matter of absolute numbers but rather a question of the balance between demand and supply of vital resources which organizations need to flourish. As such, even a relatively newly established population can theoretically have high density. As we illustrate in chapter 4, competitive pressures do shape the strategic choices of anti-corruption NGOs. However, other forces like learning effects also play a large role. Such differences between these three policy domains allow us to explore similarities and contrasts between policy domains.

2

Human Rights Vigilantes

Why is it important to begin by considering human rights in the context of an argument about the novelty and significance of vigilante NGO enforcement? International human rights law exhibits a useful series of parallels and contrasts to equivalent rules on the environment and corruption. The foundations of international human rights law were laid in the immediate post–World War II era, rather than the 1970s (international environmental law) or the 1990s (international anti-corruption law). The United Nations Declaration of Human Rights was issued in 1948, followed shortly after by the American Declaration of the Rights and Duties of Man (1948) and the European Convention on Human Rights (1950) and paving the way for a growing volume of regional and international treaties up to the present. NGOs like Amnesty International (founded in 1961) and Human Rights Watch (1978) have been at the forefront of the subsequent expansion of international human rights law and are some of the largest international NGOs—Human Rights Watch with four hundred staff and Amnesty with several thousand.[1] Since their founding they have been joined by thousands of other human rights NGOs, leading to an increasingly crowded 'market' for human rights advocacy.[2]

Human rights NGOs have often pioneered methods of enforcement later copied in other policy domains. These include such strategies as investigation and evidence gathering, as well as transnational civil litigation and private

---

1. Steinberg and Herzberg 2018: 263.
2. Cmiel 2004; Simmons 2009; Hafner-Burton 2013; Murdie 2014; Moyn 2018.

criminal prosecutions. For some observers, these tactics provide hope in light of the disappointments of the state-centred international human rights regime. Yet most commentators writing about human rights NGOs have done so in terms of an advocacy role, or somewhat less commonly in terms of service delivery.[3] Highlighting the enforcement actions of human rights NGOs thus underlines the extent to which we have for decades missed the importance, and even the existence, of transnational vigilante enforcement. Correcting this lapse not only requires a sensitivity to new NGO strategies but also requires us to rethink our understanding and classifications of what NGOs in this area have been doing for the last half century.

This chapter surveys the different approaches to vigilante human rights enforcement, looking first at actions enabled by developments in the law, then considering the impact of technological change, before finally examining inter-NGO competition. It is critical to establish that this is not a history of international human rights, or even the human rights movement, but only of one particular aspect of this struggle: autonomous enforcement of international human rights laws.

Since the foundations were laid in the early post-war years, the body of international human rights law has been continuously expanding, both in terms of the number of international treaties and conventions and in terms of the number of states that adhere to them. Yet this hasn't necessarily translated into greater protection of rights. Although the field has swung from periods of general optimism in the 1990s to more recent pessimism,[4] the gap between states' legal commitments to human rights and their actual behaviour has been a persistent, and growing, concern.

As the enforcement gap has widened, developments in international human rights law, and secondarily in national laws, have created new opportunities for enforcement beyond the state. Starting in the 1980s, NGOs in Latin America have creatively adapted the principles of international human rights law to seek justice for victims of military dictatorship through their domestic legal systems.[5] NGOs have represented victims in regional international courts, most often in the Americas but also in Europe, and most recently in Africa. A more transnational approach to human rights enforcement has depended on the legal doctrine of civil or criminal universal jurisdiction. Here courts first in the United States, then Europe, and lastly

---

3. Stroup and Wong 2017: 15; Polizzi and Murdie 2019: 253.
4. Keck and Sikkink 1998; Risse, Ropp, and Sikkink 1999; Posner 2014; Moyn 2018.
5. Sikkink 2011; Michel and Sikkink 2013.

in the developing world have increasingly played host to cases brought by NGOs, despite the original crime, the victims, and the perpetrators all being located abroad. Finally, the International Criminal Court created in 2002 has depended heavily on NGOs for investigation and evidence gathering. Yet there have also been counter-currents, such as efforts by states to narrow the scope for NGO enforcement. What goes up can come down in terms of opportunities for vigilante NGO enforcement.

Human rights NGOs have benefitted from the same advances in information and communication technology that have reduced the overall costs of transnational organization and networking. Yet they have been particularly empowered by technologies that expand the capacity for investigation and evidence gathering. These range from the leaking, dissemination, and analysis of huge data dumps to techniques for combing through social media for incriminating details, to apps for turning mobile phone photos and videos into admissible evidence, to various kinds of satellite imagery. Even tiny groups of human rights defenders today have surveillance and investigative capacities that only a couple of decades ago were the duopoly of the superpowers. Transmitted and commissioned through dense transnational networks, such niche skills feed into more general NGO enforcement efforts. Thus if the enforcement gap has provided the motive and opportunity for vigilante human rights enforcement, developments in law and technology have provided the means.

Finally there are the effects that NGOs have upon each other. The rise of Human Rights Watch in the late 1970s depended in significant part on taking up funding and campaigning opportunities left open by Amnesty. Once on the scene, competition from this group then forced Amnesty to change the nature and style of its work. Both of these large, dominant groups pioneered autonomous enforcement while still holding to a primary strategy of advocacy. In contrast, some newer, smaller, and more specialized groups have been set up as dedicated enforcers, often focusing on leveraging particular technologies or legal approaches.

The Human Rights Enforcement Gap

Even with positive trends in the observance of human rights associated with the spread of democracy,[6] and allowing for the possibility that quantitative indicators may overstate non-compliance by applying increasingly

6. Simmons 2009.

stringent standards,[7] it is hard to avoid the conclusion that a substantial human rights enforcement gap exists. Impressionistically, media coverage provides graphic illustrations of massive violations of international human rights law on a daily basis. More systematically, fundamental human rights were found to have diminished in almost two-thirds of the 113 countries surveyed for the 2018 Rule of Law Index, a negative slide that continued in 2020, as more countries degraded than improved their human rights scores.[8] Some experts find that committing to international human rights laws makes no difference to governments' likelihood of observing such laws;[9] others maintain that such commitments actually lead to *more* abuses.[10]

Assessing the enforcement gap is not just a matter of gauging the incidence of war crimes, extra-judicial killings, torture, disappearances, and so on that go unpunished (difficult enough on its own) but rather of assessing behaviour relative to an expanding corpus of international human rights law. Since the signing of the Universal Declaration of Human Rights seventy years ago, an expanding list of political, cultural, social, and economic rights has been elaborated through treaties, conventions, and declarations. Beyond the core human rights treaties which have served as a basis for further regional charters, there are more recent international conventions on the rights of women (1979), against torture (1984), on the rights of the child (1989), on the rights of migrants (1990), on the rights of the disabled (2006), and on protection from enforced disappearance (2006). Further expansion has occurred through the adoption of 'third generation rights' such as rights to a healthy environment, to self-determination, and to development. The steady expansion of international human rights standards, as well as the increasing number of states that commit to such standards, means that even if state behaviour remains the same, more and more of this behaviour is in violation of international law.[11]

Meanwhile tools of enforcement such as economic sanctions or withholding foreign aid and/or foreign investment by states and firms[12] are widely acknowledged to be lacking in both consistency and effectiveness.[13] Many observers point to a general lack of inter-state reciprocity or negative

7. Clark and Sikkink 2013.
8. World Justice Project 2020.
9. Hathaway 2007.
10. Hafner-Burton and Tsutsui 2007.
11. Dai 2013: 90.
12. Hafner-Burton 2013; Colin, Clay, and Flynn 2013; Nielsen and Simmons 2015.
13. Neumeyer 2005; Hathaway 2007; Hafner-Burton 2008, 2013; Vreeland 2008.

reputational consequences of violating international human rights commitments as another reason why so many governments can get away with human rights violations.[14] Indirect pressure on states via naming and shaming by NGOs also has a mixed record when it comes to eliciting compliance with human rights laws,[15] with some worrying that the effectiveness of 'naming and shaming' and 'boomerang' tactics focused on traditional centres of power has been further eroded by the recent rise of populism.[16] As such, there is a substantial and growing enforcement gap when it comes to human rights. The relative scarcity of public enforcement partly explains the rise of autonomous NGO enforcement in this domain.

Legal Drivers of Human Rights Enforcement

A growing enforcement gap is a driver of transnational enforcement but not a facilitating condition in and of itself. To contribute to enforcement of human rights law, NGOs must have access to appropriate legal and technological tools. The sections that follow examine how specific developments in international and domestic human rights law have enabled the creation of new NGO enforcement strategies. These strategies range from investigation and evidence gathering in order to build cases, to civil litigation or criminal prosecution, brought directly either by NGOs or by victims with the support of NGOs. Such legal action can be via domestic or international courts, though many NGO enforcers mix national and international approaches. Domestic courts are important given that the primary mechanisms for compliance with international human rights law occur at the domestic level.[17] On the other hand, the rapid proliferation in international courts and tribunals and the increasing opening of such tribunals to nonstate actors have also been recognized as an important fillip to boosting compliance.[18]

The sequence of presentation in the sections that follow moves from domestically oriented uses of international law to more purely transnational examples. Thus there is a progression from instances where the NGO, human

14. Simmons 2009; Risse and Sikkink 2013; more generally, see Dai 2002; Quintanilla and Whytock 2012; Efrat and Newman 2020.

15. Peterson, Murdie, and Asal 2018.

16. Rodríguez-Garavito and Gomez 2018, 12.

17. Remembering the lack of inter-state reciprocity and reputation effects to encourage compliance, see Simmons 2009; Risse and Sikkink 2013; Dai 2005; Quintanilla and Whytock 2012; Efrat and Newman 2020.

18. Alter 2011a, 2011b, 2014; see also Dupuy and Vierucci 2008; Mackenzie et al. 2010; Tallberg 2015.

rights abuser, and court are all in the same country (e.g., Argentina) to those where each party is from a different jurisdiction, or is an inherently international actor (e.g., international NGOs involved in the trial of Syrian war criminals in a German court, or trials before the International Criminal Court). With important exceptions, this progression to increasingly transnational enforcement is roughly a chronological trend.

DOMESTIC USE OF INTERNATIONAL LAW: PRIVATE PROSECUTIONS

Criminal prosecutions are conventionally regarded as a prerogative of the state, especially in common law countries. Yet in the countries of southern Europe and especially Latin America that made the transition to democracy in the 1970s and 1980s, private criminal prosecutions have been crucial in punishing past human rights abuses, with NGOs often playing an important role in directly bringing or supporting such cases. Of approximately 3,000 domestic human rights prosecutions in such countries between 1970 and 2010, around 750 were private prosecutions, and in most of these cases NGO involvement was vital.[19] Crucially, data gathered by the Transitional Justice Research Collaborative indicates that the frequency of private human rights prosecutions continues to rise. Thus while there were just 10 such cases between 1979 and 1988, this number jumped to 61 from 1990 to 2008.[20] Since they often involve national NGOs bringing cases against current or former officials of a national government in a domestic court in connection with crimes against citizens of that state within the borders of that same state, such prosecutions may seem to lack the transnational element that is the focus of this book. Yet often domestic human rights laws have become infused with and shaped by international human rights principles, with NGOs being crucial transmission belts.[21] Thus domestic courts often cite international human rights principles in judging cases brought with reference to national laws.

Although the first precedent-setting private human rights prosecutions were launched in Europe,[22] NGOs have been most important in directly and autonomously enforcing international human rights law in Latin America. There have been twice as many human rights prosecutions in Latin America

19. Dancy and Michel 2016: 173–74.
20. https://transitionaljusticedata.com/browse.
21. Michel and Sikkink 2013; Gonzalez-Ocantos 2014; Gonzalez-Ocantos and Sandholtz 2021.
22. E.g., the 1974 Lykourezos suit in Greece: see Roehrig 2002; Cheliotis and Xenakis 2016.

as in Europe (perhaps in part reflecting a different level of human rights abuses), and Latin American cases account for 55 percent of those world-wide.[23] A greater proportion of Latin American cases (around a third) have been private prosecutions,[24] which generally require NGO involvement to be successful.[25] Almost every human rights prosecution in Chile and Argentina has been private, usually with NGO involvement.[26] In most of these cases NGOs have been supporting victims' families, but sometimes NGOs have brought their own prosecutions.[27] More generally, NGOs have increased the capacity for private prosecutions by distributing information on how to prosecute, often introducing, disseminating, and entrenching international human rights law principles within domestic jurisprudence in the process.

Prominent examples are the Argentine NGOs *Centro de Estudios Legales y Sociales* (CELS) and the Grandmothers of the Plaza de Mayo (Asociación Civil *Abuelas de Plaza de Mayo*). Grandmothers of the Plaza de Mayo was formed in 1977 to look for missing children taken from the disappeared and adopted by military families. CELS, which was founded in 1979 to protect human rights and democracy, is unequivocal in hold-ing that 'Argentina resolved the tensions between its impunity laws and the principles of justice the country upheld by appealing to international law'.[28] During the two decades between the end of military dictatorship in 1983 and the state-led transitional justice process under the government of Nestor Kirchner from 2003, the only real enforcement of international human rights standards in relation to the thirty thousand victims of the previous regime were independent investigations and private prosecutions by these vigilante NGOs.

The main obstacle to investigating and trying thousands of human rights violations committed under the military dictatorship was a series of amnes-ties and pardons granted first by the dictatorship itself (which destroyed much of the evidence of its crimes) and in the aftermath of the transition to democracy.[29] The Grandmothers and CELS were central in challenging and overturning the impunity conferred by these amnesties, using international

23. Sikkink 2015: 357.
24. Michel and Sikkink 2013: 877, 885.
25. Dancy and Michel 2016: 174; Gallagher 2017: 1667; Michel 2018: 16.
26. Michel and Sikkink 2013: 885, 889.
27. Michel 2018: 6.
28. *Centro de Estudios Legales y Sociales* 2011: 17.
29. Sikkink 2008; Mallinder 2009; Gonzalez-Ocantos 2014.

law to create and then leverage opportunities in the Argentine court system.[30] CELS in particular propelled the enforcement process of the first crucial cases by gathering evidence, preparing witnesses, lodging private prosecutions, and arguing the cases in court.[31]

Private criminal prosecutions are not confined to a Latin American context. Scholars note 'a growing trend of the international criminal community towards private investigations, once political leaders demonstrate a lack of will to officially investigate the commission of core international crimes'.[32] This trend has been evident in places like the former Yugoslavia, Rwanda, and Syria.

NGOs AND REGIONAL INTERNATIONAL COURTS

The main role of NGOs in relation to regional international courts in Europe and Latin America has been similar to their role in the domestic courts examined above. They have served as representatives for victims in providing the evidence and legal expertise necessary to bring and win cases. The regional justice systems in question are mainly the European Court of Human Rights (from 1959) and the Inter-American Court of Human Rights (from 1979), assisted by the Inter-American Commission on Human Rights. These courts do not engage in individual prosecutions like the International Criminal Court. Instead, they issue rulings whereby governments that are found to be in breach of their obligations under the respective regional human rights convention can be publicly ordered to take remedial measures (including changing domestic law) and compensate victims. Although NGOs can bring cases directly if their rights as an association have been violated (or on behalf of 'general public interests'), it is more common for them to represent individual victims. This trend has been bolstered as existing courts have gained new members and new courts have been established, for example, the African Court on Human and Peoples' Rights, which passed down its first judgement in 2009.

Cases brought by NGOs have been most prominent in the Inter-American Court.[33] In the decade 2000–2009, around 80 percent of the judgements from this court related to cases in which NGOs were acting

---

30. DeMars 2005; O'Donnell 2009; Layus 2018.
31. *Centro de Estudios Legales y Sociales* 2011.
32. Heinze 2019: 172.
33. Haddad 2018.

for the victims.[34] A 2021 study found that since 2009, 88 of 119 cases that ended in judgements by the court were brought by regional NGOs. Given that this figure excludes NGOs not directly based in the region (including several prominent North American groups), the overall NGO involvement is likely significantly higher.[35] In contrast, the equivalent figure was only around 4 percent in Europe. The lesser role of NGOs in Europe is variously said to reflect a better-funded court less dependent on outside help, the relative reluctance of court officials to conduct field visits, and/or the fact that the European court set its procedures before NGO amici briefs were common.[36] A single group created by Human Rights Watch to litigate before the Inter-American Court, the Center for Justice and International Law (CEJIL), represented plaintiffs in almost half the cases brought before the court between 2000 and 2009.[37] Earlier, Washington-based NGOs like WOLA (Washington Office on Latin America, drawn from various Catholic and Protestant churches) and Human Rights Watch had played a key role in reviving the moribund Inter-American Human Rights Commission by presenting it with the results of their detailed investigations ahead of commission visits to offending countries.[38] Yet with time, regional NGOs have become increasingly active litigators at the Inter-American Court. Thus while CEJIL accounted for 33 of 88 cases brought by NGOs since 2009, this later period saw cases brought by NGOs based in eighteen different Latin American countries with the *Comisión Ecuménica de Derechos Humanos*, Ecuador, and Peru's *Asociación Pro Derechos Humanos* among the most active.[39]

NGOs also bring cases before regional human rights bodies in other parts of the world. From its inception in 1987 until 2010 the African Commission on Human and Peoples' Rights reviewed about 400 communications from individuals and NGOs.[40] In 2018 Asylum Access recorded a significant victory in the African Court on Human and Peoples' Rights,[41] evidencing the potential for the further spread of NGO enforcement via strategic litigation in regional international courts.

34. Mayer 2011: 931.
35. Gonzalez-Ocantos and Sandholtz 2021, 22–23.
36. Burgorgue-Larsen and Torres 2011; Heyns and Killander 2013; Haddad 2012; Haddad 2018: 99; Hillebrecht 2019.
37. Haddad 2018: 85, 104.
38. Padilla 1993; Micus 2015; Soley 2019: 356.
39. Gonzalez-Ocantos and Sandholtz 2021, 24.
40. Mackenzie et al. 2010.
41. Asylum Access 2018.

ENFORCING HUMAN RIGHTS THROUGH CIVIL LAW

Despite the importance of criminal prosecutions, civil law has also provided an important avenue for human rights enforcement beyond the state. The most important example is the U.S. Alien Torts Act. Here, and in the universal criminal jurisdiction options (domestic and through the International Criminal Court) discussed subsequently, the essentially transnational nature of vigilante enforcement comes into full view, as the locus of the trial is separated from the location of the crime, and the nationality of the court from the nationality of the victims and perpetrators.

The U.S. Aliens Torts Act declares that 'the district courts shall have original jurisdiction of any civil action by an alien for a tort only, committed in violation of the law of nations or a treaty of the United States'. Passed in 1789, the statute was re-interpreted nearly two hundred years later, perhaps an extreme example of an existing law being used in new ways. Working with the Center for Constitutional Rights, a U.S. NGO, the family of a seventeen-year-old Paraguayan national, Joelito Filartiga, who was tortured to death in Paraguay in 1976, sued the police officer responsible (who had since retired to the United States) in a U.S. court.[42] In 1980 lawyers from the Center for Constitutional Rights successfully argued for jurisdiction on the basis that human rights were now part of the law of nations, and hence within the scope of the Act.[43] The decision to let the case proceed overcame traditional understandings of the doctrine of sovereign immunity as applied to state officials. It followed several unsuccessful attempts by lawyers from the Center who had learned from previous failures, underlining the importance of NGO experimentation and the cumulation of knowledge beyond the state in enforcement strategies.[44]

Other NGOs began to specialize in the use of Alien Tort litigation. In addition to the Center for Constitutional Rights, these included the Center for Justice and Accountability, EarthRights International, and the International Labor Rights Fund.[45] These practitioners' cases raised hopes (and fears) about the creation of a de facto 'world human rights court' within the U.S. judicial system, especially in that, unlike in U.S. criminal cases, the government had less control over which actions were initiated.[46] Business

42. Danaher 1981; Claude 1983; Aceves 2007.
43. Centre for Constitutional Rights 2019.
44. Collingsworth 2002: 186; Holzmeyer 2009: 280.
45. Holzmeyer 2009: 282.
46. Su 2019: 857.

lobby groups in particular worried about the prospect of NGO plaintiffs having open season on American multinational firms.[47] These fears followed NGO-sponsored suits filed against ExxonMobile, Coca-Cola, Del Monte, TexacoChevron, IBM, Ford, General Motors, and others, which were accused of complicity in human rights violations abroad.[48] Organizations like Amnesty International and Oxfam also began to gain more legal expertise after the turn of the century because of new legal possibilities for enforcing international human rights standards through civil law, like the Alien Torts Act, and universal jurisdiction criminal prosecutions (the 'Pinochet effect' discussed below).[49]

The Unocal case gives some indication of the attraction for would-be NGO vigilantes. In the mid-1990s, Burmese villagers fled across the Thai border complaining of forced labour, torture, rape, and executions by the Burmese military associated with the building of a natural gas pipeline.[50] The Yadana pipeline was a joint venture of the military and the U.S. oil company Unocal (now a subsidiary of Chevron). The villagers had no chance of seeking redress from the Burmese government, a military dictatorship with an appalling record of human rights violations. The refugees 'had grievances, but they needed to be put in contact with someone to litigate for them'.[51] The head of the Free Trade Unions of Burma, who was in exile in Thailand, asked a Georgetown law student (Katie Redford, later co-founder of EarthRights) interning with the group for help. After some research, Redford and fellow student Tyler Giannini contacted the Washington-based International Labor Rights Fund with the plan to bring an Aliens Tort suit against Unocal.[52]

From September 1996 the Alien Torts case was filed and argued with the help of the NGOs EarthRights International, which had been largely founded to advance human rights in Burma, and the Center for Constitutional Rights.[53] One of the lawyers explained the rationale: 'I have sat through a few too many academic discussions about ideal normative standards, and I have interviewed too many victims of human rights abuses, only to feel the frustration, if not the embarrassment, of explaining that their stories will be told to the world in reports. . . . My personal obsession

---

47. Brower 2005.
48. Kurlantzick 2004: 63.
49. Ibid., 62.
50. EarthRights International 1996.
51. Kurlantzick 2004: 63.
52. Collingsworth 2002: 187; Bioneers 2015.
53. EarthRights International 2003.

has become finding ways to enforce human rights norms'.[54] The essence of the suit was that because Unocal (along with the French energy firm Total) knew of the abuses committed by the Burmese authorities and had failed to stop them, the firm shared liability. Most of the subsequent seven years of legal wrangling concerned whether the case could proceed to trial. Once the NGOs' lawyers won this point, Unocal capitulated, agreeing to settle and pay damages and compensation.

The International Labor Rights Fund later brought similar suits involving victims from Argentina, Colombia, Ecuador, Guatemala, Indonesia, Liberia, Nicaragua, and Turkey, in each case acting on complaints from local NGOs or trade unions.[55] In a manner that is highly instructive for possible reverses in the environmental and anti-corruption spheres, however, the very success in broadening the use of the Alien Torts Act, especially by NGOs against corporations, sparked a backlash. In 2013 the U.S. Supreme Court in effect decided that only those cases substantially concerned with acts on U.S. territory could proceed. Though NGOs like International Rights Advocates have continued to launch Alien Torts class actions in 2020, they have met with little success.[56] Notwithstanding arguments from Amnesty International that they are inherent in the right to reparations for victims contained in various international human rights treaties, attempts to bring equivalent cases on the basis of universal civil jurisdiction for human rights abuses in Europe and Canada have failed.[57] Recent victories in Dutch and U.S. civil suits against North Korean human rights abuses may provide a new opening for NGOs, however.[58] Similarly, France's 2017 Duty of Vigilance Law (discussed in chapter 3) provides a potential new tool for holding multinational corporations legally responsible for failing to prevent human rights abuses resulting from their activities abroad.

UNIVERSAL CRIMINAL JURISDICTION IN DOMESTIC COURTS

Perhaps even more propitious in expanding the scope for vigilante human rights enforcement than the Alien Torts Act has been the expansion of universal criminal jurisdiction, that is, the idea that certain courts can prosecute

---

54. Collingsworth 2002: 185.

55. Ibid., 187; Holzmeyer 2009: 289–90.

56. https://www.earth.live/post/terry-collingsworth; Davis 2020; http://www.iradvocates.org/cases.

57. Amnesty International 2007.

58. Guilbert and Mis 2018; Haag 2018; Stone 2018; Sang-Hun 2020b.

human rights abuses, no matter where they occur and irrespective of the nationality of the alleged victims or perpetrators. Most commonly, universal jurisdiction is asserted over grave human rights abuses such as crimes against humanity or genocide. Broadly, there are two roads to universal criminal jurisdiction. The first is via international courts and tribunals, most prominently the International Criminal Court and originally the Nuremberg Trials (1945–46) and Tokyo Trials (1946–48). The second is through national courts empowered with universal jurisdiction. NGOs have been important in exercising both options. As such 'it is an incontrovertible fact that nongovernmental organizations have become key players in the field of international criminal justice'.[59]

Human rights NGOs lobbied hard for universal jurisdiction to be included in international instruments from the Convention Against Torture to the Rome Statute of the International Criminal Court, alongside the principle of individual criminal responsibility.[60] The idea of universal jurisdiction may date back to anti-piracy campaigns,[61] but it was elaborated at Nuremberg. In the 1980s and 1990s it was used by national courts against surviving Nazi war criminals who had emigrated to the United States, Canada, Australia, or elsewhere.[62] But the most famous recent instance of this doctrine involved former Chilean dictator Augusto Pinochet in 1998.

Pinochet was arrested during a visit to London in line with a warrant issued by a Spanish judge in connection with the torture of Spanish citizens in Chile during Pinochet's rule. The original case had been lodged by lawyers on behalf of victims as a private prosecution in Spain in 1996. The British police action marked the first time a former head of state had been arrested and charged according to the doctrine of universal criminal jurisdiction. After the House of Lords upheld the warrant over his claims of sovereign immunity, Pinochet was held under house arrest in Britain until March 2000 when he was released on the grounds of ill health.[63] The former dictator then faced a series of trials upon his return to Chile for human rights and corruption offences. Although the case in Britain collapsed, the warrant had chipped away at Pinochet's impunity at home.

59. Van der Wilt 2015: 237.
60. Dietelhoff 2009; Sikkink 2011.
61. Shirk 2021.
62. Langer 2015: 248.
63. Roht-Arriaza 2005.

The Pinochet episode became an important inspiration for NGOs to adopt new, transnational legal strategies to enforce human rights laws.[64] The pursuit of Hissène Habré, dictator of Chad from 1982 to 1990, demonstrates both the potential of universal jurisdiction and the importance of NGOs spurred on by the 'Pinochet effect' in putting this doctrine to work in seeking accountability for human rights crimes. In 1999, Amnesty International, Human Rights Watch, the International Commission of Jurists, and the *Federation Internationale des Ligues des Droits de l'Homme* (FIDH) joined together to consider ways of using this new legal opportunity.[65] The answer came from an unlikely quarter: Chad. The Chadian Association for the Protection and Defence for Human Rights, led by former political prisoner Souleymane Guengueng, asked the Western NGOs for assistance in prosecuting Habré in Senegal, his place of exile after losing power. Human Rights Watch and FIDH formed a coalition with Chadian and Senegalese NGOs and victims to bring charges in Senegal, which had adopted universal jurisdiction for crimes against humanity.

An initially positive decision by the Senegalese judge in February 2000 was reversed, however, and the effort was only saved in November 2000 when the NGO coalition refiled the same case in Belgium, an example of 'jurisdiction shopping'. Belgium was chosen because at this time it had a universal criminal jurisdiction law that did not require any connection between the court or litigants and the country in which the crime had occurred. Adding to the 792 victim testimonies compiled by the Chadian Association, in 2001 Human Rights Watch discovered vital new evidence in Chad: the files of Habré's secret police, including dossiers on 1,208 people killed and 12,321 who suffered other abuses.[66] After Chadian NGOs had convinced their government to waive his sovereign immunity, Habré was indicted for war crimes and crimes against humanity in Belgium, which requested his extradition from Senegal. The Senegalese government refused.

After years of wrangling between the African Union, Belgium, the International Court of Justice, and the UN, the trial was eventually allowed to go ahead in Senegal. Beginning in July 2013, the coordinator of the NGO coalition, Jacqueline Moudeina, represented 1,015 victims as civil parties to the mixed Senegalese-African Union trial.[67] Habré was found guilty of ordering the death of 40,000 people in May 2016, marking the first time

64. Ibid.
65. Brody 2017: 8.
66. Human Rights Watch 2013.
67. Seelinger 2017: 18.

the court of one state had convicted the head of another for crimes against humanity. He was sentenced to life imprisonment and ordered to pay €123 million in compensation to victims.[68] Human Rights Watch estimated that by the time the final trial began, the campaign had cost them $2 million.[69]

Beyond the specifics of the Habré case, Belgium's involvement epitomizes the contest over universal criminal jurisdiction. In 1999 the Belgian government amended legislation in keeping with the Rome Statute to grant national courts universal jurisdiction over genocide and crimes against humanity. Furthermore, it allowed private parties to initiate such complaints as civil parties, and the government set up a special unit to investigate such international crimes. These changes led to convictions in 2001 of four Belgian residents guilty of crimes against humanity in Rwanda, Belgium's former colony.[70] Emboldened by this successful precedent, NGOs rushed to bring cases against a long list of current and former U.S., Israeli, and Chinese leaders and generals for war crimes, including George H. W. Bush and Ariel Sharon. In response the U.S. government (among others) put strong diplomatic pressure on the Belgian government, which in 2004 passed legislation to drastically narrow the scope of such cases.

However, Belgian law still provides potential for human rights enforcement beyond the state. The indictment in 2014 of Martina Johnson, a Belgian resident accused of human rights crimes in the Liberian civil war in her capacity as one of Charles Taylor's most senior officers, demonstrates the continuing relevance of the doctrine. It illustrates the crucial role of NGOs in conducting investigations and assisting victims in launching private prosecution (here first as civil parties, later joined by the Belgian state) under universal jurisdiction. In this instance the NGOs behind the effort are the Swiss-based *Civitas Maxima* and the Liberian Global Justice and Research Project.[71] However, as with the Habré case, and those of corruption discussed in chapter 4, the indictment of Johnson also highlights the slow turning of the wheels of international justice: six years after the case was filed and Johnson put under house arrest, there was still no date for hearings to begin.[72]

In line with its starring role in the Pinochet case, Spain is the jurisdiction that has perhaps most excited NGOs concerning the potential of enforcing international human rights law via universal criminal jurisdiction. The

68. Langer and Eason 2019: 806.
69. Brody 2015: 217.
70. Kaleck 2009: 932.
71. Bekou 2015.
72. Ponselet 2020.

Spanish judiciary investigated crimes committed against Spanish citizens in Argentina during the 'dirty war' of 1976–83. Guatemalan victims assisted by the Center for Justice and Accountability and *Asociación Pro Derechos Humanos de España* also lodged genocide charges against three former presidents of Guatemala. As in Belgium, the combination of universal jurisdiction, the ability of private parties to initiate criminal cases, and active, networked NGOs led to a flood of cases. Those on the receiving end included individuals from the CIA and governments such as the United States, Israel, China, Rwanda, Congo, and others.[73] As well as lodging the initial criminal complaints, 'in most cases, NGOs have driven the efforts to locate witnesses and evidence'.[74] Yet in parallel with Belgium's earlier experience, reforms in 2009 and 2014 saw Spanish authorities tighten the requirements for bringing such cases.

Nevertheless, universal criminal jurisdiction remains a powerful means for enforcing international human rights rules. Largely thanks to the efforts of NGOs, ten years after Pinochet's arrest, officials from Afghanistan, Argentina, Bosnia, Congo, Mauritania, Rwanda, Serbia, and Uganda had been convicted of major human rights abuses in European courts exercising universal criminal jurisdiction.[75] In the following decade (2008–17) there were 34 more convictions (compared with only three in the International Criminal Court in the same period).[76] But rather like NGOs' experience with the Alien Torts Act, initial hopes have been tempered by experience. This may be in part because NGOs initially overstated the legal potential of this doctrine;[77] unfulfilled expectations may also reflect the political backlash early attempts engendered.

NGOs have been entrepreneurial in seeking out new jurisdictions in which to bring this kind of case, however, and the overall effectiveness of enforcement via universal jurisdiction private prosecutions in national courts has increased over the years. Often as one door has closed (e.g., in Belgium or Spain), another has opened elsewhere. For example, in a notable reversal from earlier years, Argentine courts are currently the venues for hearing cases of Franco-era crimes in Spain, while Human Rights Watch has also lodged a private prosecution of Saudi ruler Mohamed bin Salman in

---

73. Individual targets included Ariel Sharon, George H. W. Bush, Colin Powell, Dick Cheney, and former generals Norman Schwarzkopf and Tommy Franks (Halberstam 2003).

74. Kaleck 2009: 955.

75. Ibid., 958.

76. Langer and Eason 2019: 811–12.

77. Van der Wilt 2015; Langer 2015.

connection with the murder of journalist Jamal Khashoggi.[78] The Southern African Litigation Centre has brought cases regarding human rights violations in Zimbabwe in South African courts, as well as supporting other NGOs' litigation efforts in countries including Eswatini, Lesotho, Malawi, Nigeria, and Zambia.[79] Thanks to NGO's investigative work, in Germany in April 2020 a case led by Wolfgang Kaleck of the European Centre of Constitutional and Human Rights together with the Open Society Foundation Justice Initiative on behalf of victims began against the high-ranking Syrian official Anwar Raslan for crimes against humanity.[80] In February 2021 another former Syrian official, Eyad al-Gharib, was the first to be convicted in a German court for crimes against humanity thanks to actions brought by the same NGOs.[81] In terms of numbers, in the last ten years there have been more completed universal jurisdiction trials than in the previous twenty years combined, and substantially more completed universal jurisdiction trials than completed trials at the ICC.[82]

NGOs have been the drivers behind the use of universal criminal jurisdiction at the national level.[83] Initially many of the groups bringing such cases in Europe were small and relatively unknown and inexperienced NGOs rather than the main, established human rights bodies.[84] As time went on, however, a few larger and more established groups have come to specialize in this type of strategic litigation: *Asociación Pro Derechos Humanos de España*, France's FIDH, and the German European Centre for Constitutional and Human Rights,[85] as well as Civitas Maxima and TRIAL International.[86] As a result, there has been increasing professionalization and specialization of NGOs in universal jurisdiction criminal cases.[87] Specialized brokers like the Global Legal Action Network aim to foster links among NGO litigators, journalists, and academics. Many states also have now developed a specialized capacity in investigating and prosecuting foreign war crimes.[88] The combination

78. Langer and Eason 2019: 801–3.

79. Southern Africa Litigation Centre, https://www.southernafricalitigationcentre.org/cases/precedent-cases/.

80. Hubbard 2020.

81. Hubbard 2021; Open Society Justice Initiative 2021.

82. Langer and Eason 2019.

83. Langer 2015; Langer and Eason 2019.

84. Langer 2015: 254.

85. Kaleck 2009: 977.

86. Langer and Eason 2019: 793.

87. Ibid., 782; Civitas Maxima interview 2019.

88. Human Rights Watch 2014.

of growing maturity, experience, expertise, and connections among both nonstate and state enforcers in using universal criminal jurisdiction prosecutions in national courts means that even if the hopes spurred by the Pinochet arrest have not been realized, the practical effect of this doctrine has provided a significant tool with which to pursue human rights accountability.

NGOs AND THE INTERNATIONAL CRIMINAL COURT

The biggest recent change in the international human rights landscape was the formation of the International Criminal Court in 2002 on the basis of the 1998 Rome Statute. Given the low number of convictions in the first two decades of its existence (just eight to 2020), it is an open question how much the ICC has actually done to narrow the enforcement gap.[89] The ICC is a classically inter-governmental organization, founded by and accountable to states through the Assembly of State Parties and the United Nations Security Council. The relationship between the ICC and NGOs has generally been written about in terms of advocacy.[90] NGOs were among the leading proponents of forming the ICC and endowing it with significant powers. After 2002, these groups have (generally) campaigned for states to support the ICC.[91] Yet putting advocacy efforts to one side, how is NGO enforcement relevant to the Court?

The liaison between NGOs and the ICC arises from the fact that it has few enforcement powers of its own. Instead, it depends on third parties in both legal and practical terms. In the main, these third parties are states, and sometimes inter-governmental organizations. Yet there are also many important examples of enforcement cooperation between NGOs and the ICC. Sometimes the court directly contracts one or more NGOs to deliver a service. But more commonly NGOs freely choose to make common cause with the court for particular cases.[92] Under such arrangements, although referred to as 'intermediaries',[93] the NGOs are no more subordinates of the ICC than it is of these nonstate actors.[94]

---

89. Though it may have had substantial indirect effects; see Kim and Sikkink 2010; Dancy and Montal 2017.

90. Pace 1999; Rodman 2006; Struett 2008; Dietelhoff 2009; Lohne 2017.

91. See, e.g., the 2,500-member Coalition for the International Criminal Court, http://www.coalitionfortheicc.org/.

92. De Silva 2017: 179.

93. Haslam and Edmunds 2012.

94. Baylis 2009: 122; Haslam 2011: 221; Ullrich 2016: 552; Haddad 2018: 127, 160.

For their part, international courts like the ICC may favour a greater role for NGOs to lessen their dependence on states.[95] NGOs have been more important vis-à-vis the ICC than in relation to preceding ad hoc international tribunals, which specialize in a given area.[96] However, even in the Yugoslav and Rwandan international criminal tribunals, the role of NGOs turned out to be greater than founders of these tribunals expected, especially in establishing connections with witnesses and victims.[97] In 1993, Helsinki Watch, a division of Human Rights Watch, published the report 'Prosecute Now!' Citing failure by the UN Security Council to appoint a prosecutor and judges to the Yugoslav tribunal, the report proceeded to identify twenty-nine possible defendants, linking each to specific crimes.[98] NGOs have also provided evidence for transitional justice trials in Sierra Leone, Cambodia, and elsewhere.[99]

Most often NGOs working with the ICC gather evidence and supply, protect, and liaise with witnesses (including victims) in the affected country, before and during trials.[100] For example, in the wake of the election-related violence in Kenya 2007–8 which killed over a thousand people and led to several (ultimately unsuccessful) indictments by the ICC, it was NGOs, and largely not the Kenyan authorities or the ICC itself, that collected evidence, interviewed witnesses, identified suspects, and registered victims for participation in the trial.[101] This dependence on NGOs is especially apparent where, as in Kenya, the local government is hostile to the ICC. As one ICC official put it: 'We can't just walk into the places where we think that the victims are and say "hi, here we are". We have to rely on local people to lead us to the victims and especially local people who potentially have the trust of and the knowledge of the victims'.[102] Reinforcing this point, Executive Director of TRIAL International Philip Grant argued in 2018: 'NGOs have the capacity that authorities don't have to work outside the borders of the country without needing to ask the cooperation of the country in which we are investigating . . . NGOs are more flexible than any police force. For instance, if we need to go to the

95. Haddad 2018: 13.
96. Clancy 2015: 219; Haddad 2018: 3.
97. Haslam 2011: 226–30; Heinze 2019: 169–70.
98. Human Rights Watch 1993.
99. Baylis 2009: 127–28; Heinze 2019: 170.
100. Haslam and Edmunds 2012: 50; eyeWitness interview 2020.
101. Human Rights Watch 2011; Mue and Gitau 2015: 201–2.
102. Ullrich 2016: 551.

Gambia tomorrow, we book a plane, request a visa and we are there. We can meet victims, insiders, and witnesses'.[103]

Few recent examples of the gap between international human rights laws and deeds are as graphic and widespread as those from the Syrian Civil War, thanks in significant part to Russian and Chinese vetoes in the United Nations (in 2014) barring referral to the ICC. Reflecting frustration with the limitations of the ICC, the Commission for International Justice and Accountability (CIJA) was created in 2014. Registered in the Netherlands, it now employs some 140 staff across European offices and in the field in Syria (and also Iraq).[104] CIJA's focus is to 'collect, store and analyze documentation of alleged crimes like a "proto-OTP [office of the prosecutor of the ICC]"'. So far, field staff have smuggled out a staggering 800,000 pages of largely Syrian regime-generated documents, at the cost of the lives of several activists.[105] What cannot be moved for security reasons is hidden in boxes in caves or buried in the ground to secure evidence for the future.[106] According to Deputy Director for Investigations and Operations Chris Engels, 'CIJA's focus is on collecting, corroborating, and storing . . . information that "links" superiors, national leaders and remote organizers of atrocities to the atrocity crimes committed on the ground'.[107] This evidence 'is essential to ensuring later accountability, and is the basis for multiple pre-trial legal case files developed by CIJA's legal team which a domestic or international prosecutor could present to judges before trial'.[108]

While ICC action has been blocked by high politics, CIJA's evidence has informed a number of domestic universal jurisdiction cases across Europe.[109] In September 2017, the European Center for Constitutional and Human Rights and the Caesar-Files Support Group filed a complaint with the German Prosecutor's Office against high-ranking officials of the Syrian Intelligence Services. In June 2018 the German Federal Prosecutor issued an international arrest warrant for Jamil Hassan, head of Syria's Air Force Intelligence Directorate, on charges of war crimes and crimes against humanity. The investigation was based directly on evidence submitted by CIJA (the

103. Burnand 2018.
104. Engels 2016; Burgis-Kasthala 2019: 1167–68.
105. Borger 2015a.
106. Taub 2016.
107. Engels 2016: 3.
108. Ibid., 3–4.
109. Ibid.

'Caesar files'),[110] while the trial was brought under the German Code of Crimes against International Law (enacted in 2002), which enables German courts to investigate international crimes.[111]

CIJA provides a vivid example of a private actor independently partnering with the ICC without state support or against state opposition. According to founder William Wiley, the typical response to his initial requests for funding from governments was 'What you're proposing to do is something that governments do, or the UN does, and the International Criminal Court does'—not an NGO.[112] Indicative of the scale and importance of NGO contributions to international human rights enforcement, CIJA now employs about as many investigators in Syria as the ICC has working on all its cases combined.[113] Echoing the sentiments of Philip Grant, one senior CIJA employee explained, 'This is private sector and . . . [it] functions differently than the big bureaucratic United Nations, where you have a lot of deadwood. . . . We are very flexible, our risk tolerance is higher, we can operate on short notice . . . if I get a call now, that says go to the airport, I can do that, which bureaucratic organizations cannot do'.[114]

Beyond gathering evidence, NGOs have themselves launched legal action against those indicted by the ICC. The Southern African Litigation Centre obtained a High Court order aimed at preventing the Sudanese ruler Omar Al-Bashir, indicted by the ICC, from leaving the country after a June 2015 African Union summit (the government ignored the order, however). This was only one of a number of attempts by a 'sophisticated network of local and international human rights NGOs that independently, and in coordination, followed Bashir's travel and engaged in advocacy and litigation tactics to bring about his arrest'.[115] In independently partnering with the ICC, NGOs thus provide an important, if partial, substitute in bolstering the ICC's enforcement capacity. The Office of the Prosecutor has been forthright in acknowledging this dependence: 'None of the Office of the Prosecutor's objectives could be met without this permanent interaction with NGOs at all stages of its activities: development of policies and practices, crime prevention, promotion of national proceedings, monitoring, preliminary examinations, investigations, prosecutions, cooperation, and efforts to maximize the impact of its

---

110. TRIAL International 2019; Heinze 2019: 173.
111. European Center for Constitutional and Human Rights 2016.
112. Quoted in Taub 2016.
113. Ibid.
114. Burgis-Kasthala 2019: 1182.
115. Haddad 2018: 2.

work'.[116] Such arrangements are separate from (but may complement) the effect whereby the combined impact of ICC attention and NGO pressure may stimulate domestic legal accountability.[117]

To the extent that member states insist on greater economy from the ICC, its dependence on NGOs may grow. It is important, however, to acknowledge the costs as well as the benefits of this close cooperation between the ICC and NGOs. The court's first prosecution against Congolese warlord Thomas Lubanga, for which intermediaries provided almost half the witnesses, was almost thrown out after accusations that these parties had biased the trial against the defendant. Their prominent role provoked criticism in the judge's final decision that the prosecutor had delegated investigative responsibilities to these third parties.[118] For their part, local NGOs have faced sometimes deadly retribution for their involvement with the ICC, a stark reminder of the stakes involved in the struggle for human rights accountability.[119]

NGO Enforcement and Technological Advances

For human rights abusers to be held accountable before the law, their actions must be investigated and documented. Enforcement via the courts, whether through civil litigation or criminal prosecution, depends on sufficient admissible evidence. Here technological advances have given NGOs a wide range of new tools for surveillance, investigation, and evidence gathering. Technological innovations do not merely complement the enforcement capacity created by the legal advances discussed earlier in this chapter; legal and technological advances have a synergistic and multiplicative effect on the capacity of NGOs to enforce international rules, including on human rights.

Some technologies used by NGOs may have been previously available only to leading states through their intelligence services and militaries (e.g., satellite imagery). For others, such as the means of recording and widely disseminating documents, sound, and video, capacity was previously concentrated in major media outlets.[120] Now, the wide diffusion of these technologies means that NGOs (and even individuals) have a vast new range

---

116. Quoted in Clancy 2015: 223.
117. Dancy and Montal 2017.
118. Haslam and Edmunds 2012: 58–61, 75–78.
119. Haslam 2011: 233–34; Clancy 2015: 230–32.
120. Thrall, Stecula, and Sweet 2014.

of tools at their disposal for advocating and delivering services but also to supply enforcement.

Technology rarely stands on its own; new techniques and tools generally require organizational adaptation. The technological advances surveyed in what follows here have given rise to, and sometimes been driven by, an increasingly specialized ecosystem of 'niche' NGOs which focus specifically on technology development and adaptation. Thus, a given enforcement action might see larger and more established NGOs avail themselves of advanced technological tools by collaborating with smaller and more technically specialized counterparts. The sections that follow survey the most important new technologies for the vigilante enforcement of international human rights rules and give examples of how they have been applied, but they also aim to give a sense of the rich organizational landscape that has evolved as a result.

SOCIAL MEDIA AND PHONE CAMERAS

The increasing ubiquity of mobile devices has transformed the ability of victims and bystanders to collect and share evidence of human rights abuses. In this regard, NGOs have been the incidental beneficiaries of broader technological advances, but they also have been active and highly creative in exploiting this potential. One example is the group eyeWitness to Atrocities, a British NGO spun out of the International Bar Association. It specializes in ensuring that digital photos and video of human rights atrocities can be admissible as evidence in prosecutions.[121] This group developed an app in June 2015 that verifies the time and location of photos and videos, and substantiates that the images have not been altered or tampered with, while also encrypting the material for security and establishing a legal chain of custody. The particular problem that sparked the formation of eyeWitness is that without such verification techniques, this kind of digital evidence may be disputed by defence lawyers, or judges may rule against its use in trials.[122] The group's lawyers catalogue the results to make them as user-friendly as possible for future investigators and prosecutions, whether by state or non-state actors. The group cooperates closely with the ICC and Europol, while also engaging in ad hoc collaboration with national war crimes units. Underlying the importance of the social context of technology, eyeWitness found

---

121. eyeWitness interview 2020; https://www.eyewitness.global/about-us.html.
122. eyeWitness Project 2016.

that it had to build and maintain close relationships of trust to win acceptance for the app among NGOs and human rights defenders in the field.[123]

The promise of this kind of technology use is illustrated by the collaborative work of eyeWitness, the Brussels-based NGO International Partnership for Human Rights, and Ukrainian NGO Truth Hounds, supported by the Norwegian delegation to the Organization for Security and Co-operation in Europe. This team formed to examine possible war crimes and violations of International Humanitarian Law during fighting between Russian and Ukrainian forces in Eastern Ukraine in the winter of 2016–17, with specific focus on the shelling of civilians.[124] EyeWitness was responsible for geo-coding the exact location of shell craters as other groups in the field used the eyeWitness app to ensure that the material they gathered would be admissible in any potential future legal action. This material included where shells landed relative to military and civilian facilities, the specific kind of weapon used, the exact direction from which they were fired, and hence which side was responsible for which strikes. Another example comes from the Congo, where, working together with TRIAL International, eyeWitness provided the first ever video footage admitted as evidence in a Congolese court, helping to secure the conviction of two fighters for murder, torture, and pillage.[125]

EyeWitness is just one of many groups that harness video and cellular data technologies for enforcement. Inspired by the impact of the footage of Rodney King being beaten by Los Angeles police in 1991, WITNESS was founded the following year in New York with a mission of training human rights defenders in how to produce video evidence more effectively, safely, and ethically. Once again, one aim is to ensure that evidence collected can be admissible in court, and WITNESS has provided evidential material for use by the ICC.[126] A comparative treatment of international criminal cases from the Syrian Civil War written by a former U.S. State Department official notes that many such 'groups are compiling dossiers on potential defendants, producing memoranda on key background inquiries (such as the chain of command), coding their holdings for ease of search, and authenticating digital and documentary evidence'.[127]

123. eyeWitness interview 2020.
124. eyeWitness to Atrocities 2017.
125. eyeWitness to Atrocities, n.d.
126. https://www.witness.org/about/our-story/.
127. Van Schaack 2019: 5.

Another example is Physicians for Human Rights, formed in 1986 to help hold human rights abusers accountable through medical and scientific evidence and now comprised of over forty staff members. This group created the MediCapt app, piloted in Kenya in 2018.[128] Responding to the problem that doctors and nurses in the field often recorded incomplete or inconsistent information, and that medical records were often lost or destroyed or were inadmissible, the app records forensic evidence of sexual violence in a secure, standardized digital format that is admissible as court evidence. The app also enables records to be aggregated and cross-referenced to pick up trends and patterns that may be useful in proving that violence is part of a systemic campaign of crimes.

What is striking about such technology focused groups is the high degree of specialization; interviewees freely spoke of finding 'niches' within wider 'ecosystems'.[129] There is an increasing division of labour whereby technologies for documentation, verification, archiving, and court presentation of human rights evidence are each dealt with by separate, specialized NGOs (some are discussed below). There is further specialization whereby different groups form to address different types of human rights crimes (e.g., genocide vs. labour rights), or to design technology for developed and developing country conditions.

SATELLITE IMAGERY

Satellite imagery has been invaluable in looking behind closed borders to expose mass human rights abuses, lifting 'the veil of sovereignty'.[130] Before the 1990s satellite imagery was largely limited to great power militaries and intelligence services; now it is readily available to NGOs and widely used in nonstate human rights enforcement[131] as a prominent example of the pluralization of enforcement. There is an increasingly complex ecosystem surrounding the generation and use of satellite imagery, as both state and nonstate actors buy from commercial firms, DigitalGlobe being one of the most prominent.[132] These commercial firms often do pro bono work in conjunction with NGOs and the media to advance human rights causes. Relevant enforcement technology consists not just of bespoke imagery of

128. Physicians for Human Rights, n.d.
129. eyeWitness interview 2020; Bellingcat interview 2020; Global Witness interview 2020b.
130. Witjes and Olbrich 2017: 525; Rothe and Shim 2018: 419.
131. Herscher 2014.
132. Aday and Livingston 2009: 514.

specific activities but also of access to archives of such images and, just as crucially, the diffusion of the computing power, software, and knowledge to analyze and utilize the images.[133]

As early as 2003 satellite evidence was used to supplement a report by the Washington-based Committee for Human Rights in North Korea called *The Hidden Gulag*.[134] More extensive satellite imagery provided by this group and Amnesty International enabled the mapping of North Korea's Gulag Archipelago from 2013 documenting the location, number, size, and economic activities of the labour camps.[135] In the absence of government data, satellite imagery provided by these NGOs enabled a 2014 UN Human Rights Council report to estimate that there were between 80,000 and 120,000 inmates.[136] In June 2007 Amnesty launched the Eyes on Darfur project with a direct preventive aim: to deter human rights abusers who would know their actions would be watched and recorded from afar with the aim of future prosecution.[137]

The American Academy for the Advancement of Science joined the fray in 2007 with the Geospatial Technologies and Human Rights program (funded by the MacArthur, Oak, and Open Society Foundations). This program was designed to harness geospatial technologies like satellite images, geographic information systems, and GPS to 'broaden the ability of NGOs to rapidly gather, analyze, and disseminate authoritative information' and 'provide visual proof to corroborate on-the-ground reporting on conflicts affecting human rights'.[138] Rather than forming a basis for advocacy, geospatial data and images gathered in Syria are explicitly collected as evidence of genocide to be presented to the International Criminal Court.[139] In 2010 the NGO Enough launched the Satellite Sentinel initiative with academic collaborators, again with the aim of actively deterring human rights abuses.[140]

Even where prosecutions on the basis of such evidence are currently impossible, the increasing trend towards placing individuals on human rights sanctions lists means that the officials concerned may face consequences for their actions (e.g., the United States imposed targeted sanctions

133. Baker and Williamson 2006: 6–8.
134. https://www.nkhiddengulag.org/.
135. Witjes and Olbrich 2017: 529.
136. UN Human Rights Council 2014: 15, 222, 226.
137. Parks 2009: 541; Rothe and Shim 2018: 421–22.
138. American Academy for the Advancement of Science 2006.
139. Herscher 2014: 491.
140. Ibid., 493.

against Chinese officials for human rights abuses in Xinjiang in 2020, and the UK, EU, and Canada imposed further coordinated sanctions in 2021). Evidence collected now may be crucial for prosecutions in changed political circumstances. As such, NGO surveillance and evidence gathering may serve both to deter some current abuses and to facilitate convictions and punishment through future trials, thereby functioning as tools of enforcement rather than advocacy.

OPEN SOURCE INTELLIGENCE: BIG-DATA INVESTIGATIONS

One of the most innovative NGOs in technology-based investigation is the British NGO Bellingcat, founded in 2014 by Eliot Higgins. As of spring 2021, the group had eighteen staff members.[141] Describing itself as an 'open source intelligence collective' or 'open source online investigation' agency,[142] Bellingcat is perhaps the closest thing to an NGO intelligence service. Aside from its own work, it also trains and assists other NGOs, journalists, government agencies, and general volunteers in use of crowd-sourcing and geo-location techniques.

A telling example of Bellingcat's work comes from Cameroon. In November 2018 Bellingcat was approached to verify digital footage of arson attacks by government forces earlier that same month in the town of Kumbo. The government denied the attacks, and the location was closed to foreign journalists. In the background the footage showed a building with a long, red roof across a road from some shops and an unfinished building. Google Earth satellite pictures enabled the red roof to be picked out, and Googling the shop names confirmed the exact location. These Google results led digital investigators to footage uploaded to YouTube of the same location before the fires. After posting this information, individuals from Kumbo provided additional pictures and video to Bellingcat, which enabled further verification of the extent, location, and timing of the attacks, thus undermining the government's denials. The fact that each of these online tools is free underlines the low entry barriers for this kind of work but doesn't detract from the impact it can have.[143] Also in Cameroon, Bellingcat worked with the BBC to verify online footage of soldiers executing civilians in 2018.[144] After initially dismissing the report as 'fake news', the

141. https://www.bellingcat.com/about/.
142. Bellingcat interview 2020; Janes 2020.
143. Strick 2018.
144. British Broadcasting Corporation 2018.

Cameroonian government later backtracked and charged seven of its soldiers with the murders.

As well as providing particular evidence of human rights atrocities, Bellingcat and other groups use similar digital data-analysis techniques to debunk spurious claims, notably the Russian government's attempts to deflect blame from its shooting down of the Malaysian airliner MH17 in 2014.[145] Bellingcat's painstakingly compiled analysis of video and social media evidence on the involvement of Russian armed forces in the airliner crash has played a crucial role in both the Dutch-led international Joint Investigative Team and the case pursued since 2019 by the victims' relatives against the Russian government in the European Court of Human Rights.[146] In response, Bellingcat has begun to work with other groups like the Global Legal Action Network (GLAN) and the Syrian Archive to ensure its digital evidence meets court standards.[147] It has also supplied evidence to the ICC.[148] Starting in April 2019, Bellingcat and GLAN released the results of twenty in-depth investigations into the campaign of airstrikes carried out by the Saudi-United Arab Emirates led coalition in Yemen since 2015 in the form of a searchable archive of verified open source material (yemen .bellingcat.com).[149] The evidence played a key role in a successful judicial review claim in June 2019 against the British government's decision to continue arms sales to Saudi Arabia despite the 'demonstrable risk of international humanitarian law violations'.[150]

Bellingcat is a powerful example of how dramatically technology has lowered the barriers for nonstate transnational investigators. Eliot Higgins, the group's founder, quotes a former FBI agent speaking about online open source intelligence: 'Today with OSINT [Open Source Intelligence], I'd say 98-plus per cent of everything I need to find out about someone, I don't need to pay for anymore. That's where I really jumped into the OSINT side. . . . It dawned on me that anyone can have this'.[151] It is not just that nonstate 'amateurs' can begin to perform some of the same enforcement functions as state intelligence 'professionals'. In important instances Bellingcat and others have bettered the performance of state law enforcement

---

145. Bellingcat 2019.
146. Bellingcat interview 2020.
147. Ibid.; Janes 2020.
148. https://www.youtube.com/watch?v=6muSJCSXgjY.
149. Global Legal Action Network 2019a.
150. Global Legal Action Network 2019b.
151. Higgins 2021: 6.

and intelligence agencies, for example, in determining the identity of Russian government agents responsible for assassination attempts in Britain and other countries.[152]

More esoteric examples of big-data techniques enabling NGO enforcement have involved reconstructing bullet trajectories through the combination of video footage, three-dimensional modelling and animation, and forensic oceanography. One instance involves the protests that overthrew Ukraine's Russian-backed Yanukovych government. On 20 February 2014, Ukrainian Interior Ministry police sought to clear demonstrators from Kyiv's Maidan Square, killing forty-eight protesters. Five members of the police were later put on trial, but much of the documentary and physical evidence had been destroyed. Determined to find the truth, a Ukrainian graduate student, Evelyn Nefertari, analyzed hours of digital video taken by different people of the key events and coded each element to locate it in time and space.[153] Her results were presented by prosecutors in the case at a conference at Carnegie Mellon University's Center for Human Rights Science. In the audience was the head of SITU, a U.S. firm that does for-profit architectural design but also not-for-profit 'forensic architecture' human rights work.[154] SITU and the Carnegie Center jointly took the thousands of hours of footage from four hundred separate videos Nefertari had amassed and mapped these onto finely grained three-dimensional laser scans of the street where the shootings occurred. The result was a three-dimensional model of the events that could be played forwards and backwards in time, viewed and rotated from any vantage point, and zoomed in to show details down to the centimetre.[155] They then used autopsy reports showing the angles at which bullets entered and exited protestors' bodies, as well as the timing difference between the sound of the individual gunshots and the crack of the bullet breaking the sound barrier to establish from where the fatal shots were fired. This evidence has become the prosecutors' central exhibit in the case.[156]

A similar example of forensic data analysis involves SITU's work with French human rights NGO FIDH on computer-assisted forensic oceanography. Shortly after the outbreak of fighting that overthrew Libya's Gadaffi regime in 2011, a ten-metre rubber boat carrying seventy-two African refugees left Tripoli seeking the Italian island of Lampedusa. The boat quickly ran

---

152. Schwirtz and Barry 2018.
153. Schwartz 2018.
154. SITU Research 2018.
155. http://maidan.situplatform.com/.
156. Schwartz 2018.

out of fuel and supplies and drifted through the Mediterranean for a fortnight before grounding back in Libya, resulting in the deaths of all but nine passengers. At the time, the seas off the Libyan coast were heavily patrolled by NATO forces imposing an arms blockade, and the refugees' boat had been spotted by a NATO helicopter, several fishing boats, and a warship early on in its ordeal, some getting as close as ten metres while nevertheless failing to rescue the refugees.[157] No fewer than fifteen NGOs have filed cases on behalf of survivors of what has been christened the 'left to die boat', including private prosecutions for criminal negligence, in France, Spain, Italy, and Belgium.[158] The cases hinge on establishing which ships were close enough to the distressed refugee boat to be practically able and legally obliged to render help. To answer this question, the NGO investigating team first used online information on weather and currents to reconstruct the drift path of the vessel. They then used Synthetic Aperture Radar microwave satellite data to determine which ships were in or close to this path at the relevant time.[159] In addition to forming the basis for multiple lawsuits by NGOs, the forensic report also led the Council of Europe to launch a separate inquiry to 'prevent impunity'. In its 2014 report, 'with a view to preventing the human rights violations which result from the vacuum of responsibility', the Parliamentary Assembly of the Council called on Ministers to instruct the Steering Committee for Human Rights to formulate a common approach to 'fill crucial legal gaps with regard to search and rescue in the Mediterranean Sea'.[160]

Documenting the killing of protestors in Ukraine and failure to rescue boat refugees in the Mediterranean are just two examples of how open source data analysis by NGOs can help to hold states and individuals accountable for human rights offences. In another example, the ICC specifically noted the importance of SITU's work in obtaining the 2016 conviction of Ahmad al-Mahdi for destruction of cultural monuments in Timbuktu.[161] Here the most important contribution was integrating digital evidence, much of it provided via the perpetrators' social media accounts, as well as satellite imagery into a user-friendly presentation in court. SITU Research integrated the data from different sources and formats and created an interface through which

157. Forensic Oceanography 2012.
158. SITU Research 2012a.
159. Ibid.
160. Parliamentary Assembly of the Council of Europe, Recommendation 2046 (2014), The Left-to-Die Boat: Actions and Reactions, https://pace.coe.int/pdf/449d9a4e86a94a90f65c3efd af2168bb285af8983326667a8259ffe25682ae848428feba12/recommendation%202046.pdf.
161. Stinson 2016.

judges could compare panoramic and three-dimensional before-and-after images of each monument.[162] Clearly more information is not always better (pure data dumps may simply clog the system), and NGOs' contribution in processing information and rendering it useable is at least as valuable as providing raw data.[163]

Not every technical NGO contribution is based on satellite technology or open source data gathered via the internet. One of the first questions asked in the case of atrocities is 'How many people were killed?' Getting the answer is both important and often difficult. The Human Rights Data Analysis Group (aka 'statisticians for human rights') is another specialized NGO based in California whose purpose is to provide statistical analysis for other human rights groups.[164] The group worked on the Habré case described earlier, in particular the secret police prison records found in Chad by Human Rights Watch in 2001. Included in these records were inmate death certificates. By calculating prisoners' death rate compared to the mortality rate of the general population, and adjusting for the demographic differences of the prison population (e.g., no infant mortality, relatively few women), this analysis was used in the trial to show the number of deaths attributable to the cruel and inhumane conditions of confinement.[165] By establishing the much higher death rates of the indigenous population of Guatemala versus the general population during that country's civil war, this group provided crucial evidence of a deliberate genocide against indigenous communities that led to the conviction of former general Rios Montt. In her decision the judge specifically noted the importance of the statistical evidence that killings were systematic and targeted.[166]

It is worth re-emphasizing that the link between data-gathering technologies and increasing NGO enforcement is not so much that the technology is new or unprecedented (though some of it is) but rather its increased affordability, availability, and diffusion and the fact that the resulting data can be shared widely and instantly. In an example of this new availability, Bellingcat responded to the need for a particular satellite image with a successful crowd-sourced appeal for the modest sum of £1,435.[167]

---

162. Ibid.
163. See also Brody 2017; SITU Research 2012b.
164. https://hrdag.org/.
165. Human Rights Data Analysis Group 2010.
166. Betts 2017.
167. Higgins 2021: 93.

Of course, at the same time as they have facilitated enforcement, new technologies have also provided a massive boost to NGO service delivery and advocacy. For example, while satellite imagery and online data are important sources of evidence for prosecution, they are also used widely as new aspects of traditional NGO awareness-raising and naming and shaming strategies by groups such as Human Rights Watch and Amnesty International.[168] Thus, the 'turn to enforcement' is explained not only by advances in technology but also by legal opportunity structures and by specific organizational incentives to focus on enforcement rather than advocacy or service delivery.

Competition and Differentiation among Human Rights Groups

The last three to four decades have seen a growing role for NGOs in enforcement of international human rights standards. Yet not all NGOs have been equally active in enforcement. Many legal and technology-assisted advances in human rights enforcement beyond the state have been driven by small, specialized groups, often reflecting technical expertise that would be difficult or costly for larger, generalist groups to replicate. To be sure, the dominant groups in international human rights law, Amnesty International and Human Rights Watch, have incorporated the use of satellite imagery in their reports, just as they have engaged in strategic litigation, especially as a result of the 'Pinochet effect' at the turn of the century. Nevertheless, in doing so, they have often partnered with smaller groups like eyeWitness, Bellingcat, SITU, and others to draw on their technical skills rather than replicate these capabilities. When engaging in litigation, dominant human rights groups have often targeted high-profile defendants like Pinochet or geopolitical struggles that enjoy high visibility with public and political audiences, whereas universal jurisdiction investigations and trials by other, smaller NGOs have often focused on less conspicuous, 'low-cost' defendants.[169]

What evidence is there of inter-NGO competitive dynamics in the field of human rights, and what does this have to do with enforcement, if anything?

One driver of the rise of enforcement has been the sheer growth in the number of human rights NGOs, which accounts for a significant part of the overall global growth in NGOs. The take-off point was the end of the Cold War, which led to a rapid expansion in transnational human rights groups in

---

168. See 'Our Story', https://www.hrw.org/about/about-us.
169. Langer and Eason 2019.

both numerical and geographic terms.[170] This rise in the population reflected the spread of democracy and the increased political space for civil society. It was also powered by increased funding from governments and private foundations.[171] Yet even with these additional opportunities and resources, large and small NGOs in this area confronted a new era of growing competition.

Founded in 1961 in Britain, Amnesty International was the first international human rights NGO. Based on mass membership, it was self-consciously an advocacy group whose strategy was focused on shaming governments to observe international human rights standards by mobilizing popular pressure on the basis of careful fact-finding and reporting. Until 1978, when Helsinki Watch, the precursor to Human Rights Watch (HRW), was formed and also adopted a focus on 'naming and shaming abusive governments', Amnesty enjoyed a 'virtual monopoly' in this area.[172] Yet even at this early stage, there was a strategic and inter-dependent aspect to NGO development. According to its co-founder, Human Rights Watch arose in part to fill policy, strategy, and financial space left unoccupied by Amnesty.[173] First, Amnesty defined violations of the laws of war as outside its scope of interest. Second, it did not pass judgement on or lobby with regards to the foreign policy of the United States or other countries; to this extent at least, Amnesty was 'apolitical'. Third, it eschewed funding from U.S. foundations like Ford and Rockefeller, and the private sector more generally, and governments too.[174] The component parts of what in 1988 became a unified Human Rights Watch filled each one of these vacant spaces. Speaking of the laws of war in the 1980s, Aryeh Neier suggests that 'if it [Human Rights Watch] had not had this field to itself in that era, it might have had far more difficulty building its rapidly growing reputation'. After much debate, Amnesty also began scrutinizing this area, in part to defend 'its very strong brand',[175] but Neier believes 'the fact that it [Amnesty] took so long contributed to the emergence of Human Rights Watch as an effective competitor in its capacity to influence public policy'.[176]

The rise of Human Rights Watch and the strategy it employed was thus in significant part a result of the 'gap in the market' left by Amnesty, to employ

---

170. See Smith, Pagnucco, and Lopez 1998; Sikkink 2011; Neier 2012; Hafner-Burton 2013.

171. Hafner-Burton 2013: 154; https://www.hrw.org/our-history.

172. Hopgood 2006: 54.

173. Neier 2012: 204–5.

174. Hopgood (2006: 144) attributes a general 'anti-money' orientation to there being 'too many academics' in the organization.

175. Ibid., 75.

176. Neier 2012: 194.

a common and telling metaphor. At key turning points Amnesty was forced to change tack by competitive dynamics, for example, dropping its earlier reluctance to give immediate public reactions on human rights crises. In this regard, as in others, Hopgood relates: 'Amnesty was forced to confront the logic of the market. By the 1990s, with the mass media now transformed into something extraordinary, where speed, clarity, and punch were essential, Amnesty found itself confronted by a more agile competitor for publicity and money: Human Rights Watch'.[177] These two giants of the human rights sector still clearly feel that they are in competition. For example, one of our interviewees observed that Amnesty has measured its success by a monthly comparison of the press coverage it received relative to Human Rights Watch on particular topics.[178]

Yet despite the important differences between them, at the broadest level both Amnesty and Human Rights Watch remain defined by their advocacy role. As Neier puts it: 'With rare exceptions, Human Rights Watch does not engage in litigation. Its principal means of promoting rights is by documenting abuses, calling attention to the discrepancies between the practices of a government and its commitments and obligations under international law; and publicizing its findings widely in order to embarrass the authorities responsible for the abuses and, thereby, to persuade them to change their ways'.[179] Clearly signalling priorities for Human Rights Watch, he argues that 'the most significant practical contribution of international human rights law has not been the actual enforcement of its statutes'.[180]

The 'What We Do' section of Amnesty's website presents the same logic: 'Human rights change starts with the facts. Our experts do accurate, cross-checked research into human rights violations by governments and others worldwide. . . . We use our analysis to influence and press governments, companies and decision-makers to do the right thing'.[181] It is very clear here that Amnesty's mission is to pressure 'the people and institutions who can make change happen', not to pressure for change directly themselves. Thus there is a notable contrast with the idea of direct and autonomous enforcement. The equivalent section of the Human Rights Watch website is remarkably similar: 'Investigate: Our researchers work in the field in 100 some countries, uncovering facts that create an undeniable record of human rights

177. Hopgood 2006: 107–8.
178. Amnesty International interview 2020.
179. Neier 2012: 80.
180. Ibid., 114.
181. https://www.amnesty.org/en/what-we-do/.

abuses. Expose: We tell the stories of what we found, sharing them with millions of social media and online followers each day. News media often report on our investigations, furthering our reach. Change: We meet with governments, the United Nations, rebel groups, corporations, and others to see that policy is changed, laws are enforced, and justice is served'.[182]

According to these mission statements, change happens through meetings, persuasion, and media attention but not through direct enforcement by NGOs. Certainly both Amnesty and Human Rights Watch do engage in a variety of other activities, including litigation, but their dominant strategic rationale centred on advocacy is clear.

What, then, about the many smaller and newer human rights groups? As might be expected, the effects of competition are even more pronounced for NGOs that do not have the public reputation and extensive financial and political support enjoyed by the giants of the field's growing population density, and competition can drive sameness via herding as NGOs strive to appeal to the same group of major donors. Others have christened this phenomenon 'the NGO scramble'.[183] However, it can also encourage differentiation as groups seek to reduce competitive pressures and insecurity by searching for unoccupied niches.[184]

Certainly there is some evidence of 'market pressures' leading to conformity and sameness among human rights NGOs. As foreign funders of groups in the Congo herded towards the priority of sexual and gender-based violence (SGBV), so too did NGOs because 'there is a common perception that, in order to receive international funding, [NGOs] must have a SGBV component to their work', even when NGOs had little aptitude for work in this area and when the money would have been better spent elsewhere.[185] The same dynamic was observed in Kenya, where one local noted, 'There is a scramble for victims so everyone wants to grab them to do this and that and the next pet project is SGBV'.[186]

In our story, however, competition is just as likely to lead NGOs to differentiate their strategies.

A clear example of strategic differentiation is the Commission for International Justice and Accountability (CIJA), discussed earlier in connection with the ICC, which has explicitly sought to distinguish its enforcement role

---

182. https://www.hrw.org/about/about-us.
183. Cooley and Ron 2002.
184. Bush and Hadden 2019; Eilstrup-Sangiovanni 2019.
185. Lake 2014: 523.
186. Ullrich 2016: 550.

from larger advocacy groups like Human Rights Watch and Amnesty by eschewing publicity, even to the point of not having a website. The founder and director of CIJA, William Wiley, has asserted the need for a unique 'selling point': 'we don't want to be called a foundation that starts to do what other NGOs do, we have our space'.[187] In part this reflects a low opinion of much of the service delivery work in this area. Wiley says of the human rights training projects to which Western governments allot hundreds of millions of dollars each year: 'Human rights training . . . it's a waste of time and money. Everybody's doing it and it's bullshit'.[188] In line with our general thesis about inter-NGO competition, one activist within the organization suggests that there is 'massive pressure on anyone in the industry [international criminal law] to . . . adapt or innovate', and as a group 'your ability to survive is based on how well you can sell yourself and the product meeting their [funders'] expectations'.[189] In this context, selling the organization and product requires having something that stands out from other NGOs, especially the dominant ones; for CIJA, and for many other smaller NGOs, this novel selling point is enforcement.

For the more technologically advanced specialized groups this sort of differentiation comes naturally. As the examples in this chapter attest, these groups tend to partner with others from the non-profit, corporate, government, or university sector in contributing their unique capabilities and skills. They see their role as filling an important niche and, by being the best at what they do, making a valuable contribution to a broader network or ecosystem of human rights activists. For other groups, small size and a relative lack of bureaucracy can provide a distinct advantage when it comes strategic innovation. As Simmons notes, there is some criticism that 'Some HROs [human rights organizations] are now too professionalized and bureaucratized to respond nimbly to emerging human rights violations'.[190] Being free of organizational constraints and political and donor oversight allows smaller groups to experiment more freely with new strategies. Insofar as growing market pressures produce differentiation among NGOs, rather than a dysfunctional scramble this may lead to an overall increase in effectiveness thanks to increasing specialization and collaboration, a question explored further in the concluding chapter of the book.

187. Burgis-Kasthala 2019: 1165.
188. Borger 2015a.
189. Quoted in Burgis-Kasthala 2019: 1176, 1180.
190. Simmons 2014: 192.

Conclusion

This chapter has illustrated NGO enforcement of human rights law.

It is once again important to note that there is often a good deal of overlap between problems and solutions in international human rights, environmental, and anti-corruption matters. Human rights abuses might be the precursor to or result of environmental damage. Governments and leaders that engage in mass atrocities are often guilty of major corruption crimes as well.[191] As much of the rest of the book sets out, there are strong parallels in NGO enforcement strategies across all three policy domains. Some of the most creative NGO solutions have sought to cross-fertilize or combine responses from these different domains, as when human rights law becomes the basis for climate change litigation (see chapter 3). In many respects, however, the pioneers of vigilante NGO enforcement have been groups seeking to uphold international human rights law, in part because the relevant body of international law predated that related to the environment and corruption, in part because universal jurisdiction rules for human rights crimes have facilitated transnational litigation. What are the main lessons from this on-going struggle?

The first is to underscore the interactive effects of technological and legal changes in facilitating the pluralization of human rights enforcement, beyond the monopoly of the state. Given the scale of human rights abuses, and the codification of ever more human rights, would-be enforcers confront a proverbial target-rich environment. In combination legal and technological demand- and supply-side trends have driven the rise of transnational vigilante enforcement by human rights NGOs. Although these actions span a wide spectrum, they are genuinely autonomous, rather than being directed by governments. They are also increasingly occurring across borders, thanks to the rise of universal jurisdiction and the proliferation of international courts. This trend towards enforcement involves contestation between NGOs and governments but also competition between NGOs themselves, which has led some established groups to focus increasingly on enforcement and has served to fuel the rise of a new category of smaller NGOs formed with dedicated enforcement missions.

191. Cardona, Ortiz, and Vazquez 2018.

3

Vigilante Environmentalists

Like human rights, environmental protection has been the focus of intense transnational advocacy for many decades. From the Sahelian droughts in the 1960s and 1970s and depletion of stratospheric ozone in the 1980s to destruction of tropical forests, extinction of species, and anthropogenic climate change, NGOs have rallied to call attention to mounting global environmental crises and pressure governments to deliver solutions. In recent years, more and more NGOs have moved beyond seeking to educate, lobby, and shame governments into action to directly enforcing environmental rules themselves. Whether they are blocking supertrawlers from fishing in protected marine areas, intercepting illicitly trafficked wildlife, or suing governments and multinational corporations for their contributions to climate change, activists are increasingly taking matters into their own hands in compelling compliance with environmental law.

Observers of global governance have long recognized that environmental NGOs are crucial suppliers of environmental governance alongside states and inter-governmental organizations.[1] Throughout the post-war period (and even before) environmental NGOs have worked to mobilize public concern, produce scientific knowledge, and advise governments and international organizations during treaty negotiations. As a result, much international environmental legislation bears the direct imprint of NGOs. Starting in the 1990s, NGOs have launched private accreditation schemes and forged

---

1. Raustiala 1997; Keck and Sikkink 1998; Andonova 2010; Green 2014; Green and Colgan 2013; Hale 2020.

partnerships with governments and private corporations to develop and implement environmental standards and 'best practices'.[2] Great strides have been made in enlisting nonstate actors as partners in environmental protection programs worldwide through assigning them formal roles of implementation and monitoring.[3] But while these expanding governance roles have attracted much attention,[4] the role of NGOs in enforcing environmental rules has been largely overlooked.

This is surprising given the pervasiveness of transnational environmental enforcement. Compared to NGOs working on human rights and anti-corruption, environmental NGOs have engaged in a broader range of hard and soft methods of enforcement. Perhaps more so than in other domains enforcement has taken a cross-border form, involving NGOs based in one country directly enforcing rules in another, or international NGOs helping victims seek redress for local environmental damages caused by multinational corporations—often by petitioning courts in jurisdictions separate from where the damage occurred.[5] The wide range and volume of transnational environmental enforcement make this domain a prism and a crucial laboratory for exploring wider questions concerning the evolution of transnational enforcement.

The chapter surveys a spectrum of approaches to transnational environmental enforcement: from direct action and litigation to more indirect methods of surveillance and evidence gathering; from the global oceans, rainforests, and wildlife markets to the courtroom. Given the wealth of examples in this domain, cases are chosen with a specific view to showcasing the breadth of environmental enforcement strategies and to illustrate the development of increasingly sophisticated and specialized enforcement tools in line with the evolution of legal frameworks and new technologies.

As in the case of human rights, transnational environmental enforcement has been driven by a proliferation of international legal frameworks. Since the first global Earth Summit in Stockholm in 1972 more than 1,300 multilateral and 2,300 bilateral environmental agreements have been signed,[6] making environmental policy the densest area of global rule-making after international trade.[7] A 2019 United Nations Environment Report declared:

---

2. Cashore, Auld, and Newsom 2004; Najam, Papa, and Taiyab 2006.

3. Raustiala 1997; Najam, Papa, and Taiyab 2006; Abbott, Green, and Keohane 2016.

4. E.g., Betsill and Corell 2001; Andonova and Mitchell 2010; Betsill 2014.

5. Gwynn 2018.

6. International Environmental Agreements Database Project (https://iea.uoregon.edu).

7. Susskind and Ali 2014.

'we now have "treaty congestion"'.[8] Meanwhile, the membership of major multilateral environmental agreements, like the Convention on International Trade in Endangered Species of Wild Fauna and Flora (CITES), has expanded to become almost universal.[9] Yet state enforcement has largely failed to keep up with expanding commitments. Governments often lack motivation to enforce rules on transboundary environmental issues given limited pressure from domestic constituencies.[10] Environmental crimes frequently cross borders, whereas state enforcement agencies are limited to operating within national jurisdictions.[11]

As the enforcement gap has widened, developments in law have created new opportunities for transnational enforcement. First, there has been a sharp increase in the number of environmental dispute settlement mechanisms around the world.[12] Second, whereas international courts have traditionally been limited to inter-state disputes, many have today expanded participation rights for private actors, granting environmental NGOs the right to intervene on behalf of specific third parties or 'general public interests'. Third, both national and regional courts show a growing willingness to admit cases brought by environmental NGOs even when the crime, victims, and perpetrators are located in foreign jurisdictions.

Along with developments in law, vigilante environmental enforcement has also been stimulated by advances in technology which reduce the costs and risks to NGOs of monitoring compliance in remote areas. These range from commercial satellites to infrared camera traps, and from forensic DNA analysis to big-data analysis of illegal wildlife trade. While NGOs have long played a role as environmental watchdogs at the national level, pursuing states and corporate actors through the courts, these combined developments in law and technology have provided the means for an increasingly direct and increasingly cross-boundary approach to environmental enforcement.

The final section of the chapter considers why environmental NGOs take different stances towards enforcement. Recent decades have seen an explosive growth in the number of transnational environmental groups. As environmental NGOs have multiplied, both financial resources and strategic room for maneuver have become tighter, encouraging strategic

---

8. Also Najam, Papa, and Taiyab 2006: 46; International Union for Conservation of Nature 2008.

9. Mitchell et al. 2020.

10. McCormick 2010.

11. United Nations Environment Programme 2016.

12. Alter 2011a; Preston 2016.

differentiation.[13] Perhaps more so than in other policy areas, environmental enforcement can be politically costly given the contested nature of many environmental norms.[14] For NGOs that have invested heavily in gaining access to decision makers and/or in cultivating an image as trusted sources of scientific knowledge, vigilantism may be damaging to their broader agenda. For groups that lack such resources, however, enforcement can be a means to eschew expensive 'inside' lobbying strategies or costly publicity campaigns in favour of more direct action that allows them to achieve something with their scarce resources. As larger groups swallow up a growing portion of available funding and political attention, many new groups have been founded with a specific and increasingly specialized focus on enforcement.

The Environmental Enforcement Gap

Although environmental awareness has grown since the 1960s and 1970s, a significant gap remains between states' commitments to environmental protection and actual results. Since 1980, 35 percent of the world's mangroves have been lost and more than a quarter of coral reefs destroyed.[15] Three decades after 168 countries signed the Biodiversity Convention at the Rio Earth Summit in 1992, the species extinction rate remains 1,000 times higher than what would be occurring without human impact.[16] Aggregate carbon emissions continue to rise, fuelling destructive climate change. In short, despite growing awareness of environmental problems, rapid ecological degradation continues globally.[17]

The environmental enforcement gap exists not only in terms of spiralling ecological destruction but also relative to an expanding body of law which today regulates everything from hunting, fishing, and logging to air pollution, pesticide use, and climate change. Compared to human rights, international environmental law is of relatively recent origin. Most accounts of treaty-based environmental cooperation begin with the 1972 Stockholm Earth Summit.[18] Prior to this date, during the 1950s and 1960s, limited international agreements were adopted on narrow issues such as conserving

13. Eilstrup-Sangiovanni 2019.
14. Eilstrup-Sangiovanni and Phelps Bondaroff 2014.
15. Sanderman et al. 2018; https://wwf.panda.org/our_work/oceans/coasts/coral_reefs/coral_threats.cfm/.
16. Pimm et al. 2014.
17. Najam, Papa, and Taiyab 2006: 45.
18. Berny and Rootes 2018; Hale 2020.

specific species of commercial value (e.g., whales and fur seals) or preventing oil pollution. The Stockholm summit broadened the agenda by creating the United Nations Environment Programme (UNEP) as the leading global authority in environmental agenda setting and by delivering the first environmental framework convention: the CITES. This was soon followed by other 'flagship' conventions on migratory species (1979), long-range transboundary air pollution (1979), tropical timber (1983), and depletion of the ozone layer (1985).

Twenty years after Stockholm, the 1992 Earth Summit in Rio presented another watershed moment by introducing the Convention on Biological Diversity, the UN Framework Convention on Climate Change (UNFCCC), and the Convention to Combat Desertification and by creating another focal institution for global environmental cooperation: the UN Commission on Sustainable Development. Fast-forward to 2002 and the Johannesburg Summit on Sustainable Development produced agreement among governments to restore the world's depleted fisheries and galvanize the private sector by introducing some three hundred 'Type-II Partnership Initiatives' featuring collaboration between governments, the private sector, and civil society actors.[19] At the UN Conference on Sustainable Development in 2012 governments agreed to further expand cooperation with the private sector through new public-private partnership initiatives aimed to strengthen implementation of inter-governmental commitments.[20]

Since the turn of the century, the fastest-growing area of international environmental law has been climate change. During the 1990s, governments adopted two legal frameworks as the scaffold of the international climate change regime: the UNFCCC (1992), which serves as a framework forum for climate dialogue and cooperation, and the Kyoto Protocol (1997), which sets out legally binding emission reductions for developed countries. Since then, the number of national and international climate change laws has increased from just 60 in 1997 to more than 2,100 in 2021—a thirty-five-fold increase.[21] This body of international law forms a substantial basis for transnational litigation.[22]

Despite growing commitments to environmental sustainability, however, the gap between states' stated ambitions and actual behaviour continues to

19. As opposed to 'Type I Partnerships', which are the traditional outcome of international treaties.

20. https://sustainabledevelopment.un.org/index.php?menu=1500-

21. Grantham Research Institute on Climate Change and the Environment 2021.

22. Setzer and Nachmany 2018; Bouwer and Setzer 2020.

be a concern. According to a recent UNEP report, governments often lack the desire to implement environmental laws due to the potentially negative impact on domestic livelihoods, lands, properties, and profits. Environmental crime often carries minimal risks for criminals, as probabilities of detection are low in most countries, and penalties for violations are also low.[23]

Among barriers to enforcement UNEP and Interpol list lack of data, limited use of legislation, lack of institutional will, lack of capacity in the enforcement chain, and corruption.[24] A lack of enforcement capacity is not only a problem in so-called weak jurisdictions. A 2015 survey of environmental crime in the EU found that much such crime goes undetected due to the reticence or inefficiency of law enforcement agencies.[25] In the UK alone, public agencies tasked with enforcing environmental standards saw their funding halved between 2009 and 2019 and their staff reduced by one-third, resulting in an 80 percent reduction in prosecutions over the period.[26]

The continuing gap between the formal obligations accepted by states on the one hand, and the limited willingness and capacity to enforce environmental rules on the other hand, has led to treaty fatigue among many NGOs.[27] While many groups continue to lobby for stronger legislation, others have shifted their focus to improving compliance with rules already in place. As Wietse van de Werf, founder of the small maritime conservation NGO The Black Fish, puts it: 'We have all the laws we need. What we need to do is to ensure that they are actually respected'.[28] Paul Watson of the Sea Shepherd Conservation Society agrees: 'The oceans are dying in our lifetime and it's not for want of laws and regulations. The problem is enforcement. Governments are not enforcing the laws, so we have to'.[29]

Legal Drivers of Environmental Enforcement

Along with exasperation at the widening enforcement gap, vigilante environmental enforcement is stimulated by legal and technological developments which facilitate intervention by NGOs, as well as by growing NGO

23. United Nations Environment Programme 2019; United Nations Environment Programme 2016.

24. United Nations Environment Programme 2019; United Nations Environment Programme 2016.

25. Europol 2015.

26. Rose 2020.

27. International Union for Conservation of Nature 2008.

28. Black Fish interview 2015.

29. *Telegraph* 2009.

competition which encourages organizational differentiation. This section explains how recent developments in law have enabled new NGO enforcement strategies. These range from autonomous evidence gathering to support court proceedings to a sharp rise in legal cases brought by NGOs against corporations and governments before domestic and international courts.[30] A crucial driver of the surge in environmental litigation is changes to procedural law which expand NGOs' access to courts in many jurisdictions. Also important is the growth in international judicial forums with the power to resolve environmental disputes,[31] along with national courts' growing willingness to accept jurisdiction for extra-territorial environmental offences and, more broadly, to cite international law in domestic rulings.[32]

WIDER ACCESS TO COURTS

To sue either a government or a corporation for an environmental offence an NGO must be entitled to bring a case in court—it must have 'standing'. Rules governing standing traditionally require that claimants can demonstrate a direct interest in a case, for example by showing that they have been (or may be) personally harmed by the (in)action being challenged in court. This can present a significant hurdle for plaintiffs in environmental cases concerning climate change or transboundary pollution, which often involve diffuse harms to large numbers and where cross-border effects of pollutants can make it hard to link an injury to a particular defendant's actions. For example, in 2016 a case filed by Senior Women for Climate Protection against the Swiss Federal Environment Department for failing to protect fundamental rights to life and health through inadequate climate action was thrown out, as the court ruled that senior women are not specifically affected by climate change and that the group therefore lacked standing to have their case heard.[33]

Rules restricting standing remain a significant barrier to environmental litigation in many countries. However, recent procedural reforms mean that standing is increasingly granted to NGOs as an act of law across many jurisdictions.[34] In a European context, the Aarhus Convention which came into force in 2001 grants participatory rights to private individuals and groups

30. Humby 2018; Saiger 2020; Peel and Osofsky 2018; Bouwer and Setzer 2020.
31. Ulfstein 2009; Preston 2016.
32. Boisson de Chazournes 2004; Ulfstein 2009; Harrison 2014; Gwynn 2018.
33. https://klimaseniorinnen.ch/english/; Climate Change Litigation Databases 2016.
34. Peters 2009; Tallberg 2015; United Nations Environment Programme 2019.

to challenge violations of national environmental laws.[35] The Convention also expands rights for NGOs to institute challenges against acts of EU institutions, bodies, or agencies, both via the Court of Justice of the European Union and via member states' courts.[36] On this basis, many European countries have widened access for NGOs to engage in domestic litigation on behalf of under-represented third parties or general 'public interests'.

The Aarhus Convention has played a crucial role in giving teeth to existing environmental law across Europe. Two pillars of conservation law were introduced across EU member states prior to 2001: the Birds Directive of 1979 and the Habitats Directive of 1992. Given the limited enforcement powers of the European Commission, however, member states were left to enforce rules at the national level, raising the question of how to hold national governments accountable for non-compliance with EU environmental laws.[37] While in theory citizens could bring cases in domestic courts to enforce EU directives, in practice, restrictive standing rules mitigated against this in many member states.[38] By granting participatory rights to private actors the Aarhus Convention unleashed a tsunami of judicial review cases where NGOs have asked national courts to review the legality of governments' administrative decisions in light of European law.[39]

For example, in 2013 the Swedish Society for Nature Conservation successfully challenged the Swedish government in the Stockholm Administrative Court over a 2010 law allowing Sweden's Environmental Protection Agency to license the hunting of wolves in violation of the EU Habitats Directive.[40] An analogous case was brought in 2017 by the Association for Nature Conservation Tapiola against the Finnish government.[41] In 2017 the NGO France Nature Environment successfully filed a suit in the Administrative Court of Pau against the Prefect of Hautes-Pyrénées for permitting bird hunting in violation of the EU Birds Directive.[42] The same year Friends of the Earth won a case before the Northern Ireland Court of Appeal to stop sand-dredging on Lough Neagh, an area protected under the EU's

---

35. Officially the United Nations Economic Commission for Europe Convention on Access to Information, Public Participation in Decision-making and Access to Justice in Environmental Matters.

36. Popoola 2017; European Commission 2019.

37. Goodman and Connelly 2018.

38. European Commission 2019; Goodman and Connelly 2018.

39. Ryngaert 2013; Goodman and Connelly 2018; Gwynn 2018; Peel and Osofsky 2018.

40. Epstein and Darpö 2013.

41. ClientEarth 2019.

42. France Nature Environment 2017.

Birds Directive.[43] In addition to working through domestic courts, NGOs increasingly also use regional courts to challenge national and EU policy. For example, in 2016 ClientEarth successfully brought a case before the EU Court of Justice to force the Polish government to stop logging in Białowieża Forest, a protected area under the EU Habitats Directive.[44]

Wider opportunities for NGOs to sue governments for environmental offences are not limited to Europe. So-called 'open standing' provisions which allow any person to seek remedy for violations of environmental law without having to prove direct personal harm from such violations exist in many non-European countries including Australia, Canada, the Philippines, Ecuador, and Uganda.[45] Overall, as of 2017, 117 countries worldwide provided for public participation in environmental laws, and 46 countries provided for public participation in laws governing public administration, which may have environmental impacts.[46]

In addition to more permissive rules, legal scholars also point to a change in courts' interpretations of rules governing standing. In the pioneering case *Stitching Urgenda v. The Netherlands Government* (2015), the Hague District Court granted an NGO, Urgenda, standing to sue the Dutch government for its inadequate CO_2 emission reduction targets. Urgenda argued that this failure violated the government's constitutional 'duty to protect' and 'to provide a healthy environment', as well as the right to life and well-being enshrined in the European Convention on Human Rights (ECHR).[47] In a landmark decision, the court allowed the case to go forward based on Urgenda's specific aim of 'promoting sustainability' and on the right to defend the rights of future generations. In 2018, after the government appealed the verdict, the Dutch Supreme Court confirmed Urgenda's standing, citing specifically the Aarhus Convention and the ECHR:

> Urgenda . . . represents the interests of the residents of the Netherlands with respect to whom the obligation [to take appropriate measures against climate change] applies. After all, the interests of these residents are sufficiently similar and therefore lend themselves to being pooled. . . . Especially in cases involving environmental interests, such as the present case, legal protection through such pooling of interests is highly

---

43. Friends of the Earth 2017.
44. https://www.clientearth.org/saving-bialowieza/; Neslen 2018.
45. International Bar Association London 2020.
46. United Nations Environment Programme 2019.
47. www.ibanet.org/Climate-Change-Model-Statute.aspx.

efficient and effective. This is also in line with Article 9(3) in conjunction with Article 2(5) of the [Aarhus Convention], which guarantees interest groups access to justice in order to challenge violations of environmental law, and in line with Article 13 of the European Convention on Human Rights.[48]

In addition to confirming a wider notion of standing the Dutch Supreme Court's decision to allow the case is illustrative of a growing willingness by courts to consider cases of environmental harms in light of human rights laws, as we discuss in the following section, and is broadly credited with having fuelled a wave of similar cases around the world.[49]

Access to environmental justice for private individuals and groups has also been expanded by developments in constitutional law. Since the 1990s, many countries have introduced constitutional rights to a clean and healthy environment.[50] Like the Dutch Civil Code, the constitutions of Ecuador, Kenya, India, Nigeria, Norway, and South Africa all contain clauses which oblige governments to protect and promote a clean environment.[51] For example, Greenpeace's lawsuit against the Norwegian government for its contributions to climate change (*Greenpeace v. Norway* [2017]) was based on a clause (Article 112) inserted in Norway's constitution in 2014 which establishes a 'right to an environment that is conducive to health and to a natural environment whose productivity and diversity are maintained'. In Latin America the Ecuadorian and Bolivian constitutions (enacted in 2008 and 2009, respectively) present a 'social contract' between humans and nature whereby nature itself becomes entitled to rights.[52] As of 2015, the constitutions of more than 76 countries explicitly guaranteed environmental rights,[53] increasing opportunities for NGOs to bring public interest environmental lawsuits.[54]

---

48. European Convention on Human Rights (www.ibanet.org/Climate-Change-Model-Statute.aspx_). In practice *Urgenda* was facilitated by the Dutch Civil Code (Art 3:305a), which allows anyone to establish a foundation mandated to protect a public interest. However, by confirming NGOs' standing under the Aarhus Convention to challenge national climate change policy, and by recognizing the relevance of international human rights law for environmental litigation, the Dutch Supreme Court's ruling fuelled a wave of similar cases across Europe and beyond. Mission 2020; International Bar Association London 2020.

49. Boyle 2012, 2018; Burns 2016; Peel and Osofsky 2018.

50. Burns 2016.

51. Gwynn 2018; International Bar Association London 2020.

52. Burns 2016; International Bar Association London 2020.

53. Burns 2016.

54. Boyle 2012; Setzer and Nachmany 2018; Bouwer and Setzer 2020.

The widening of judicial access for environmental NGOs is neither a universal nor an irrevocable trend. NGOs are frequently denied standing to bring cases to court. Cases are often struck down for lack of evidence of a direct link between a defendant's actions and environmental harms or due to a lack of suitable remedies to redress such harms. Nevertheless, as we illustrate in following sections, environmental groups are becoming increasingly adept at navigating national and international legal systems, choosing the most accommodating venues in which to bring cases.

THE 'HUMAN RIGHTS TURN'

As we have already alluded to, a remarkable development in environmental enforcement is the growing trend of linking environmental harms to international human rights law.[55] An early example is the 2005 Inuit Circumpolar Petition brought against the United States before the Inter-American Commission on Human Rights by the Center for International Environmental Law and Earthjustice together with the chair of the Inuit Circumpolar Conference, Sheila Watt-Cloutier.[56] The petition claimed that, as the largest contributor to global greenhouse gas emissions, the United States was responsible for global warming in the Arctic, which violated the Inuit's human rights and endangered their survival.[57] Although the court declined to proceed with the petition citing insufficient evidence, the case helped to establish a link between climate change and human rights law, and thereby opened a new avenue for holding governments responsible for greenhouse gas emissions.

More recently this link has been strengthened by an increasingly wide interpretation of international human rights instruments. In an advisory opinion in 2018 the Inter-American Court of Human Rights interpreted the American Convention on Human Rights to recognize a human right to a healthy environment and a corresponding duty of states to prevent significant environmental harm to individuals inside or outside their territory.[58] The European Court of Human Rights has held that while the European Convention on Human Rights does not enshrine an explicit right to a healthy environment, 'the exercise of certain Convention rights may be

55. Boyle 2012, 2016; Burns 2016; Peel and Osofsky 2018.

56. http://www.inuitcircumpolar.com/inuit-petition-inter-american-commission-on-human-rights-to-oppose-climate-change-caused-by-the-united-states-of-america.html.

57. Earthjustice 2005.

58. Inter-American Court on Human Rights 2017; Banda 2018.

undermined by the existence of harm to the environment' and therefore 'public authorities may be obliged to take measures to ensure that human rights are not seriously affected by adverse environmental factors'.[59] The inclusion of the right to a 'satisfactory environment conducive to develop-ment' in the African Charter on Human Rights also widens the scope to seek redress for environmental harms citing human rights.[60]

Seizing upon these opportunities, environmental NGOs have launched a cascade of rights-based claims before national courts.[61] In 2005 represen-tatives for the Iwherekan Community in the Niger Delta sued the Nigerian government and Shell in Nigeria's Federal High Court for harms caused by gas-flaring by oil companies.[62] Siding with the plaintiffs, the court ruled that gas-flaring violates fundamental rights of life and dignity protected by the African Charter on Human and Peoples' Rights. Human rights principles also form the basis for a string of climate lawsuits against European govern-ments.[63] In 2014 Klimaatzaak (a Belgian NGO) and 9,000 Belgian citizens sued the Belgian government for failing in its duty of care under the Belgian constitution and the European Convention on Human Rights through insuf-ficient efforts to combat climate change. The claimants have demanded that the authorities reduce greenhouse gas emissions by at least 55 percent of 1990 levels by 2030. Since the case began in 2014 more than 60,000 Belgian citizens have joined as co-plaintiffs, making it the biggest court case in the country's legal history. Similar cases have been launched in Austria, France, Germany, Holland, Ireland, Norway, and Sweden.[64]

The 'human rights turn' also widens opportunities for environmental litigation before international courts. As discussed in chapter 2, it is widely accepted that states may be held responsible for human rights violations beyond their territory. Linking environmental harms to human rights thus entails a recognition of state responsibility for environmental harms abroad[65] and widens the venues in which redress can be sought from national courts to regional and international human rights courts and tribunals. Among regional bodies, the European Court of Human Rights has issued by far the most extensive judgements on the linkages between individuals' human

---

59. Council of Europe 2012: 8; European Court of Human Rights 2020.
60. Peel and Osofsky 2018.
61. Setzer and Higham 2021: 32.
62. *Gbemre v. Shell Petroleum Development Company Nigeria Ltd and Others.*
63. Mission 2020.
64. Peel and Osofsky 2018; Mission 2020; Sabin Center for Climate Change Law 2021.
65. Boyle 2012.

rights and environmental harms,[66] but regional human rights courts in the Americas and Africa also play host to a growing number of cases alleging violations of human rights resulting from adverse environmental factors.

A recent example involves a case brought by Sakala Community Centre for Peaceful Alternatives before the Inter-American Commission on Human Rights on behalf of Six Children of Cité Soleil, claiming that health harms from toxic trash disposals in their residential districts violates Haitian children's human rights. In a European context, the 'People's Climate Case' is being brought in the European Court of Justice by Climate Action Network Europe on behalf of ten European families.[67] The plaintiffs are suing the European Parliament and the EU Council for allowing unacceptable levels of greenhouse gas emissions to continue until 2030, thereby failing to heed the customary no harm principle in international law.[68] Another illustrative case was brought in September 2020 by the NGO Portuguese Youth before the European Court of Human Rights against thirty-three member states of the Council of Europe. The complaint alleges that the governments' inaction on climate change is likely to result in future violations of the children's human rights under the European Convention on Human Rights and seeks an order requiring them to take more aggressive action.[69] Environmental litigation cases also come before international courts. One example is the pending case against the Australian government before the United Nations Human Rights Committee. The plaintiffs, eight Torres Strait Islanders, argue that Australia's failure to mitigate and adapt to climate changes constitutes a violation of the government's obligations under the International Covenant on Civil and Political Rights.[70]

These are just a few examples of the fast-growing volume of lawsuits before domestic and international courts seeking to link environmental harms to international human rights violations in the wake of the Dutch *Urgenda* case, providing a vivid illustration of how NGOs have moved to take advantage of new legal opportunities.[71] While the majority of rights-based claims are brought against governments, a growing number are also brought against corporations, as we discuss in subsequent sections.

66. Council of Europe 2012.

67. https://peoplesclimatecase.caneurope.org.

68. Setzer 2018.

69. *Youth for Climate Justice v. Austria et al. 2020.*

70. Petition of Torres Strait Islanders to the UN Human Rights Committee Alleging Violations Stemming from Australia's Inaction on Climate Change, 2019.

71. Setzer and Byrnes 2020: 1; Setzer and Higham 2021: 32.

THE PARIS AGREEMENT AND CLIMATE CHANGE LITIGATION

The effects of changing legal opportunity structures for NGO enforcement are perhaps nowhere more visible than in regard to climate change. As already discussed, the proliferation of national climate change laws and the link to international human rights law have widened the basis for holding governments responsible for CO_2 emissions. Equally important, however, has been states' acceptance of international obligations under the 1992 UN Framework Convention on Climate Change (UNFCCC) and the 2015 Paris Agreement on Climate Change.[72]

As a non-binding accord the Paris Agreement acts not so much as a direct legal basis for climate litigation but rather as a 'force multiplier' for lawsuits based on national legislation and international human rights law. It does so, first, by establishing benchmarks for acceptable state behaviour and, second, by shifting standards of scientific evidence. Although the Paris Agreement establishes a clear goal of limiting global warming to below 1.5–2 degrees Celsius compared to pre-industrial levels, it does not oblige governments to meet this goal or stipulate how they must do so. Instead, each state party is obliged to formulate its own mitigation commitments at the national level. In turn, this means that domestic courts are often called upon to interpret the agreement.[73]

Thanks to the momentum created by the Paris Agreement, climate change litigation is growing rapidly worldwide. The first such case was brought in the United States in 1986; the first non-U.S. case was tried in Australia in 1994. Today there are 1,387 on-going or concluded cases in the United States alone and 454 cases involving 39 other countries and 13 international or regional courts or tribunals.[74] Of these cases, 843 were filed between 1986 and 2014 while 1,006 have been filed in the six years since 2015, demonstrating the accelerating impact of the Paris Agreement.[75] Cases are targeting a variety of alleged offenders, from governments to private sector and financial actors.

The majority of climate change cases (about three-quarters) have been brought against governments (often by NGOs) to establish the unlawfulness of specific administrative policies and actions that fail to take into account international obligations. An illustrative example involves a small NGO, Plan

---

72. Bouwer 2020; Bouwer and Setzer 2020; International Bar Association London 2020.
73. Saiger 2020: 44.
74. http://climatecasechart.com (30 March 2021); Setzer and Higham 2021.
75. Setzer and Higham 2021: 9–10.

B, which sued the UK government for failing to consider its obligations under the Paris Agreement when authorizing a third runway at Heathrow.[76] In a similar case the South African NGO Earthlife successfully challenged the government's authorization of a project to construct a coal-fired power station by arguing that failure to duly consider South Africa's commitments under the UNFCCC and the Paris Agreement made the authorization unlawful.[77] Comparable cases have been filed in France by Oxfam and other French NGOs, as well as in Austria to prevent the government from permitting another runway at Vienna's main airport.[78] A common element in these cases is that domestic courts are called upon to rule on the duty of competent national authorities to interpret domestic administrative law in light of the Paris Agreement's long-term temperature stabilization goal.[79]

A second way in which the Paris Agreement has boosted transnational climate litigation is by clarifying and shifting standards of evidence. Successful climate change litigation often turns on complex scientific and technical issues which can present insurmountable barriers for individual claimants.[80] By mandating governments to publish evidence on climate change, international climate accords provide a source of public evidence that can be referenced by NGOs before the courts. As noted by the International Bar Association: 'Being required to prove scientific matters in every climate claim . . . should be unnecessary in government-related proceedings when the position has been recorded in, for example, the Paris Agreement or Reports of the Intergovernmental Panel on Climate Change (IPCC) . . . IPCC assessment reports have been recognized as "the most authoritative sources available for information on climate change"'.[81]

As stated, the majority of climate change cases are filed against governments. Yet private corporations have also come under fire despite not being party to the UNFCCC or Paris Agreement. In April 2019 seven environmental and human rights organizations in the Netherlands and 17,000 individual co-plaintiffs filed suit against Royal Dutch Shell for its failure to align its

76. *Plan B Earth and Others v. Secretary of State for Transport*, 2020.

77. *Earthlife Africa Johannesburg v. Minister of Environmental Affairs & Others*, Case No. 65662/16: http://cer.org.za/wp-content/uploads/2017/03/Judgment-Earthlife-Thabametsi -Final-06-03-2017.pdf; https://climate-laws.org/cclow/geographies/south-africa/litigation_cases /earthlife-africa-johannesburg-v-minister-of-environmental-affairs-others.

78. Fältbiologerna 2016; Brun 2019.

79. Saiger 2020.

80. International Bar Association London 2020.

81. Ibid.

business model with the goals of the Paris Agreement.[82] The plaintiffs asked Shell to adjust its business model to keep the average global temperature rise below 1.5 degrees Celsius as recommended by the UN's Intergovernmental Panel on Climate Change, arguing that by failing to do so, Shell is flouting its own public commitment to the Paris Agreement and international human rights conventions. In May 2021 the District Court of the Hague ordered Shell to reduce its CO_2 emissions by 45 percent from 2019 levels by 2030 as a way to secure that global warming stays below 1.5C. This marks the first time a major energy company has been held legally responsible for its contribution to global climate change and ordered to reduce emissions.[83]

A similar case seeking to hold a company accountable for insufficient climate action was filed in January 2020 by five French NGOs and fourteen local authorities against fossil fuel giant Total.[84] Brought under France's 2017 Duty of Vigilance Law, which requires French companies and their foreign subsidiaries to prevent risks to the environment and human rights as a result of their activities, the case illustrates how NGOs use the Paris Agreement to bolster their claims against state and corporate targets. Sandra Cossart, director of French NGO Sherpa, which is among the plaintiffs (and a pioneer in anti-corruption enforcement), says: 'It's really a paradigm shift. . . . This is the first legislation anywhere in the world that pierces the corporate veil'. The main objective 'is to compel Total to adopt a climate strategy consistent with the Paris Agreement'.[85] At the time of writing there are at least 33 on-going climate cases worldwide against major fossil fuel companies.[86]

ENFORCING ENVIRONMENTAL RULES THROUGH CIVIL LAW

Whereas public international law forms the basis for many recent climate change lawsuits, private international law—law applicable to private relationships containing a foreign element—provides another important avenue for transnational enforcement directed at corporations. A number of high-profile cases against major energy companies are sought in tort, for example, public nuisance, private nuisance, and negligence.[87] Procedural rules typically dictate that actions under civil law must be brought in the

82. *Milieudefensie v. Shell,* 2019; Kottasová 2019.
83. Setzer and Higham 2021: 32.
84. Friends of the Earth 2019; Reuters Staff 2019.
85. Vetter 2020.
86. Setzer and Higham 2021: 28.
87. Setzer and Byrnes 2020.

country where the damage occurs. However, liability may transcend borders if actions by a subsidiary can be connected with its parent company in a different jurisdiction or if the action itself has cross-border impacts.[88]

Barriers to transnational tort litigation are generally lower in civil law systems than in common law jurisdictions.[89] For example, the U.S. Supreme Court in 2013 restricted extra-territorial application of the Alien Torts Statute, preventing victims of tortious actions abroad from seeking redress in U.S. federal courts (see discussion in chapter 2). Nevertheless, creative uses of tort law have found ways around such barriers, for example, by framing a case involving a subsidiary of a multinational corporation as one of wrongful conduct in a defendant's home jurisdiction. In effect, 'it is the tort of negligent supervision of a foreign subsidiary'.[90] Such strategies have enabled a range of 'foreign direct-liability' cases in which NGOs file claims on behalf of victims in country X against the parent company of a multinational corporation in country Y, suing it for damages caused by its subsidiaries abroad.[91] One such case was brought by villagers in Lago Agrio in eastern Ecuador against Texaco Petroleum in a U.S. federal court for water pollution, soil contamination, and deforestation caused by oil exploitation.[92] When the U.S. court refused to hear the case, the plaintiffs instead brought a class action lawsuit in Ecuador against Chevron (of which Texaco became a subsidiary in 2001), which led to the company being ordered to pay $8.6 billion in damages.[93] In the end Texaco never paid the damages, so the case was ultimately a disappointment. It nevertheless highlights the transnational nature of vigilante enforcement and shows how creative use of law by NGOs can widen the scope of corporate liability.

European courts generally take a more accommodating stance on torts by habitually accepting jurisdiction for cases involving foreign subsidiaries of corporations domiciled in the EU.[94] For example, Popoola documents the frequent transfer of environmental lawsuits from Nigerian to European courts to circumvent legal obstacles at the national level where litigation against multinational companies is often blocked by high legal costs and restrictive standing rules.[95] Two examples illustrate the trend. In November 2008 four

---

88. Gwynn 2018.
89. International Bar Association London 2020; Setzer and Higham 2021.
90. Archer 2020: 109.
91. Archer 2020; Boyle 2018; Gwynn 2018.
92. *Aguinda v. ChevronTexaco.*
93. Gwynn 2018: 11.
94. Gwynn 2018; Ulfstein 2009: 137; Boyle 2018.
95. Popoola 2017.

Nigerian individuals and Friends of the Earth filed claims against Royal Dutch Shell and its Nigerian subsidiary, Shell Petroleum Development Company, before the District Court in The Hague where Shell has its global headquarters. Since this was a tort case, the court held that the applicable law was Nigerian tort law.[96] In a related case, Akpan, a Nigerian farmer, and Milieudefensie, a Dutch NGO, filed a claim against Shell for damages caused by oil spills in Nigeria between 2006 and 2007.[97] Both cases were successful, meaning that a Dutch court found Royal Dutch Shell liable for environmental harms caused by its Nigerian subsidiary under Nigerian law.

In another tort case, Saúl Luciano Lliuya, a Peruvian farmer, brought a civil case against RWE, a German electric utilities company, in a regional court in Essen in 2016 with the support of the NGO Germanwatch in respect to environmental damage incurred in Peru.[98] Lliuya sued RWE for a financial contribution to safety measures to reduce the risk to his land from flooding from a glacial lagoon as a result of anthropogenic climate changes to which he claimed the company had contributed. Lliuya based his claim on paragraph 1004 of the German Civil Code, which deals with interference and damage to property.[99] By accepting the case, the German court acknowledged that a private company can in principle be deemed responsible for its share in causing climate damages. These and similar tort claims—like the one brought by farmers in Zambia against the UK parent company of Konkola Copper Mines for water pollution[100]—demonstrate that, despite legal barriers, multinationals can successfully be held to account in their home jurisdictions for torts committed by their subsidiaries abroad.[101]

PROMISES AND PITFALLS OF ENVIRONMENTAL LITIGATION

Environmental litigation has advantages and drawbacks. When cases brought by NGOs win in court and stand up on appeal, they hold a reasonable prospect of having a direct positive impact on environmental outcomes, often delivering faster and more conclusive results than protest or advocacy.

96. For tort cases Article 4(1) of the Rome II Regulation states that 'the law applicable to a non-contractual obligation arising out of a tort/delict shall be the law of the country in which the damage occurs'.

97. *Akpan and Vereniging Milieudefensie v. Royal Dutch Shell PLC and Shell Petroleum Development Company of Nigeria Ltd.*

98. 'Saúl versus RWE (The Huaraz Case)', https://germanwatch.org/en/huaraz.

99. Setzer and Benjamin 2020.

100. *Lungowe and others v Vendata Resources Plc*, 2017.

101. Grossman 2003; Popoola 2017; Gwynn 2018: 19–20.

As Bouwer and Setzer note, cases like *Save Lamu v. NEMA* in Kenya (coal) or *Earthlife Africa Johannesburg v. Minister of Environmental Affairs and Others* (Thabametsi) in South Africa (coal) are effective because they literally prohibit the construction of high carbon infrastructure.[102] Yet far from every lawsuit against governments or corporations is successful. In 2018 an Oslo court dismissed Greenpeace's suit against the Norwegian government for issuing licenses for Arctic oil drilling, ruling that this did not breach constitutional rights to a healthy environment. Among cases that do proceed to court, many fail to deliver the hoped-for outcomes. Looking at climate cases outside the United States, 58 percent have been found to have outcomes favourable to climate change action, 33 percent unfavourable outcomes, and 9 percent no discernible likely impact.[103]

Some observers point to a high number of unsuccessful cases and warn against a backlash.[104] Others point out that even winning in court doesn't guarantee success. Despite a widespread assumption that judicial rulings will shape policy, scholars have found compliance with international court rulings tends to be patchy and slow.[105] Court-mandated emission cuts may not have the same democratic legitimacy as measures introduced through ordinary legislative procedures. As a result, governments may be reluctant to follow court orders in a cooperative fashion.[106]

Yet legal victories are not the only measure of success for NGO litigators. According to many activists, whether or not it succeeds, litigation can be an important tool to push environmental issues into a central position in legal and political discourse.[107] Similarly, litigation against private corporations can serve to directly disrupt the risk profiles of major companies.[108] Beyond potential awards of damages, litigation can have indirect financial impacts for companies through increasing premiums under liability insurance policies and negative impacts on market valuation and share prices.[109] Enforcement action may have advocacy payoffs as well. Litigation presents a way to hold governments publicly accountable for violating environmental commitments. '[We are] highlighting the huge gap between the commitments

---

102. Bouwer and Setzer 2020.
103. Setzer and Byrnes 2020.
104. Miller 2010; Mission 2020.
105. Von Staden 2018; Pérez-Liñán, Schenoni, and Morrison 2021.
106. O'Neill 2020.
107. Ibid.; Bouwer and Setzer 2020.
108. Hsu 2008.
109. Setzer and Byrnes 2020.

made in international climate agreements and our government's actions', says Serge de Gheldere of Klimaatzaak, the NGO suing the Belgian government for climate inaction.[110] By taking the battle to the courts in pursuit of binding injunctions, however, NGOs' efforts to expose enforcement gaps through litigation go far beyond traditional 'naming and shaming' strategies.

As testimony to the allure of litigation, a number of NGOs have emerged which focus exclusively on environmental enforcement through the courts. Once such group is ClientEarth, founded in 2008 by James Thornton and modelled on U.S.-based environmental litigation organizations like Earthjustice and the Natural Resources Defense Council, where Thornton previously worked.[111] Initially limited to the UK, ClientEarth now operates in London, Brussels, Warsaw, Berlin, and Beijing and has a staff of over 150 lawyers. Since its founding just over a decade ago, ClientEarth has defeated the UK government in court on three occasions for illegal levels of air pollution and launched a string of successful cases across Europe.[112] In 2017 ClientEarth was named the most effective environmental NGO in the UK by its peers,[113] eclipsing traditional heavyweights like Greenpeace, the Royal Society for the Protection of Birds, and Friends of the Earth, which tend to focus more on protest, lobbying, and mobilizing public support.[114]

ClientEarth is not alone in favouring litigation. UK-based Plan B was established with the explicit mission 'to support strategic legal action against climate change'.[115] Similar groups in other countries include the Bangladesh Environmental Lawyers Association, the World Organization for the Protection of the Environment (France), the Environmental Law Association (South Africa), and the Lawyers' Environmental Action Team (Tanzania). There are also many examples of groups traditionally focused on protest and advocacy (such as Greenpeace) embracing litigation. A good example is Both ENDS, a small NGO that seeks to promote environmental justice and human rights in developing countries. As the group explicitly states in its 'theory of change', enforcement has not been its focus thus far.[116] Nevertheless, it has recently become co-plaintiff in a lawsuit against Royal Dutch Shell, a move it explains in these terms: 'In the 30 years during which,

110. Climate Case Ireland 2018.
111. https://www.clientearth.org/what-we-do/.
112. Carrington 2016; ClientEarth 2017; Harvey 2018.
113. Miller, Cracknell, and Williams 2017: 5.
114. Berny and Rootes 2018.
115. https://planb.earth/about/.
116. Both ENDS 2019: 7.

together with partner organizations around the whole world, we have fought for climate action, we have seen that nothing has changed. . . . In our opinion, therefore, taking legal action is necessary to compel companies such as Shell to take real action'.[117]

NGO Enforcement and Technological Change

Along with developments in law, vigilante environmental enforcement has been advanced by new technologies which expand NGOs' capacities for surveillance, investigation, and evidence gathering. High-resolution remote-sensing devices, commercial satellite imagery, and supporting tools such as Geographical Information Systems enable NGOs to document environmental crimes in previously inaccessible areas. Closer to the ground commercial drones, acoustic sensors, and camera traps help to expose poachers, while advances in DNA technology allow activists to conduct detailed forensic investigations of conservation and wildlife offences, yielding evidence for court cases. Meanwhile, data mining and machine learning enable activists to identify hotspots for internet wildlife trade, for example, by building computational models that can mine hundreds of commercial sites for protected wildlife.

The following sections survey the most important technologies for vigilante enforcement of environmental law. While some of these technologies are new, others—such as camera traps and video recording—are much older but have been refined over time through organizational adaptation and a growing focus on meeting exacting standards for legal evidence. As in the domain of human rights, technological advances have given rise to, and have also sometimes been driven by, an increasingly specialized ecosystem of 'niche' NGOs that focus narrowly on technology development and adaptation. Thus, enforcement actions often see 'field-based' NGOs with long-standing expertise in an area team up with newer tech-savvy groups who supply advanced technological tools for the mission. In 'ecological' terms, technology thus fuels strategic differentiation while also encouraging collaboration and exchange.

SATELLITE IMAGERY

Perhaps the most powerful technological boost to NGO enforcement capacity has been the growing quality and declining cost of commercial satellite imagery, as discussed in the previous chapter. Many NGOs, including global

117. Both ENDS, n.d.

heavyweights like the World Wildlife Fund and Greenpeace, but also smaller groups like Imazon in Brazil, today use satellite data to document deforestation and other large-scale environmental destruction from space[118] or to expose and intervene against illegal fishing. While bespoke satellite surveillance may be possible only for larger and wealthier NGOs, many smaller groups rely on publicly available satellite imagery such as Google Earth or on crowd-sourced data from Geographic Information Systems for enforcement.

One of the first examples of large-scale environmental satellite surveillance is Global Forest Watch, an online platform established by World Resource Institute in 1997 to monitor global forests in real time.[119] Originally an NGO initiative, Global Forest Watch today provides a platform where NGOs and leading businesses in remote sensing (Airbus, DigitalGlobe, Esri, and Google) collaborate with governments and inter-governmental organizations to monitor and manage the world's forests.[120] While providing surveillance data to governments and inter-governmental organizations like UNEP, Global Forest Watch is also a crucial resource for independent monitoring and data gathering by NGOs. The platform allows users anywhere to scroll data, zoom in on any location, and visually combine a broad range of social, economic, and environmental databases. Like many similar monitoring tools, it also includes an element of crowd-sourcing via its smartphone application which allows users to share evidence on deforestation based on local observations. The data, in turn, become the basis for targeted interventions by NGO enforcers.

A similar platform focused on monitoring the world's oceans, Global Fishing Watch, was launched in 2016 by SkyTruth, a small NGO specializing in the use of high-resolution satellite imagery to monitor threats to the environment, in partnership with Oceana (another NGO) and Google. Analogous to Global Forest Watch, Global Fishing Watch strives to combat illegal fishing by providing a real-time map of industrial fishing activities via an Automatic Identification Signal (AIS) system that tracks commercial vessels anywhere in the world. While countries can restrict fishing by foreign vessels within their Exclusive Economic Zones, enforcing such restrictions requires substantial surveillance and enforcement capacity, which many states lack. Global Fishing Watch aims to improve compliance among the global fishing fleet by closing this gap. Soon after its launch in 2016 evidence provided by Global Fishing Watch analysts was used to reach a $2 million

118. Rothe and Shim 2018: 428.
119. www.globalforestwatch.org.
120. Rothe and Shim 2018.

settlement for Kiribati from the Central Pacific Fishing Company, which owned and operated a Marshalls Islands–flagged vessel shown to be fishing illegally in the Phoenix Islands Protected Area established in 2006 by the small island nation.[121]

The AIS system is discerning enough to defeat attempts at misdirection, as in August 2000 when a fleet of Chinese 'ghost ships' tampered with their automatic identification system transponders to falsely broadcast their location as being within New Zealand waters while in reality they were fishing close to a protected marine reserve near the Galapagos Islands.[122] SkyTruth broadcast the location data on its online platform, where it was picked up by a Sea Shepherd vessel which decided to check it out. When the Sea Shepherd vessel arrived, the fishing vessels took flight, leaving their illegal fishing gear behind to be confiscated by activists. The revelation raised diplomatic tensions between Beijing and Quito, Ecuador's capital, and led U.S. secretary of state Mike Pompeo to accuse China of 'illegal and unregulated over-fishing'.[123]

Like Global Forest Watch, Global Fishing Watch focuses on boosting governments' enforcement capacities. However, by making data freely available to use and interrogate, these platforms also assist NGOs in their independent enforcement efforts. The same is true of Skylight, which also uses satellite-based analytics to provide real-time visualization and alerts of illegal fishing. Developed by Vulcan (a company started in 1986 by Microsoft cofounder Paul G. Allen and Jody Allen) in collaboration with maritime NGOs, Skylight focuses specifically on enforcement of maritime laws through identifying incursions by commercial fishing vessels in or near marine-protected areas and exposing transshipments of illicit goods.[124] Along with several other high-tech conservation tools developed by Vulcan, Skylight is licensed under Creative Commons license, which permits non-commercial use and sharing of its content among conservation NGOs.

Satellites are useful not only for round-the-clock surveillance but also for evidence gathering. In 2010 SkyTruth, in partnership with Florida State University, used satellite images to document the magnitude of the oil spill caused by the Deepwater Horizon accident in the Gulf of Mexico. The group was the first to publicly challenge British Petroleum's reports of the rate of the oil spill.[125] Currently the group is working on a system that will provide

121. https://sustainability.google/progress/projects/fishing-watch/.

122. Vance 2020.

123. SkyTruth interview 2020.

124. https://skylight.global/.

125. http://skytruth.org/issues/oceans/#sthash.Kxqo8LDO.dpuf.

alerts of illegal bilge dumping, whereby ships bypass costly pollution pre-vention equipment by simply flushing the bilge water directly into the sea. SkyTruth is seeking to identify individual dumping vessels by correlating sat-ellite imagery of oily slicks with Automatic Identification System broadcasts from the ships. 'Once we have reliable data that links pollution to individual ships, we can make information freely available to actors that have the means to do something about it, either NGOs or government authorities', says the group's founder.[126]

OPEN SOURCE INTELLIGENCE: BIG-DATA INVESTIGATIONS

Along with high-resolution satellite imagery, many environmental surveil-lance tools depend on big-data analysis. To detect pairs of vessels meeting at sea, analysts at SkyTruth and Google apply machine learning algorithms to more than thirty billion Automatic Identification System messages from boats to find tell-tale signs of illicit transshipments.[127] The ability to collect, share, and analyze vast amounts of data is also vital to other types of enforce-ment tools like WildLeaks, a global 'whistleblower' platform launched in 2014 by Earth League International (ELI) to gather and evaluate anonymous information on environmental crime. Staffed by former intelligence, law enforcement, and security professionals specializing in high-tech security and defence systems, ELI styles itself as the 'First Intelligence Agency for the Planet', operating 'at the nexus of civil society and law enforcement'.[128] Rely-ing on crowd-sourcing, WildLeaks collects information on wildlife crime via an online platform that offers users full anonymity. Unlike many leaks-based websites (e.g., WikiLeaks), WildLeaks does not upload unfiltered data but verifies and evaluates information through data analysis and investigation which analysts use to prepare detailed intelligence reports for other NGOs and law enforcement agencies around the world.

ELI's intelligence-driven approach to exposing and prosecuting environ-mental crime provides a vivid illustration of how legalization has fuelled a new approach to environmental protection. As Andrea Costa, ELI's founder, explains: 'Most environmental crime is now not an environmental conserva-tion issue but a crime issue. That's what many environmental NGOs fail to grasp. They want to make it about emotions when it's about crime'.[129] Since

---

126. SkyTruth interview 2020.
127. Bladen 2018.
128. WildLeaks interview 2020; https://earthleagueinternational.org/wildleaks/.
129. WildLeaks interview 2020.

2014, ELI has launched investigative field operations in fourteen countries throughout Africa, Asia, and Latin America to uncover criminal wildlife supply chains, resulting in at least twelve arrests. In 2017, undercover investigations by ELI allowed the Thai police to arrest high-profile wildlife traffickers, while the groups' intelligence briefs on illegal fishing in Mexico 'pushed Mexican, Chinese and US authorities to crack down on the main traffickers'.[130]

Despite its stated aim of facilitating action by other NGOs by sharing 'actionable intelligence', ELI's work also highlights the challenges of NGO cooperation. Since its launch in 2014 WildLeaks has received hundreds of confidential submissions. The volume of information is so large that Costa decided to reach out to other NGOs to get involved in analysis and investigation. But, he says, 'Nobody wants to cooperate. They don't want to share visibility or credit'.[131] Cut-throat competition for donor funding creates the problem, he argues: 'Everyone wants to look as if they are in charge of a project and responsible for the results'.[132] These observations about donor visibility confirm wider findings that cooperation can leave NGOs, especially small NGOs, vulnerable by undermining their ability to attract resources.[133]

As we emphasized in chapter 2, the link between online data-gathering and data-sharing tools and increasing NGO enforcement is not so much that the technology is unprecedented, but rather that its growing sophistication and diffusion empowers ordinary individuals to supply and access information on environmental crime on an unprecedented scale. This trend facilitates decentralized enforcement through field action and prosecution. At the same time as they empower nonstate enforcers, satellite imagery and online data also support more traditional strategies of awareness-raising, information provision, and naming and shaming. Rather than favouring one strategy over another, technology is a catalyst for transnational activism generally.

GPS TRACKERS, SMARTPHONES, DNA, AND DRONES

Satellite-based surveillance and big-data analysis constitute the high end of environmental investigation tools. But NGO enforcers have also benefitted from advances in cheaper technologies such as mobile phones, infrared and thermal cameras, and commercial drones. These technologies often allow

130. https://earthleagueinternational.org/wildleaks/; https://earthleagueinternational.org/our-impact/.
131. WildLeaks interview 2020.
132. Ibid.
133. Bloodgood and Clough 2017.

less wealthy NGOs to develop innovative, targeted enforcement strategies. A good example is Paso Pacifico, a small NGO founded in 2005 to protect the Pacific Slope ecosystems of Central America. Poachers regularly steal the eggs of endangered sea turtle species that nest on Mesoamerican beaches. In response Paso Pacifico invented the InvestEGGator, an artificial sea turtle egg produced with a 3D printer which contains a covert GSM-GPS tracking device.[134] Eggs are placed in nests at high risk of poaching and, once poached, their movement can be tracked, revealing domestic and international smuggling routes.

Another example of using cheap technologies to devise local enforcement solutions is the Instant Detect Program, a wildlife threat monitoring system developed by the Zoological Society London in cooperation with the Kenya Wildlife Service. Combining low-power sensors, camera traps, and military-grade acoustic sensors, Instant Detect provides early warning of poaching in protected wildlife areas. Animals' movements and poachers' guns and knives trigger the system's hidden metal and acoustic detectors, which activate a camera camouflaged in a bush. Alerts are sent via radio to a base station and then via a communications satellite to park rangers so they can respond immediately to threats.[135] In a parallel project, the Zoological Society has worked with scientists since 2017 to develop underwater acoustic sensors for detecting illegal fishing vessels in remote archipelagos and coral lagoons within the British Indian Ocean Territory.[136]

Vigilante environmental enforcers also make use of everyday technologies such as smartphones. Planet Indonesia uses a simple mobile app to allow users to easily and inconspicuously collect evidence of illegal trade in Indonesian bird markets. While pretending to send a text, users can collect standardized data on species, price, and origin of bird species which are collected in a central database and shared with enforcement authorities. Similar apps are used by indigenous groups in Cambodia to defend against illegal logging, habitat destruction, and poaching.[137] Cheap to operate and posing low risks to investigators, such widely available technologies allow local groups to fight back against organized illegal wildlife trade.

DNA analysis is yet another low-cost technology in the tool kit of vigilante enforcers. The small conservation NGO Bosque Antiguo protects endangered wildlife in Mexico, Guatemala, Honduras, and Costa Rica by

134. Paso Pacifico, [2021a].
135. Zoological Society London, n.d. [2021b].
136. Zoological Society London, n.d. [2021a].
137. https://preylang.net/about/plcn/.

providing DNA evidence for criminal prosecutions. International Animal Rescue also uses forensic analysis to tackle illegal animal trafficking in Indonesia.[138] Both groups collect blood samples from confiscated animals, which they analyze to identify their origin (and thus identify hot spots for poaching) and to provide evidence against poachers and traders in court. A more sophisticated DNA-testing system funded by the Paul G. Allen Family Foundation uses a shark's DNA to create a unique barcode for different species and combines this with a portable mini polymerase chain reaction (PCR) testing device to allow instant identification of shark species. While wildlife forensics tools like DNA barcoding are widely used by customs officers to detect illicit wildlife trade, the PCR test offers a quick and reliable tool that can be used by activists away from the laboratory.[139]

Lastly, wildlife conservation groups have benefitted greatly from declining costs of commercial drones. Small NGOs like the Cobra Collective and Conservation International use 'eco-drones' to detect environmental crime and collect evidence for use in court.[140] More broadly, a growing number of environmental NGOs—from small, specialized enforcement groups like the Wildlife Justice Commission to global titans like the World Wildlife Fund—work directly with rangers around the world to build technologies that deliver real-time alerts of poaching activity, using drones, remote sensing, acoustic recording devices, and simple on-the-ground camera traps. As we discuss in a following section on direct-action enforcement, such alarm systems often become the basis for direct interventions by NGOs seeking to make up for insufficient enforcement capacity among official rangers.

ENFORCEMENT TECHNOLOGY AS A NICHE

Technology use by most NGOs is growing. However, recent years have seen the emergence of a new type of NGO that specializes narrowly in enforcement technology. Conservation Drones, a small Swiss non-profit founded in 2012, specializes in developing low-cost drones for use by conservation groups in developing countries.[141] SoarOcean uses commercial drone technology to build aerial monitoring platforms for maritime conservation, while TRACE promotes the use of forensic science in the investigation of wildlife

---

138. https://www.internationalanimalrescue.org/about-us.
139. Cardeñosa et al. 2018.
140. Gommers 2015.
141. Conservation Drones interview 2020; https://conservationdrones.org/.

crime.[142] Other groups in this niche include Wildlife Protection Solutions, which specializes in 'use [of] technology for the conservation of endangered species and ecosystems',[143] and WILDLABS, an online platform created in 2015 by the Spatial Monitoring and Reporting Tool Partnership with funding from Google to facilitate open sharing of information about the development and use of technology to fight illegal wildlife trade.[144]

One of the most successful environmental tech organizations is Sky-Truth. Started in 2002 by geologist John Amos, the group today has a global team of researchers, volunteers, and funders. As already mentioned, in 2016 SkyTruth launched Global Fishing Watch in collaboration with Google and Oceana, creating what is now a stand-alone global non-profit working with researchers and governments around the world to inform and empower fisheries management and enforcement. Earlier SkyTruth projects have included the use of satellite and aerial imagery to study environmental impacts of natural gas drilling in the Rocky Mountains and to reveal oil spills and illegal mining and the effects of fracking. The organization's current headline project, 'Conservation Vision', focuses on using artificial intelligence to analyze the ever-increasing torrent of satellite imagery and other data on the global environment.[145]

ShadowView (since 2017 SmartParks) is another niche NGO devoted to the use of surveillance technology for environmental enforcement. The group has used drones to monitor wildlife parks with thermal cameras and has developed a range of ground-based anti-poaching surveillance systems for use in southern Africa.[146] It also supports animal welfare NGOs with criminal and observational investigations, gathering images and film for use in prosecution and investigation of environmental crimes. It advertises its 'tech services' to other NGOs as follows: 'Sometimes a flying camera alone won't be enough to get you the evidence that you need. . . . Following criminals, interventions, GPS tracking, field observations, beacon placing, you name it and we'll figure it out!'[147]

The work of these and many other groups illustrates how advanced technologies empower transnational vigilantes to contribute directly to law

142. https://www.tracenetwork.org/about-trace-network/.

143. https://wildlifeprotectionsolutions.org/wpswatch/.

144. https://www.wildlabs.net/about.

145. SkyTruth interview 2020; https://skytruth.org/about/.

146. https://www.ft.com/content/cc0e0e8e-7fbe-11e4-adff-00144feabdc0; https://www.smartparks.org/story/.

147. https://www.traceinternational.org/.

enforcement. Intervening effectively against environmental crime requires detailed knowledge of where and when it occurs and reliable evidence for potential court cases. While many groups use real-time surveillance and data gathering as a basis for direct interventions against law-breakers, others use technology to provide hard evidence to public authorities which can facilitate arrests and prosecutions. Importantly, however, both types of action are self-directed and autonomous, funded by charitable donations rather than by governments or inter-governmental organizations. Furthermore, many 'investigatory' groups are prepared to take independent action when enforcement agencies decline to act. As we discussed earlier in the chapter, evidence of environmental crimes or negligence gathered by NGOs is often used against governments in court. The importance of autonomy from government authorities was highlighted by many groups we spoke to. The director of one small enforcement NGO explained: 'Governments don't want to fund us. They want to give grants for democracy projects but not for wildlife enforcement'. His organization receives funds from private foundations in Europe and the United States but, he says, rejects more donations than it accepts: 'We want to be fully independent. We don't accept directions. We don't even take advice'.[148]

Direct-Action Enforcement

In leveraging new (and old) technologies to gather evidence for use in court, the work of environmental NGOs mirrors that of many activists working to enforce human rights. Compared to human rights and anti-corruption activism, however, environmental activism also provides many examples of NGOs taking direct punitive action against law-breakers. Prominent cases involve groups like the Sea Shepherd Conservation Society, Greenpeace, and The Black Fish, which have confiscated and sabotaged illegal fishing equipment and blockaded or 'ship-jacked' vessels exporting toxic waste, or EAGLE, which intervenes directly against wildlife poaching.

Direct-action enforcement by environmental groups reflects a longer tradition of direct confrontation in the environmental movement. But although it doesn't operate through courts, direct enforcement is still aided by the expansion of environmental law. As discussed in chapter 1, directly intervening against environmental harms in the absence of binding regulations can leave groups vulnerable to state reprisal and legal counter-measures.

---

148. EAGLE interview 2020.

By contrast, direct action cast as law enforcement can shield groups against public and political backlash by signalling 'just cause'. In this way, the proliferation of environmental law has provided fertile ground for recasting many forms of direct environmental action as enforcement.[149] Indeed, while direct environmental action as such has a long history, direct *enforcement* is a more novel phenomenon.[150]

Leveraging legal and technological opportunities to supply direct enforcement has been a learning process for many environmental groups. Environmental direct action first took off in the 1970s when, fed up with the tame approaches of legacy organizations like the Sierra Club, newly founded Greenpeace and Friends of the Earth adopted a more confrontational approach.[151] During anti-whaling campaigns in the 1970s and 1980s both groups sent boats into direct clashes with Japanese and Soviet whalers.[152] When entering the 'seal wars' in the 1970s, Greenpeace activists used inflatable boats to block hunters' vessels and sought to prevent the clubbing of seals by spray-painting their fur.[153] While these combative tactics brought significant media attention, they also proved politically costly given the absence of a formal ban on seal hunting. Preventing the lawful slaughter of seals invariably meant threatening the livelihood of hunters, including vulnerable indigenous Inuit communities. As a result, the campaign sparked a powerful counter-protest by groups such as Codpeace and the Society for the Retention of Our Sealing Industry.[154] In 1978 Michael Amarook, president of the Inuit Tapirisat, released a press statement saying that 'thanks to the hysterical propaganda of [NGOs] Inuit hunters face economic ruin'.[155]

During the 1980s such political backlash caused many NGOs to pull back from direct confrontation.[156] In 1985 Greenpeace publicly retracted its call for a ban on seal hunting and issued a formal apology for its campaign activities.[157] In the following decade the organization lost almost 1 million members and suffered a 40 percent drop in donations.[158] As Greenpeace and Friends of the Earth withdrew from direct confrontation to focus more

149. Eilstrup-Sangiovanni and Phelps Bondaroff 2014.
150. Eilstrup-Sangiovanni 2019.
151. Keck and Sikkink 1998: 129; McCormick 2010: 99; Zelko 2013: 41.
152. Day 1987; Keck and Sikkink 1998: 129; Darby 2007.
153. Coish 1979; Khatchadourian 2007.
154. Barry 2005: 52.
155. Coish 1979: 194.
156. Wenzel 1991: 47; Page 2004; McCormick 2010: 103; Zelko 2013: 233.
157. Kerr 2014.
158. Dowie 1996: 46–47.

on moderate forms of public protest, the baton of radical environmentalism passed to new groups like Earth First! and the Sea Shepherd Conservation Society (SSCS).[159] The latter group was founded in 1977 by Paul Watson (a co-founder of Greenpeace) with the explicit mission of 'shutting down illegal whaling and sealing operations'.[160] Seeking to establish itself in opposition to mainstream groups, the Sea Shepherds adopted a manifestly radical agenda, branding themselves as 'eco-pirates' 'going where others won't'.[161] During its first campaign in 1979 the group went after a notorious pirate whaling ship, the *Sierra*, which they took more than a year to hunt down, then rammed at full speed ripping open its hull.[162] After the *Sierra*'s owners spent $1 million on uninsured repairs, Sea Shepherd activists blew holes in its hull with mines, sinking it dockside in a Portuguese harbour. The Sea Shepherds went on to sink three Norwegian whaling ships, two Icelandic whalers, and half the Spanish whaling fleet. They also caused more than $6 million in damages to a whale-processing plant in Reykjavik.[163]

Despite its radical beginnings, Sea Shepherds portrays itself squarely as a law enforcement organization. In the early 1990s, rather than simply claiming the side of morality, the group began to assert legal authority for its actions, dropping their image as questionable 'do-gooders' in favour of an image as defenders of the law. For this, Watson cited mainly the UN World Charter for Nature adopted by the General Assembly in 1982, which states that 'States and, to the extent they are able, other public authorities, international organizations, individuals, groups and corporations shall . . . safeguard and conserve nature in areas beyond national jurisdiction'. On this basis, argues Watson, an 'NGO has as much right to operate on the high seas as any government'.[164]

In line with its growing focus on law enforcement, the Sea Shepherd's anti-whaling campaigns have shifted over time from Norway and Iceland to Japan which—unlike the former two countries—was until 2019 formally bound by the International Whaling Commission's Moratorium on Commercial Whaling.[165] Since 2002 the group has focused on shutting down Japan's

159. Zelko 2013.

160. Hoek 2010: 177.

161. https://seashepherd.org.

162. Day 1987: 53; *Telegraph* 2009.

163. https://www.nytimes.com/1986/11/20/world/around-the-world-whaling-ships -refloated-in-iceland.html.

164. https://seashepherd.org/mandate.

165. Eilstrup-Sangiovanni and Bondaroff 2014.

disputed scientific whaling program,[166] widely deemed to be in violation of an International Moratorium on Commercial Whaling, and on enforcing whaling bans within the Southern Ocean Whale Sanctuary (established in 1998) and the Australian Whale Sanctuary (1999).[167]

There can be little doubt that environmental law plays a growing role for many environmental direct-action groups. Not only has asserting a legal basis for direct interventions helped to restore favour with the public, but legality has often played a role in shielding groups against charges of criminal damage—allowing activists to argue that their interventions were necessary to prevent greater damages being caused by law-breaking. Paul Watson says, 'You have to look at our record. We've never been convicted of a felony. We've never been sued'. (This is in fact not true.) Why not? 'Because all those vessels were operating illegally and criminals do not generally want to go to court, and because we have the legal authority to do what we do'.[168] That Watson and his crew are both keen students of the law and shrewd tacticians is evidenced by their campaigns. Onboard Sea Shepherd ships are experts in international law who advise on the legality of specific interventions and brief crew members prior to press announcements on how to present the legal case for campaign actions.[169]

Whether or not direct-action groups like the SSCS have the authority to intervene, stretched public law enforcers often appear to welcome a helping hand when it comes to policing the high seas. 'Sea Shepherd is doing what no one else will', said Peter Whish-Wilson, an Australian senator in reference to the groups' interventions against illegal fishing. 'The urgency of this problem has grown . . . but the government response, from all governments really, has fallen'.[170]

Another area for direct enforcement at sea has been illegal tuna fishing. A string of formal resolutions by the International Commission for the Conservation of Atlantic Tunas has failed to reduce unregulated fishing in the Mediterranean due to the commission's inability to enforce compliance through formal penalties.[171] In turn, this has opened an opportunity for NGOs to intervene. In May 2010 Greenpeace deployed the *Rainbow Warrior* and *Arctic Sunrise* to block the French port of Frontignan to prevent fishing

166. Hoek 2010: 174; Phelps Bondaroff 2011.
167. EPBC Act §3(2)(e)iii 1999.
168. *Telegraph* 2009; Sea Shepherd Conservation Society interview 2019.
169. Anonymous source.
170. Urbina 2015.
171. Sturtz 2001; Valero 2003.

vessels from leaving port.[172] The Black Fish and Sea Shepherds also sent boats to the Mediterranean, but unlike Greenpeace, whose blockade of registered fishing vessels drew sharp condemnation from the European Fisheries Commission, Sea Shepherd activists only took action once the European Fisheries Commission announced on 9 June 2010 that annual fishing quotas had been exhausted. Laurens De Groot, director of the Sea Shepherds Netherlands, explained his organization's strategy: 'We are waiting to pounce upon the criminals, and when the time is right and the evidence supports it, we will make our move'.[173] On 17 June five Sea Shepherd divers entered the water and cut the nets of the *Cesare Rustico*, an Italian vessel, releasing eight hundred illegally caught bluefin tuna back into the ocean.[174] A subsequent press release by SSCS clearly distanced itself from Greenpeace's tactics: 'SSCS does not believe that publicity stunts and harassment of legal fishing operations is the answer to the problem of saving the bluefin tuna from extinction. . . . Our job is to investigate, identify, and intervene against illegal fishing operations. . . . We are an anti-poaching organization and not a protest group'.[175]

A similar approach is taken by The Black Fish, whose founder, Wietse van de Werf, sailed with SSCS from 2006 to 2009. Like the Sea Shepherds, The Black Fish embraces direct action while emphasizing legal evidence gathering as a means to shed the 'alternative image' of many environmental NGOs. 'No one can ignore hard evidence!' says van de Werf.[176] 'We don't see ourselves as witnesses, more as enforcers of law. We want evidence of illegality and we are prepared to take direct action'.[177] In 2012, The Black Fish staged a daring raid on a heavily protected fish farm near the island Ugljan in Croatia when divers sliced through a huge underwater wire net to release hundreds of juvenile tuna into the sea.[178] Such tactics have been emulated by other groups like the Blue Seals, which describes itself as 'a rapid response conservation strike team'.[179] The group deploys Albatross seaplanes, helicopters, and specially designed boats 'to spot environmental crimes from the air, to record them, expose them, and to coordinate with our land and sea direct action activists to intervene'.[180]

172. *Times of Malta* 2010.
173. Sea Shepherd Conservation Society 2010.
174. Vidal 2010.
175. Sea Shepherd Conservation Society, 17 May 2010.
176. Black Fish interview 2015.
177. Vidal 2010.
178. Ibid.; Green 2016.
179. https://www.blueseals.org/index/home.
180. Ibid.

Direct-action enforcement is not confined to the high seas. A land-based parallel is the International Anti-Poaching Foundation (IAPF), founded in 2009 by former Australian soldiers, which trains and operates armed rangers to hunt down and arrest poachers in Zimbabwe and other southern African countries. Although Zimbabwe has anti-poaching rangers of its own, wildlife conservation is not a priority for the current government, which faces economic collapse and is burdened by tough sanctions imposed by the United States and the EU. In 2017 IAPF introduced its Akashinga program, the first all-female, armed anti-poaching unit in the world trained in an abandoned trophy hunting reserve in Zimbabwe. In the first three years of operating Akashinga the IAPF claims to have driven an 80 percent downturn in elephant poaching in Zimbabwe's Lower Zambezi Valley. Building on this success, the organization trained a further 160 women as full-time rangers in 2020.[181]

Eco Activists for Governance and Law Enforcement (EAGLE) is another example of an anti-poaching organization that provides the full spectrum of enforcement activities—from investigation to arrest and prosecution.[182] The group's mission is to 'hunt down' and 'bring about the prosecution and subsequent imprisonment of wildlife traffickers'.[183] Founded in Cameroon in 2009, EAGLE today operates in eight countries with a legal team in each country that assists in prosecuting the cases arising from its operations. Across these countries EAGLE claims to have helped—or in many cases, pushed—local authorities to put more than 2,000 traffickers in jail. The group's founder and director, Ofir Drohi, explains his philosophy: '[Our aim] is enforcement. We have a legal unit at EAGLE [that] employs private prosecutors. We hire private prosecutors, not to represent us—the NGO—but to represent the government. We say to the government: We'll pay 25 percent of the prosecutor's honorarium you pay 75 percent. But the government never pays. So de facto they [prosecutors] work for me. They follow my strategy. Our lawyers instruct them what to do'.[184]

EAGLE works mainly in countries governed by dictatorship where corruption is rife. In this context, Drohi is emphatic that his group does not provide a 'service' to low-capacity public enforcement authorities but rather ensures that conservation laws are enforced in spite of a corrupt public system that has little interest in doing so:

181. Engel Rasmussen 2014; https://www.iapf.org/news/akashinga.
182. EAGLE interview 2020; http://www.eagle-enforcement.org/crisis.
183. https://www.eagle-enforcement.org/arrest-operations.
184. EAGLE interview 2020.

[Our work] is fully independent. We plan the sting operations to the last detail, including contingency plans. We then go to the police. They don't know the plan. They don't even know where they are going. We tell them what to do. Eighty-five percent of the time they try to obstruct it. They don't act. We end up doing the fighting, the chasing. They only put on the handcuffs. Often, we even fight physically with police officers when they try to sabotage an arrest because they just got a call from their superior. Eighty-five percent of the time that happens.[185]

Direct environmental enforcement highlights chronic problems of lack of capacity and lack of political will to enforce environmental laws. This is perhaps best illustrated by the capture of the *Thunder* described in this book's introduction. Interpol issued a Purple Notice (a 'most wanted' notice) for the *Thunder* in 2013 based on the vessel's illegal fishing activities across at least fifteen countries.[186] Yet no government took action to apprehend it. During the winter of 2014–15, the Sea Shepherds spent 110 days and more than $1.5 million in chasing the Nigerian-flagged vessel across three oceans before finally halting its journey and seizing its fishing gear as evidence.[187] In bringing *Thunder* to justice, an NGO did what governments were seemingly unwilling to do: 'They are maritime ship-trackers fighting fishing crime', said an anonymous Interpol official, 'and they are getting results'.

Like direct action more broadly, direct enforcement has limits. The Sea Shepherds' 'loveable pirate' image has earned the group much media attention, but over time its leadership has also sought to develop closer cooperation with government authorities. Following the high-profile chase of the *Thunder*, Sea Shepherd has been approached by several countries looking for an injection of cash and manpower to boost their scarce enforcement capacity.[188] In April 2016 SSCS signed a ship-rider agreement with the government of Gabon by which it agreed to provide a ship, crew, and fuel, while Gabon would provide an armed detachment under whose authority the ship would operate. Since February 2017, the group has been working in partnership with Liberian authorities in Operation Sola Stella on joint sea patrols.[189] Similarly, in 2019, SSCS entered into a partnership with the

185. Ibid.
186. Interpol 2015.
187. Sea Shepherd Conservation Society, https://seashepherd.org/news/poaching-vessel-kunlun-is-detained-in-thailand/ and https://seashepherd.org/news/poaching-vessel-thunder-sinks-in-suspicious-circumstances/.
188. Berube 2021.
189. Ibid.

Namibian Ministry of Fisheries and Marine Resources to patrol Namibia's Exclusive Economic Zone.[190]

Asked why his organization is suddenly partnering with public authorities, Omar Todd, Global Director of Special Operations, reflects, 'Sea Shepherds were getting more and more critical press. . . . We needed to shake off the pirate image. We seek legitimate partnership with governments to engage in law enforcement. . . . We bring the enforcement, they authorize'.[191] Regarding the benefits of partnering with under-resourced coast guards versus the vigilante approach adopted vis-à-vis Japanese whalers and elsewhere, he elaborates: 'In the Southern Ocean, well, that should have been enforced by Australia. . . . And a local court acknowledged that. . . . But you know, on the high seas, it's mainly a question of who has a ship and is able to do something about it. What we do in Africa is in territorial waters. So, when you operate in local waters you need permission'.[192]

Competition and Differentiation among Environmental NGOs

As discussed in chapter 1, organizational ecology factors—the number, density, and interaction of different groups in a population—often play a role in shaping organizational strategy. In this context, a remarkable trend is the explosive growth of environmental NGOs since the 1970s.[193] The World Directory of Environmental Organizations lists over 2,500 environmental NGOs across 190 countries. Yet these are mainly larger organizations that are sufficiently established to be recorded in official databases. The real number is likely much larger.[194]

Another trend is the growing size of some individual environmental organizations. Until the late 1980s, most of today's leading environmental organizations had fewer than ten employees. Today, the same organizations employ hundreds of professional staff who formulate strategy, oversee fundraising, and nurture corporate partnerships.[195] For example, the World Wildlife Fund (WWF), which was founded by six volunteers in 1961, today has more than 5,000 staff, 5 million members globally and an annual

190. https://www.seashepherdglobal.org/latest-news/namibia-partnership/.
191. Sea Shepherd Conservation Society interview 2019.
192. Ibid.
193. Sikkink 2002: 41.
194. Murdie and Davis 2012b: 180.
195. Zelko 2013: 271; Stroup and Wong 2017; Berny and Rootes 2018.

budget of $66 million. Another heavyweight, Greenpeace, has increased its membership from 1.4 million in 1985 to over 3 million in 2020 and has a $40 million annual budget.[196]

Growing institutional density imposes resource constraints on a sector and pushes individual organizations to adopt either generalist or niche strategies to survive (see discussion in chapter 1).[197] This strategic choice is not random but depends on underlying organizational factors. As legally incorporated organizations with large professional staff and complex administrative infrastructures, today's leading environmental NGOs have inevitably lost some agility.[198] As they have become more professionalized, governments have granted such NGOs wider access to participate in the negotiation and implementation of environmental accords, and businesses have grown keener to exploit the 'green-washing' potential of NGO-business alliances.[199] Having invested heavily in nurturing relationships with policymakers, corporations, and wider publics, many 'legacy' NGOs have increasingly gravitated towards 'soft' strategies and moderate statements which are compatible with maintaining political access and avoid alienating donors or the wider publics whose support keeps them politically and financially afloat.[200] Co-founder Bob Hunter's statement during a Greenpeace board meeting in the 1970s that 'I don't give a fuck who I take money from! I'll take it from child molesters or the CIA. I'm just trying to save whales'[201] would hardly be conceivable today.

The constraints that come with having a large public membership or privileged political access were highlighted by many activists we spoke to. Referring to the large environmental NGOs that receive the bulk of government and corporate funding, one NGO representative said: 'They cannot do real work because they take zero risk. If the World Wildlife Fund were to support intelligence-gathering they'd be kicked out of China. They have to focus on capacity-building'.[202]

There may also simply be less pressure on 'legacy' organizations to innovate strategically. Referring to leading NGOs as the 'seven sisters' of the environmental movement, one enforcement activist told us: 'The seven

---

196. https://www.activistfacts.com/about/.
197. Hannan and Freeman 1977.
198. Berny and Rootes 2018: 949.
199. Raustiala 1997; Green 2016.
200. Page 2004; McCormick 2010; Zelko 2013: 316; Stroup and Wong 2017.
201. Zelko 2013: 263.
202. WildLeaks interview 2020.

sisters have a monopoly. And they seek to stifle all competition and innovation. They are a cartel swallowing 90 percent of the funding. They are not receptive to ideas from small, innovative groups because they are not under pressure: the funders are always there'.[203]

But while some environmental groups have grown increasingly embedded in powerful state institutions, others have staked out more radical, independent positions. For groups that lack financial resources or political access, enforcement can be a means to eschew expensive 'inside' lobbying or costly publicity campaigns in favour of more direct actions which are cheaper to execute and less reliant on political access and media exposure. At the same time, enforcement presents a way for these groups to establish themselves in opposition to mainstream competitors and to create a 'niche' in which they can escape direct competition with larger incumbents. It is no coincidence that enforcement-focused groups are often smaller, poorer, and administratively lighter on their feet. To quote one of the pioneers of vigilante environmental enforcement, the Environmental Investigation Agency: 'as a small organization we have also often been able to voice what larger groups feel unable to say, and our size allows us to mobilize in ways bigger organizations cannot'.

The choice between advocacy and enforcement is not either/or.[204] Nevertheless, for many groups, the challenges of funding and competition from other groups mean that there is considerable pressure to emphasize one or the other strategy. Thus, as newer and smaller groups have found a niche in enforcement, older incumbents have continued to consolidate their positions as trusted advisors and providers of services to governments.[205] Even among direct-action groups there is a visible division of labour whereby some groups carefully style themselves as law enforcers working within the confines of the law, while others, like Greenpeace, embrace civil disobedience as a form of protest. Arrests and imprisonment of Greenpeace activists are commonplace, and Greenpeace's leadership is explicit in describing these as part of its strategy to call attention to governments' complicity in environmental harms. Indeed, Greenpeace has unusually deep pockets to pay legal fees and is distinguished from other NGOs by enjoying a strong base of public support for its civil disobedience. Given that Greenpeace has cornered the 'public-protest' segment of the market, many other

203. Ibid.
204. Eilstrup-Sangiovanni and Sharman 2021.
205. Berny and Rootes 2018; Eilstrup-Sangiovanni 2019.

direct-action groups have sought out a different niche, seeking to leverage the opportunities offered by expanding legal frameworks. The following quote from a Sea Shepherd press release succinctly captures the difference between the two groups: 'Greenpeace breaks laws through the practice of civil disobedience. Sea Shepherd does not break laws, we uphold them. We intervene against illegal activities'.[206]

Conclusions

Environmental NGOs are increasingly supplying the kind of enforcement that one might expect of governments: carrying out independent monitoring and investigation, facilitating arrests, and taking law-breakers to court. As in human rights, vigilante environmental enforcement has been driven by three processes. First, environmental governance has become increasingly legalized worldwide, creating a vast web of poorly enforced law. Second, technological and legal advances have put new tools in the hands of transnational activists to engage in independent monitoring and investigation and to litigate. Third, an increase in the number, size, and professionalization of NGOs worldwide has led to growing competition for political access and funding, causing some groups to abandon advocacy in favour of enforcement. As with human rights vigilantism, transnational environmental enforcement both substitutes for ineffective or missing state action and challenges recalcitrant governments to up their game.

The organizational profiles showcased in this chapter hint at growing division of labour among environmental groups. While they sometimes engage in enforcement, large, resource-rich organizations like the World Wildlife Fund, the Nature Conservancy, Friends of the Earth, and Greenpeace today tilt overwhelmingly towards advocacy and/or public protest. Given their large public constituencies, these organizations often find it difficult to adopt and sustain a radical agenda.[207] By contrast, smaller organizations can afford to worry less about their public image and are therefore relatively freer to experiment with new strategies—including enforcement. At the same time, given their limited resource base, they are also more dependent on innovation.

During the last twenty years, NGO enforcement has led to a series of victories against environmental crime and has helped to close urgent

---

206. Sea Shepherd Conservation Society UK, n.d.
207. Thrall, Stecula, and Sweet 2014; Stroup and Wong 2017; Eilstrup-Sangiovanni 2019.

enforcement gaps in regard to vulnerable ecosystems. However, foreshad-
owing our discussion in the concluding chapter, vigilante enforcement raises
a number of thorny questions regarding legitimacy and effectiveness—both
for individual NGOs and for the larger causes for which they work. Although
some governments and inter-governmental organizations are content to let
vigilante enforcers do their job for them, too prominent an intervention by
NGOs can trigger considerable anxiety among governments who fear that
uninvited actions may disrupt on-going diplomatic processes or undermine
other policy goals. Another concern is that transnational enforcement leaves
the underlying reasons as to why governments are failing to enforce environmental law unaddressed and may even invite public enforcement authorities
to 'lean back' and let NGOs pick up the slack. Asked whether he worries
that by doing the authorities' job for them his group provides an incentive
to invest less in official enforcement, Wietse van der Werf, founder of The
Black Fish, shrugs, 'We are effectively doing their job for them. . . . It's not
ideal but the issue is urgent'.[208]

208. Black Fish interview 2015.

4

Vigilantes against Corruption

Corruption is as old as the distinction between public and private. Policies to counter corruption go back centuries. According to Article 2 of the U.S. Constitution, one of the few grounds on which the president can be impeached is bribery. The most common definition of corruption was coined by Transparency International: the abuse of public office for private gain. Though no one definition can capture all aspects of such a varied phenomenon, this rendering has become fixed in the policy landscape and in general understanding. Yet rather than corruption per se, or the domestic responses, here we are interested in international rules to counter cross-border corruption and vigilante efforts to enforce them.

The complex system of hard and soft international rules to combat cross-border corruption is surprisingly new. As late as the year 2000, in many European countries it was not only legal to bribe foreign (but not domestic) officials, the bribes were in fact tax deductible as a legitimate business expense. The decade 1995–2005 saw a complete transformation whereby international corruption moved from being a barely discussed taboo subject to a staple trope of policy-makers' speeches. It is now cast as a central obstacle to development and a pressing threat to the integrity of the global financial system. Regional anti-corruption conventions in the latter half of the 1990s were capped by the United Nations Convention Against Corruption (UNCAC) in 2005. Since this time, the transnational corpus of international anti-corruption rules has diffused and deepened. Along with these rules has come the parallel development of international anti-corruption NGOs.

The first order of business in this chapter is to give a brief account of the relevant international rules. What is the global regime to counter corruption, and how is it meant to work? After presenting a thumbnail sketch of these rules, the next task is to explain the rise of vigilante enforcement in this domain. The broad trends parallel those in human rights and the environment: more rules have not been matched by proportionate state enforcement, and hence a gap has opened, creating the demand for greater anti-corruption enforcement. This gap reflects the fact that countering corruption involves especially acute challenges of enforcement. Corruption often takes place in secret, the victims are seldom obvious, and governments may face political pressure to turn a blind eye or may themselves be the guilty party.

On the supply side, an incongruous combination of legal innovations, from new ways of bringing criminal prosecutions to civil law remedies for commercial cases that have been repurposed to pursue dirty money, has also expanded the opportunities for vigilante enforcement. Technology has again been important in boosting enforcement beyond the state. Increased computing power and the internet have made it much easier to investigate corruption through the ability to leak, process, and analyze vast amounts of financial data. Rather than parallel trends, legal and technological changes often interact in facilitating enforcement beyond the state.

Why have these changes prompted some anti-corruption groups, but not others, to take enforcement of international standards into their own hands? In answering this question the main contrast is between Transparency International, the dominant advocacy group, and Global Witness, which has specialized in investigation. In many ways Transparency International is the epitome of the establishment NGO. Its well-connected founders have deliberately opted for a consensual approach in networking with big business and governments to advocate for policy change. Global Witness and other, smaller, groups are more outsiders, with little or nothing to lose from more confrontational strategies. They have often drawn directly on earlier experience in the environmental and human rights sectors in their strategies for enforcing international anti-corruption standards. There has also been a notable trend of NGOs from other fields taking important roles in anti-corruption enforcement.

The International Anti-Corruption Regime

Perhaps the most surprising feature of the global anti-corruption regime is its novelty, especially compared to the human rights and environmental equivalents. As noted, although domestic prohibitions against bribery, embezzlement, nepotism, and related abuses are long-standing, equivalent international rules against cross-border corruption date only from the second half of the 1990s. Broadly speaking, these rules aim to counter two main forms of corruption. The first is the bribery of foreign government officials by multinational firms. The second is the movement of funds looted by government officials in one country across borders to be stashed or spent in another country. Foreign bribery was first addressed in the 1997 OECD Anti-Bribery Convention. The second prohibition on the cross-border laundering of looted funds was enshrined in the 2005 United Nations Convention Against Corruption. From around the turn of the century, international anti-corruption rules have been reproduced in a slew of hard and soft law standards at the regional and global level, the main provisions of which have then been incorporated into domestic law. Denunciations of international corruption by policy-makers, until recently taboo, are now almost a platitude.

The reasons for the rapid development of the global anti-corruption regime are largely beyond the scope of this book.[1] In brief, change was driven by a combination of domestic and international factors. The mid-1990s saw a spate of corruption scandals that brought down governments around the globe. More generally, the failure of development policy, especially in Africa, led the World Bank and national development agencies to portray corruption as a stumbling block to ending poverty. In addition the end of the Cold War meant that the West was less willing to support kleptocratic but reliably anti-Communist client governments in the Third World. As a result, under the rubric of 'good governance' (the prevailing euphemism for those unwilling to use the C-word), increasingly strict conditions were put on development aid and lending from Western governments and institutions like the World Bank and the International Monetary Fund. Feeding into the international policy response were more general worries (often exaggerated) about a 'dark side of globalization', the idea that as finance became ever more borderless, states were losing the power to counter transnational financial crime.[2] Finally, the United States had long supported a tougher common international line against corruption and foreign bribery in particular after precociously introducing its own ban on such practices in 1977.[3]

---

1. See Wang and Rosenau 2001; McCoy and Heckel 2001; Abbott and Snidal 2002; Vogl 2012; Sharman 2017.
2. Andreas 2011; Jakobi 2013; Shelley 2014, 2018.
3. Davis 2019.

The first global legal agreement occasioned by this change in sentiment was the December 1997 OECD Anti-Bribery Convention (officially the OECD Convention on Combatting Foreign Bribery of Public Officials in International Business Transactions; an Inter-American Convention had been signed the year before).[4] The Convention committed members to criminalize the bribery of foreign officials by their citizens and companies, as well as offering, aiding or abetting such a transaction (Article 1). The Convention was revised to include ambitious new features in 2009 and was reviewed again to further strengthen its terms in 2019.[5]

The second and much more wide-ranging international anti-corruption treaty, in terms of both the number of states that have signed up and the breadth of its provisions, is the United Nations Convention Against Corruption (UNCAC). Opened for signature in 2003, the Convention came into force in 2005 and currently covers 187 states.[6] Many of its provisions replicate those of earlier regional treaties, as well as the OECD Convention and the UN Convention on Transnational Organized Crime. The UNCAC mandates a list of domestic measures, including criminalizing a range of forms of corrupt behaviours, creating a dedicated anti-corruption agency, reiterating the need for anti–money laundering laws, ensuring officials are appointed on a transparent and meritocratic basis, and making public finances transparent and accountable. It has a standard set of provisions encouraging international legal cooperation. Perhaps the most novel element of the Convention is the principle of asset recovery: money corruptly taken from a 'victim' country and transferred to a different 'host' country must be confiscated by the latter and returned to the former (Chapter V).

NGOs have had a central role as advocates in building this system of international anti-corruption law. They have campaigned for the creation of various conventions, pressed governments to sign up, and then tried to make governments honour the promises they have made through naming and shaming—the classic accountability politics.[7] Much of this activity has been carried out on a state-by-state basis by purely domestic groups, yet international NGOs have also been prominent. For example, the UNCAC Civil Society Coalition, founded in 2006, is an umbrella group of 350 different organizations fighting corruption, ranging from the Albanian Institute of Science to the Zero Corruption Coalition of Nigeria.

4. Abbott and Snidal 2002.
5. https://www.oecd.org/corruption/2019-review-oecd-anti-bribery-recommendation.htm.
6. United Nations Convention Against Corruption 2004.
7. Keck and Sikkink 1998.

The Anti-Corruption Enforcement Gap

Compared with human rights and environmental rules, enforcing international anti-corruption laws is especially difficult, and the enforcement gap is correspondingly large, for several reasons. One reason is that corruption is a crime that usually happens behind closed doors and that the victims are typically unaware of their loss. Unlike human rights abuses, there are seldom definite individual victims of corruption, and the costs of violations are typically widely dispersed (similar to many environmental offences). Another reason is that much international anti-corruption law faces a fundamental contradiction: it relies on corrupt governments to somehow police their own corruption. Even democratic governments generally operating under the rule of law are hardly immune to mixed motives in this area; the Trump administration provided a multitude of colourful examples from the United States.

Less obvious, yet probably just as important, are the legal and technical obstacles to fighting international corruption. Even clean and capable governments find it hard to obtain convictions for cross-border financial crime. In common law countries it is difficult for prosecutors to prove a case beyond a reasonable doubt. Where prosecutors do not think they will be able to reach this standard, they usually opt not to prosecute at all. All countries face difficulties in managing cases that sprawl across borders, including the mundane process of getting information from one country to another in a form that is admissible as evidence. Investigating cross-border corruption requires advanced accounting and legal skills that are very scarce in the public sector and generally very expensive in the private sector. As such, there is little mystery as to why so few international corruption crimes are solved and so few of the criminals involved held to account.

What is the actual evidence of an enforcement gap in international anti-corruption law? Where is the evidence that this gap is growing? The legal position is relatively clear. Before the mid-1990s there simply was no international anti-corruption law, and hence no 'enforcement gap'. If it is easy to show that there is currently more international anti-corruption law, measuring the effectiveness of laws and policies against corruption is much harder. Because corruption itself is so difficult to measure, there is no credible 'before' and 'after' picture.[8] Yet there is little doubt that in only a small minority of cases are perpetrators ever brought to justice.

8. Reuter 2012; Forstater 2018.

Transparency International has monitored enforcement of the OECD Anti-Bribery Convention in a series of reports.[9] The latest is unequivocal: 'the Convention's fundamental goal of creating a corruption-free level playing field is still far from being achieved, due to inadequate enforcement'.[10] Only seven of forty signatory countries assessed were judged to be actively enforcing the Convention in the period 2014–17 (the United States, Germany, the UK, Italy, Switzerland, Norway, and Israel).[11] Even among this virtuous subset, only the United States, the UK, and Germany had actually applied substantial penalties over the four-year period in question. In contrast, according to Transparency International, twenty-seven signatory countries had not concluded a single enforcement action with substantial penalties.[12] While some countries had increased their enforcement, in others enforcement had actually declined. By the OECD's calculation, twenty-one signatories had never concluded a single enforcement action.[13] Further supporting the idea of a conspicuous enforcement gap, an academic review of 137 articles published on bribery in international business during 1992–2019 holds that 'laws and regulations against corruption exist but are largely ineffective due to weak judicial systems and the indifference of governments'.[14]

Of course from a baseline of zero, by definition there is an upwards trend in enforcement; the OECD notes that 621 individuals were sanctioned for foreign bribery among signatory states to the Convention during 1999–2018.[15] Yet no one disputes that this total is only a tiny fraction of those bribing foreign officials. Furthermore, relative to the toughened requirements of international law on bribery, the enforcement gap is almost certainly widening. For example, because the United Nations Convention also bans bribing foreign officials (Article 16), since 2005 around 140 additional states are bound by this requirement, almost none of which have ever prosecuted a cross-border corruption case. If OECD governments find this sort of case a daunting challenge, what are the chances for their counterparts in poorer countries?

9. https://www.transparency.org/exporting_corruption.

10. Transparency International 2018: 1.

11. Ibid., 9.

12. Ibid., 10.

13. Organization for Economic Cooperation and Development 2018: 5.

14. Bahoo, Alon, and Paltrinieri 2020: 5.

15. Organization for Economic Cooperation and Development 2019: 2.

The same mismatch is apparent in recovering looted wealth and combatting cross-border grand corruption. Here the relevant international law is even more recent,[16] and if anything the enforcement gap is even more conspicuous, although again exact data are hard to come by. In terms of stolen wealth returned to victim countries, the last synoptic survey was published by the World Bank-UN Stolen Asset Recovery (StAR) Initiative in 2014 (at time of writing a sequel is in the works). The title of the survey, *Few and Far: The Hard Facts on Asset Recovery*, gives away the punch line. The report concludes that 'there is a disconnect between high-level international commitments and practice at the country level' and that 'ultimately, a huge gap remains between the results achieved and the billions of dollars that are estimated stolen from developing countries'.[17] Looking at cross-border illicit financial flows more generally, a United Nations report estimates that perhaps only around 0.2 percent of these tainted funds are seized by the authorities.[18]

The point here is not that international anti-corruption laws are never effective, that those guilty of corruption never face consequences, or that there has been no progress in enforcement. Clearly there has been some progress in enforcement, if only because until relatively recently there simply was no international law to enforce in the first place. Nevertheless, despite the impossibility of putting a precise number on it, there is general agreement that only a tiny fraction of the perpetrators and proceeds of corruption is ever detected, let alone apprehended. With the proliferation of hard and soft international anti-corruption law, and the enthusiasm of states in signing on to these rules, the result is a large and growing enforcement gap. NGOs have been vocal in identifying and decrying this enforcement gap and in demanding action. The sections below illustrate how legal and technological changes have made it easier for such actors to take a further step to supply enforcement beyond the state.

Legal Drivers of Anti-Corruption Enforcement

Though NGOs have been enthusiastic and at times influential allies in getting international anti-corruption standards off the ground, their role has been seen by scholars and policy-makers alike as some combination of

16. United Nations Convention Against Corruption 2004.
17. Stolen Asset Recovery Initiative 2014a: 2.
18. United Nations Office on Drugs and Crime 2011: 7.

cheerleaders and gadflies. Yet recently, changes in the law, or in some circumstances the discovery of new ways to use old laws, have allowed nonstate actors to play an important role in directly and autonomously fighting international corruption. While in some instances states have deliberately created these new opportunities, perhaps seeking to 'orchestrate' NGOs into action, in most cases they have been largely unanticipated. Sometimes these new opportunities have been taken up by dedicated anti-corruption groups, sometimes by activists from different fields, especially human rights but also those focused on protecting the environment.

While some NGOs' efforts to take legal action against corruption have been purely domestic, most have had a transnational aspect. This is because either the crime itself was cross-border or international NGOs were key players, or because the case was based on a direct appeal to international law. After a brief comment on international law, these new strategies are discussed in terms of first criminal and then civil law.

The principle of nonstate actors using the courts to fight corruption finds support in the UN Convention Against Corruption, which holds that 'each State Party shall take such measures as may be necessary, in accordance with principles of its domestic law, to ensure that entities or persons who have suffered damage as a result of an act of corruption have the right to initiate legal proceedings against those responsible for that damage in order to obtain compensation' (Article 35). As detailed below, many NGOs have taken action in accord with this principle (which was in many countries' legal codes long before the UN Convention). The important caveats in this formula, however, are first 'in accordance with domestic law' and second the requirement that only parties who have suffered damage have standing to initiate action.

Explicit anti-corruption laws are not the only basis in international law for fighting corruption. Most governments that are guilty of human rights abuses are guilty of corruption crimes as well,[19] and so in practice enforcing either set of international standards often means converging on the same states and the same individuals. As a result, human rights NGOs have increasingly ventured into the area of anti-corruption enforcement, and vice versa. In terms of international criminal law, the International Criminal Court (ICC) has no jurisdiction over corruption or financial crimes.[20] However, the ICC

---

19. Carranza 2008; Roht-Arriaza and Martinez 2019.

20. Though there have been proposals to expand the ICC's remit to include such crimes or to establish a dedicated international anti-corruption court; e.g., Wolf 2018.

and some other international human rights courts have had a secondary role in fighting financial crime. The ICC can levy fines against those convicted of human rights crimes, can impose the forfeiture of wealth derived from such crimes, and mandate reparations be paid to victims.[21] Each of these prerogatives requires investigating and confiscating funds across borders. As discussed previously, however, the ICC itself has relatively little capacity for investigations, financial or otherwise. Given the existence of NGOs straddling the areas of human rights and anti-corruption activism like Conflict Awareness Project (U.S.), the Sentry (UK), Civitas Maxima (Switzerland), APDHE (Spain), *Poder Ciudadano* (Argentina), and others, it is not hard to see why links between these domains have been made.

The following sections examine two paths by which NGOs enforce international anti-corruption law through domestic courts. The first is by directly targeting the corrupt and their assets through private prosecutions; the second, more indirect strategy works at one remove: NGOs sue governments to force the state to enforce anti-corruption obligations.

CRIMINAL ANTI-CORRUPTION ENFORCEMENT BEYOND THE STATE

The most prominent uses of private criminal law prosecutions in grand corruption are parallel cases launched in Spain and France against the ruling Obiang family of Equatorial Guinea. As evidenced throughout this chapter, the Obiang example illustrates the range of NGO vigilante actions, from initial investigations and gathering evidence, to funding court challenges, to autonomous prosecution.

Teodoro Obiang came to power in 1979 after overthrowing and executing his psychopathic uncle, whose human rights abuses had earned Equatorial Guinea the sobriquet of 'the Dachau of Africa'. The desperately poor country later struck it rich in the 1990s with the discovery of oil. While the majority of the population remained mired in poverty, however, the Obiang family went on an incredible overseas spending spree. At the forefront was son (and from 2012 vice president) Teodorin Obiang. Seemingly unconstrained by his $80,000 official salary, Obiang Jr. spent $314 million on various luxury items in the period 2004–11 alone (not counting another $250 million on two yachts).[22]

---

21. International Criminal Court 2017.
22. Adams 2012.

The starting point for the process that led to Obiang's conviction for corruption and money laundering in Paris in 2017 was in 2003. Information released jointly by Global Witness and Ken Silverstein of the *Los Angeles Times* revealed that between $300 and $500 million of Equatorial Guinea's oil wealth was held in Riggs Bank in Washington, D.C., under the personal control of Teodorin's father, President Obiang (whose autobiography is entitled *My Life for My People*).[23] This information sparked a highly critical U.S. Senate investigation into Riggs Bank.[24]

Building on their earlier investigation, in 2006 Global Witness obtained and published the property and company records showing that Obiang Jr. had bought a $35 million mansion in Malibu, California, next door to Britney Spears.[25] This evidence was important in stimulating and sustaining government action, especially from the anti-kleptocracy group formed within the U.S. Department of Justice in 2006. Whether deliberately or otherwise, a 2007 Department of Justice document and PowerPoint presentation on Obiang Jr. were leaked to a group of NGOs, confirming and extending the NGOs' accusations.[26] Later the Justice Department brought a civil action against Obiang's assets in the United States, ending with the confiscation of his Malibu mansion in 2014. Both Senate and Department of Justice staff singled out Global Witness as giving them the initial 'thread to pull on' in pursuing the case.[27]

While the Obiang clan began to attract unfavourable attention in the United States from 2003 (causing a transfer of some of their wealth to Spain), in France the first clouds on the horizon appeared with a 2007 report by the NGO *Comité Catholique contre la Faim et pour le Développement*. The report estimated that various African dictators had between them looted over $200 billion, with a good deal of this money transferred to France.[28] The report was the opening for three French NGOs, Sherpa (also active in human rights and environmental enforcement), Survie, and *Fédération des Congolais de la Diaspora*, to lodge a criminal complaint against the ruling families of Equatorial Guinea, Congo-Brazzaville, and Gabon.[29] In practice, the case came to focus on Obiang Jr., the most brazen of those in the frame.

23. Silverstein 2003; Global Witness 2003.

24. United States Senate Permanent Subcommittee on Investigations 2004; Bean 2018.

25. Global Witness 2006, 2009.

26. United States Senate Permanent Subcommittee on Investigations 2010: 25–26.

27. U.S. Department of Justice interview 2014; U.S. Senate Permanent Subcommittee on Investigations 2014.

28. https://ccfd-terresolidaire.org/IMG/pdf/biens-mal-acquis.pdf.

29. Perdriel-Vaissiere 2017: 3–4.

In France, private parties who can show they are victims of a crime can initiate a criminal complaint to an investigating magistrate. Here, as in the private human rights prosecutions, NGOs needed to work through a victim, in this case interpreted broadly as citizens of the affected country.[30] The charges in question related to the offence that 'anyone who maintains assets on French soil that were acquired through the commission of an offence (i.e., embezzlement) is punishable by law, no matter where the principal offence took place' (Articles 321-1 and 432-15 of the French criminal code).[31] The criminal origin of the money from outside France creates the derivative money-laundering crime in France. After the initial criminal complaint there followed a three-year see-saw battle between Sherpa and other NGOs (joined by Transparency International-France), on the one hand, and the French authorities on the other, over whether the case could go ahead, a struggle fought in both the courts and the media.

Having won their battle for standing against the French government in late 2010, the NGOs drew first blood in September the following year, as a collection of fifteen of Obiang Jr.'s luxury sports cars were confiscated from his €110 million Paris mansion (which housed another €49 million worth of furniture). In 2012 the mansion itself was seized. The Equatorial Guinean government struck back, however, maintaining that both Obiang Jr. and the mansion were covered by diplomatic immunity. On this basis they took France to the International Court of Justice. Undeterred, in October 2017 a French court convicted Obiang in absentia of corruption and embezzlement; his appeal was rejected in February 2020.[32] The French Obiang case is the single most successful instance of vigilante NGO enforcement of international anti-corruption standards so far.

In terms of the broader significance, following the French court decision on legal standing in November 2010, anti-corruption NGOs were for the first time given the right to bring criminal corruption complaints without relying on victims to gain standing, mirroring a prerogative already enjoyed by environmental NGOs (discussed in chapter 3).[33] This prerogative was then legislated in 2013, entrenching this important precedent. In addition to Equatorial Guinea, French NGOs have now used this right to make criminal complaints in relation to alleged proceeds of corruption held in France by the ruling families of Angola, Burkina Faso, Congo-Brazzaville, Egypt,

---

30. Ibid., 14–15.
31. Perdriel-Vaissiere 2011: 26; Sherpa interview 2017.
32. Gagné-Acoolon 2020.
33. Perdriel-Vaissiere 2017: 6.

Gabon, Libya, Syria, and Tunisia.[34] This is another important example of how pioneering vigilante action by a few leading groups can increase and institutionalize opportunities for others following in their wake, a pattern familiar from enforcement by human rights and environmental groups.

French courts have not been the only venue for pursuing the Obiang family. As noted in chapter 2 in connection with human rights, Spanish criminal law allows any citizen, non-citizen, or NGO to bring a criminal complaint to a magistrate, without having to show that they themselves have been harmed by the crime.[35] Article 125 of the Spanish constitution allows NGOs standing to bring action under the UNCAC and European law, as well as Spanish law.[36] *Asociación Pro Derechos Humanos de España* (APDHE), a human rights group formed after the transition to democracy in the 1970s, used this opportunity to bring a private criminal prosecution in October 2008 against the Obiang family for moving proceeds of corruption through Spain.[37] In 2015 the Spanish authorities detained three Spanish-based enablers suspected of laundering Obiang funds.[38] The same Spanish NGO and the U.S. group EG Justice jointly lodged a complaint at the African Commission on Human and Peoples' Rights, arguing that Obiang's corruption was a violation of the African Human Rights Charter.[39]

Beyond Obiang, a second major corruption victory, again involving French NGO Sherpa, was that of Rifaat al-Assad, brother of Syria's former ruler Hafez al-Assad and uncle of current ruler Bashar al-Assad. Rifaat had been exiled after a failed coup in 1984, dividing his time between London, Paris, and Spain (the three host governments apparently had no qualms about receiving a guest widely linked to massive human rights abuses in Syria, especially the massacre of 10,000–20,000 people in Hama in 1982; France awarded him the *Legion d'Honneur*). Rifaat had not left Syria empty-handed, departing with $300 million, of which €90 million was spent on mansions in France. After an unsuccessful first attempt in July 2011, in March 2014 Sherpa (once again, not the French government) brought an embezzlement and money-laundering complaint against Rifaat and his associates to the prosecutor, as they had earlier against Obiang and Francophone

---

34. United States Senate Permanent Subcommittee on Investigations 2010: 24; Perdriel-Vaissiere 2017: 10.

35. Stephenson 2016: 13.

36. Sanz and Sese 2013: 299; Open Society Foundations interview 2015, 2017.

37. Sanz and Sese 2013.

38. Open Society Justice Initiative, n.d.

39. Marshall 2013: 13–14.

African ruling families, arguing that the conduct was in violation of France's obligations under the UN Convention Against Corruption.[40]

The corruption trial in France began in December 2019 with Rifaat maintaining that his wealth represented gifts from the Saudi royal family. Yet in June 2020 he was found guilty of embezzlement, money laundering, and tax evasion and sentenced to four years in jail, forfeiting his wealth, and ordered to pay the rather modest sum of €30,000 to Sherpa.[41] A separate case in Spain in 2017 saw his real estate empire comprised of 503 separate properties worth $735 million seized. Adding to Rifaat's legal woes was a human rights criminal complaint lodged in Switzerland by TRIAL International in 2013.[42]

ANTI-CORRUPTION ENFORCEMENT AT ONE REMOVE: NGOs CONSCRIPTING THE STATE

Even where NGOs cannot legally or practically bring their own criminal prosecutions directly like those in France and Spain, they may be able to sue in order to compel governments to do so, in some sense conscripting or forcing the hand of the authorities. In the UK, two NGOs, the Corner House and the Campaign Against the Arms Trade, took action against the British government's decision to drop a bribery investigation of arms firm BAE Systems. The latter had signed a lucrative agreement with Saudi Arabia to sell and then service fighter planes. In a long and sordid story that epitomizes the failure of democratic governments to uphold their international anti-corruption commitments, first Conservative and then Labour governments had conspired to prevent investigations of BAE's bribery, reflecting both the sensitivity of the relationship with Saudi Arabia and the money and jobs at stake in the deal.[43] In 2006 the NGOs challenged the UK Serious Fraud Office's decision to drop the investigation. An initial NGO victory in the High Court saw the judge harshly critical of the government, but the verdict was reversed on appeal in the House of Lords in 2008.[44]

Yet other cases have been more successful. The Corner House had the year earlier won a case against the British government's efforts to stop the Export Credit Guarantee Department refusing credit to firms involved in

40. Sherpa 2016.
41. Salaun and Irish 2020.
42. TRIAL International 2017.
43. https://www.theguardian.com/baefiles/page/0,,2095831,00.html.
44. Stephenson 2016: 15–16.

bribery and corruption.[45] The case was brought in conjunction with law firm Leigh Day, which took the work on a 'no win, no fee' basis. The Corner House had also succeeded in obtaining a Protective Costs Order for the case, meaning that even if the NGO (and Leigh Day) lost, they would not have to pay the government's legal costs. The logic of the court's decision was that the Corner House could not hope to pay the bill, given that the group rejected almost all outside funding, but that it was nevertheless in the public interest that the suit proceed.[46] The combination of the 'no win, no fee' arrangement with the private law firm and the precedent of Protective Costs Order set a precedent for similar litigation, though larger NGOs with more money are less likely to qualify than smaller ones that can more convincingly plead inability to pay.[47] The Corner House won the case against the government, which as the losing party paid Leigh Day's costs.[48] By directly targeting the government this case provides a clear example of autonomous enforcement, rather than some form of public campaigning, let alone service delivery.

There are many similar cases of NGOs successfully challenging governments for omission or wrongful conduct (as opposed to going after individual criminals). In 2013, the Corner House teamed up with Global Witness, the Italian NGO Re:Common, and an individual Nigerian anti-corruption campaigner to challenge a British government decision not to take action against funds suspected of being the proceeds of bribery. After discussions with the police Overseas Corruption Unit, the Crown Prosecution Service was initially inclined to take the case but later got cold feet (NGO sources speculate that the change of heart was due to intervention by the UK Foreign Office). In response, these three organizations applied to the High Court to force the Crown Prosecution Service to take action in relation to $215 million in the British banking system from a corrupt Nigerian oil deal.

The scam itself was relatively simple. In 1998 Nigerian Oil minister Dan Etete awarded a lucrative oil field (OPL 245) to a shell company he controlled, Malabu Oil and Gas. In 2011 Royal Dutch Shell and Italian oil company ENI paid the Nigerian government $1.3 billion for the concession. Days later the government then bought the concession from the minister's company for $1.1 billion. A middleman described the government's role as a

---

45. Lester and Jaffey 2005.

46. https://swarb.co.uk/corner-house-research-regina-on-the-application-of-v-secretary-of-state-for-trade-and-industry-ca-1-mar-2005.

47. Corruption Watch interview 2020; Global Witness interview 2020b.

48. Corner House interview 2020.

'condom', insulating the Western oil firms from direct contact with Malabu.[49] Proceeds from the deal were allegedly kicked back to President Goodluck Jonathan and other middlemen. The Nigerian public had lost an amount greater than the entire annual Nigerian health budget at the time.[50]

The NGO court challenge sought to force an investigation but most immediately to freeze $215 million of the suspect funds held in Britain. In March 2014 the judge refused their request because the Crown Prosecution Service said it was still deciding whether to proceed. The British authorities then opted not to freeze the stolen assets until a separate request was later made by Italy. By this time more than half of the money had been spirited out of Britain.[51] At this point the NGOs considered taking independent legal action to recover the funds themselves but ultimately decided that it was financially too risky.[52] However, Global Witness continued its pursuit of the OPL 245 case and the $1.1 billion diverted from the sale via a criminal complaint that led to the trial of Italian oil firm ENI and to the provision of further evidence that became the basis for separate prosecutions against Royal Dutch Shell.

Global Witness had been following Malabu and its beneficial owner Etete since 2002 and were sceptical of the companies' denials of any knowledge that they were complicit in a corruption scheme.[53] Together with the Corner House and Re:Common (the same combination behind the attempted UK asset freeze), Global Witness lodged a criminal complaint with the Milan public prosecutor on 9 September 2013.[54] The Italian police began investigating shortly afterwards, raiding ENI's offices in 2014. Shell's headquarters in the Netherlands were raided as part of the same investigation in 2016.[55] The Milan public prosecutor brought charges against both companies and thirteen individuals (including the Italian firm's CEO) in 2016, and the trial opened in 2018.[56] Global Witness founder Simon Taylor also gave extensive evidence at the trial.

By this time, emails leaked to Global Witness had demolished the firms' story that they had no knowledge that Malabu/Etete were the real

49. Faull, Jeory, and Doward 2017.
50. Turner 2019.
51. Corner House 2014.
52. Global Witness interview 2020c.
53. Ibid.
54. Global Witness 2018b.
55. Global Witness 2017: 4.
56. Global Witness 2018b.

beneficiaries of the deal. Thus an email to Shell's CEO by the company's head of exploration stated that the $1.3 billion paid by the two firms 'will be used by the FGN [Federal Government of Nigeria] to settle all claims from Malabu'. Even earlier, in 2010, an email between senior Shell executives surmised that a letter from Nigerian president Jonathan confirming Malabu's ownership of OPL 245 was 'clearly an attempt to deliver significant revenues to GLJ [President Goodluck Jonathan]. . . . This is about personal gain and politics'.[57] Shell's CEO (who personally signed the agreement) received an email immediately prior to the deal being finalized saying that 'Etete can smell the money'.[58] The same day the Global Witness report containing this information was released, Shell admitted that it had known Etete was the beneficiary of the deal all along.[59] ENI's own due diligence report on the deal in 2010 also confirmed 'whatever the formal ownership structure of Malabu, all of the sources to whom we have spoken are united in the opinion that Dan Etete is the owner of the company'.[60] This trove of damning evidence, together with the accompanying testimony from Global Witness, has greatly complicated Shell and ENI's on-going legal defence against bribery charges in trials in Italy and Nigeria.

Another attempt at a lawsuit to force authorities to undertake a criminal prosecution was that by the NGO TRIAL in Switzerland. The case related to a Swiss company, Argor-Heraeus, accused of refining three tons of gold illegally taken from the Ituri region of the Congo via Uganda, in violation of UN sanctions. Following a UN investigation of illegal gold mining, the Open Society Foundations (OSF) had funded further investigations by the U.S. NGO the Conflict Awareness Project, whose leader, Kathi Lynn Austin, had led the earlier UN probe. This group is devoted to building prosecutions, and in this case it had prepared an extensive dossier for anticipated cases in Britain, Jersey, and Switzerland.[61] These investigations suggested that Argor-Heraeus must have known about the illegal provenance of the gold they were refining, given UN reports and widespread media coverage, and hence that they were guilty of pillage and money laundering.

Taking the results of the investigation, OSF then made common cause with the Swiss group TRIAL, indicating the ability of international groups

---

57. Global Witness 2017: 5.
58. Ibid., 6.
59. Global Witness 2017.
60. Global Witness Investor Briefing, April 2017, p. 2.
61. Austin 2013.

to 'shop around' for local collaborators.[62] TRIAL's primary aim is to support and mount legal action against mass human rights abuses, but this has also led to an interest in associated financial crimes. Acting on a criminal complaint from TRIAL, the Swiss police raided the company and seized documents in 2013.[63] Other Swiss NGOs, the Bern Declaration and the Bruno Manser Fund, have each amassed dossiers of evidence on corruption and money laundering in the past and have formally requested Swiss prosecutors bring criminal charges on several occasions, but all have so far met with refusal.[64]

Very different in its nature but similar in its strategy is Hermitage Capital, the investment vehicle of billionaire Bill Browder. Initially it operated as an 'activist investment' fund exposing corruption for profit in Russia from 1996. After the murder of Hermitage's lawyer Sergei Magnitsky by corrupt Russian government officials in 2009, however, Browder turned his considerable energy and resources to tracking down the killers' stolen assets in a quest for justice. This priority has subsequently expanded into a campaign against Russian overseas corruption more generally.[65] Hermitage Capital is not an NGO, but there are some relevant similarities in campaigning for policy change and being independent of the government, and in this respect at least not for profit. Browder and his associates have also been highly effective advocates. His campaign prompted the passage of the Magnitsky Act targeting corrupt Russian officials, first through the U.S. Congress and then Britain, Canada, the Baltic States, and the European Union. But in true vigilante style, Browder and his colleagues have also sought to take the fight against Russian corruption abroad into their own hands, including by lodging criminal complaints in an attempt to force the authorities to take action.

Browder maintains a highly skilled team of investigators and lawyers simultaneously pursuing dozens of separate investigations into Russian corruption and overseas money laundering,[66] probably representing more capacity than any state law enforcement agency outside of the United States. On the basis of the evidence obtained, Hermitage has been active in seeking to prompt criminal actions against both individuals and banks that have

---

62. Open Society Foundations interview 2020.

63. de Moerloose 2016.

64. Bern Declaration interview 2015; Bruno Manser-Fonds interview 2015.

65. The Russian government has responded by convicting Browder in absentia for tax evasion and making him the subject of an Interpol Red Notice international arrest warrant. Browder 2015.

66. Williams 2019.

laundered corruption proceeds in fifteen countries.[67] In 2018–19 alone Hermitage lodged detailed and widely publicized criminal money-laundering complaints against Danske Bank, Nordbank, and Swedbank in Denmark, Sweden, Finland, Latvia, and Estonia.[68]

ENFORCEMENT THROUGH CIVIL LAW

Given that international corruption is a crime, why isn't it dealt with exclusively in the criminal justice system? Why is civil law relevant? In general, criminal law has been a disappointment in fighting international corruption. Aside from the inherent difficulty of proving complicated cases beyond a reasonable doubt (in common law countries at least), there are the political sensitivities, technical problems of state-to-state mutual legal assistance, and bureaucratic disincentives for law enforcement and prosecutors already referenced. The limited international asset recovery that has occurred has very rarely relied on standard criminal prosecutions.[69] Law enforcement agencies have increasingly sought to take the profit out of crime in general without relying on criminal convictions.

Instead, law enforcement agencies have increasingly resorted to civil law actions.[70] To start with, this reduces the burden of proof to the balance of probabilities. In common law countries, it often does away with the jury, with the case made to a (hopefully) informed and financially literate judge.[71] But most importantly for vigilantes, civil law is designed to be used by nonstate actors, originally corporations and private individuals. There are still questions of standing that constrain NGO involvement, the United States being particularly inhospitable, but these are less constraining than in criminal law.[72] This section examines how NGOs can provide autonomous international anti-corruption enforcement via civil litigation. Few if any of these changes were designed with NGO enforcement in mind; instead, these groups have incidentally been the potential or actual beneficiaries.

New civil law powers have often been developed for use in commercial disputes (e.g., insolvency), but their financial nature may mean that they

67. Bill Browder, Transparency International-UK talk, Zoom, 29 April 2020.

68. Vaish and Gelzis 2019; Milne 2018.

69. Stolen Asset Recovery Initiative 2014a: 2; Sharman 2017.

70. Fenner-Zinkernagel, Monteith, and Gomes Pereira 2013; Marshall 2013; Stolen Asset Recovery Initiative 2014b, 2019.

71. Private asset recovery lawyer interview 2019.

72. Stephenson 2016.

can be re-purposed by nonstate actors looking to pursue and confiscate the proceeds of corruption. Those investigating financial crime are commonly faced with the need to compulsorily obtain documents and records from the defendant. Police and prosecutors may be equipped with such powers, but what about nonstate actors? Since the mid-1970s, under some conditions private parties can apply to courts for search orders (also known as Anton Piller orders). These are court orders for the defendant to produce specified documents and records, with refusal equivalent to being in contempt of court.[73]

Another civil law instrument is freezing orders, also known as Mareva injunctions, which can freeze assets with worldwide effect. Such freezing orders and search orders have been referred to as the 'nuclear weapons of English commercial litigation'.[74] The rationale for the former is that if one party loses a commercial dispute to another, the winner must be able to ensure that the loser's assets cannot be removed or spent in order to frustrate any award.[75] Freezing orders have been used in relation to kleptocrats as far back as 1989, with a freezing order in the UK against the assets of 'Baby Doc' Duvalier of Haiti.[76] Freezing orders may also be used to immobilize money held by third parties, again with worldwide effect, even when these parties are not themselves targets of the legal action.[77] This third-party application is especially useful when, as is commonly the case, the proceeds of corruption are held in the name of a front man or shell company.

Though the trend towards the pluralization of enforcement is unmistakable, all of these tactics have their limitations. Perhaps the elephant in the room with civil law is cost. If governments and law enforcement agencies are often deterred by the expense of corruption cases, especially in using civil law, how can not-for-profit actors hope to afford them? The advanced legal and accounting skills often needed to take advantage of these options can be hugely expensive, especially considering that these cases tend to run for years.

The first response is that although most NGOs do not have much money, some do. In 2017 George Soros transferred $18 billion to the Open Society Foundations (OSF) he had created. Not only does this body have an annual budget of $1.2 billion,[78] it has taken a keen interest in funding efforts to enforce international anti-corruption rules. It has provided money and

73. Oliver 2011.
74. Alexander 1997.
75. Jeyaretnam and Lau 2016: 504.
76. Davis 2011: 79.
77. Oliver 2011: 174.
78. https://www.opensocietyfoundations.org/who-we-are/financials.

legal expertise to exposés of various corruption schemes and, as discussed, supported criminal prosecutions brought or requested by NGOs in France, Spain, and Switzerland; it continues to search for additional anti-corruption lawsuits to fund.[79] In doing so, OSF has developed a role as perhaps the leading funder of enforcement NGOs, evidence of the organizational differentiation and division of labour among such groups. As already discussed, Bill Browder's Hermitage Capital has also spent millions of dollars investigating the trail of corruption funds from Russia on a not-for-profit basis since 2009. However, Open Society Foundations and Hermitage Capital are the exceptions rather than rule, being vastly wealthier than their peers. What about the typical NGO on a shoestring budget?

Just as important as new legal options are the corresponding financial innovations. New legal strategies in business litigation will not be much use unless people can pay for them. Once again, although recent advances in litigation financing have been made with for-profit actors in mind, some are also available to not-for-profits. A simple example is when a lawyer or team of lawyers works on a contingency 'no win, no fee' basis, being paid only a share of the money won. Enrico Monfrini, a Swiss lawyer who worked from 1999 to 2014 to recover money stolen by former Nigerian dictator Sani Abacha, was commissioned by the Nigerian government on this basis. Upon recovering $321 million of the missing money from Luxembourg, Monfrini was paid $5 million plus 2.8 percent of the money recovered.[80] Usually the share of the money taken in the event of success is far higher. As discussed above, UK law firm Leigh Day also has taken NGO anti-corruption cases on this basis, while Protective Costs Orders also insulate smaller NGOs against the costs of an unsuccessful lawsuit.

Clearly, if most or all of the expense of a legal team can be covered out of corruption assets recovered (if any money is recovered), this makes it easier for financially poor NGOs to take this route. Such an arrangement may raise vexed moral issues, however. Some NGOs have spoken out against such deals, on the grounds that all stolen assets should be returned to their rightful owners.[81] Contingency arrangements have long been allowed in the United States but have only been permitted in countries like the UK relatively recently, and they are prohibited in many other European countries.[82]

79. Open Society Foundations interview 2020.
80. Sahara Reporters 2017.
81. Bern Declaration interview 2015; Transparency International-UK interview 2017.
82. Civitas Maxima interview 2019.

In 'no win, no pay' contingency arrangements the law firm assumes all the financial risk, which is considerable. International corruption cases are long, expenses are high, and failure is common. Even the successful cases in France against Obiang and al-Assad took around a decade. Many firms cannot or will not take on such a risk. However, it is increasingly common for risk to be passed to third parties by insuring against loss with specialized litigation insurance.[83] Another option is that dedicated litigation financing firms pay for the case, with these firms seeking money from other third-party investors; litigation has become a new and very much sought-after investment class of its own.[84] These recent developments significantly lower the financial barriers to NGOs' ability to engage sophisticated legal teams to pursue civil enforcement.

Finally, not all legal options are hugely expensive. Our interviewees confirm that many lawyers are willing to put in at least some work pro bono on major corruption cases, and many NGO activists are themselves lawyers or ex-lawyers. As an example of anti-corruption legal action on the cheap, a rare success in the efforts to recover stolen assets in the wake of the Arab Spring revolutions was the one-man campaign that led to the confiscation of Saadi Gaddafi's (the late dictator's son) £10 million mansion in London via a civil suit in March 2012. Local lawyer Mohamed Shaban was one of many private individuals who was granted permission to act (unpaid) on behalf of the Libyan National Transitional Council government in pursing the overseas corruption proceeds of the Gaddafi family. The mansion was owned via a British Virgin Islands shell company, Capitana Seas Limited, with the company in turn owned by Saadi. Saadi had neglected to pay the $500 annual renewal fee on the company, however, and because at the time he had fled Libya for Niger, there was no one to represent him, and the case went through unopposed. The judge ruled that the property was bought unlawfully with funds properly belonging to the Libyan state.[85]

Anti-Corruption Enforcement and Technology

Although relatively recent, the technological revolution whereby billions of people now have access to massive amounts of information at their fingertips is easy to take for granted. For the same reason, it is easy to miss

83. Mather 2017.
84. La Croix 2018.
85. See https://www.globalwitness.org/en/archive/10m-house-expensive-london-suburb-recovered-libya/; Global Witness interviews.

the implications of this revolution. Anyone with the ability to connect to the internet now has more investigative capacity than any law enforcement agency before the mid-1990s. It is not just the volume of information (which by itself would be overwhelming) that is the key change but also the availability of computing power to search and process this information. This information and processing power are available cheaply, often for free. Each of these facts is well-known, almost banal, yet the significance for NGO enforcement has not yet been appreciated. Jointly, they have created an open source investigation and enforcement revolution.[86] The section below spells out the consequences for vigilante enforcement in terms of investigating and gathering evidence on transnational corruption crimes.

OPEN SOURCE INTELLIGENCE AND INVESTIGATIONS

Drawing the line between what counts as NGO enforcement and what does not can be difficult. It is particularly challenging when it comes to investigation and evidence gathering, the 'softer' end of the enforcement spectrum. In this context it is also sometimes far from simple to draw the line between NGOs and other actors. Some of the most effective investigators of corruption are located in the grey area between journalism and NGO work, such as the Organized Crime and Corruption Reporting Project, the International Consortium of Investigative Journalists (ICIJ), and Bellingcat. Aside from their own actions, each group has boosted the capacity of other NGOs to begin their own corruption investigations. As well as reflecting the reduced costs of supplying enforcement in this domain, these groups lower costs even further, creating a positive feedback loop which strengthens the investigative infrastructure and momentum, akin to the dynamics observed in environmental and human rights enforcement.

As discussed in chapter 2 in connection with human rights enforcement, Bellingcat, founded in 2014, perhaps best epitomizes the potential of open data and new technology in investigations. Initially funded through the crowd-sourcing website Kickstarter, subsequently it has received grants from the Open Society Foundations, among other bodies. Like many other new technology-enabled groups, Bellingcat does not see itself as being in the advocacy business and resolutely rejects the traditional journalistic prohibition on cooperating with law enforcement.[87] Bellingcat has partnered with

86. Higgins 2021.
87. Bellingcat interview 2020; Higgins 2021: 98–99.

Transparency International-UK to investigate the laundering of corruption funds from Moldova and other former Soviet republics in and through Britain.[88] The information demands of unravelling such scandals can be grasped by the fact that one such scheme used around 5,000 separate companies, partnerships, and other legal entities and involved 70,000 individual banking transactions across 96 different countries.[89] Because of the inherently slow and bureaucratic nature of state-to-state international legal cooperation, where a single international request for information generally takes months, it is easy to see both how powerless state law enforcement might be in the face of such complexity and how an informal, more networked investigative response may be more effective.

The International Consortium of Investigative Journalists (ICIJ) is another group that shows how technological advances have enabled nonstate investigation and evidence gathering. Formed in 1997 as a part of the Center for Public Integrity, the ICIJ became an independent non-profit organization in 2017. It functions as both a small core team and a much larger network of investigative journalists working at for-profit media outlets collaborating on particular projects on an ad hoc basis.[90] It has a range of funders, from the Open Society Foundations to Meryl Streep.[91] This network is best known for a series of leaks of offshore financial information, the most prominent of which is the Panama Papers in 2016.[92] An unknown individual at the Panamanian law firm Mossack Fonseca leaked a huge amount of information on shell companies and bank accounts. This example provides strong pointers as to how technology has enabled investigation beyond the state.

The sheer volume of information that can be copied and transported on USB sticks and external hard drives and through uploading to websites is easy to take for granted, as the pre-computer, paper-only world recedes from memory. The Panama Papers comprised 2.6 terabytes of data on 214,000 companies, 11.5 million documents, including 4.8 million emails, 3 million database entries, 2.2 million pdf documents, and 320,000 text files. But for technology, it would have been impossible to leak this volume of information, equivalent to truckloads of paper files. The same tendency to forget the world before the internet obscures the importance and the novelty of being able to communicate and share documents with people in many different

88. Transparency International-UK and Bellingcat 2017.
89. Ibid., 7.
90. International Consortium of Investigative Journalists interview 2013.
91. https://www.icij.org/about/our-supporters/.
92. Obermaier and Obermayer 2017.

countries for free, instead of making expensive international phone (or fax) calls or having to physically send documents back and forth.

But by itself the huge amount of information leaked is immaterial. To be useful to either state or nonstate enforcers, investigators need to be able to find the needle in a very large haystack. The initial naive hope was that those combing through the leaked Panama Papers would simply be able to type in a name, press 'search', and see what information came up.[93] In fact, to be useable, the different file formats first had to be converted so as to be able to be read by a common search function, and then specialized search software had to be designed. The legacy of this work (including other leaks in addition to the Panama Papers) is an online free database of 785,000 offshore companies, trusts, and other corporate entities (the Offshore Leaks Database) hosted by the ICIJ searchable by company or personal name and jurisdiction.[94]

As little as a decade ago, this kind of information was a closely guarded secret. In the best case, getting access would have required travelling to the jurisdiction where the shell company was incorporated to look at the paper records. However, the most valuable information, that is, the identity of the real owners behind the shell companies, would have been entirely unavailable to all but law enforcement and regulators. Even they may have had to go to court to get access and then negotiate the slow and arduous process of international mutual legal assistance. Usually, such hurdles meant that enquiries were rarely made, and investigations simply stopped or were never started. Thus this sort of online database is a profound transformation in the capacity of NGOs, and even just private individuals, to investigate financial crime.

An even larger database along the same lines was set up by the NGO Open-Corporates, which since 2010 has aimed at 'total corporate transparency'.[95] It too has used data from the leaks but more so website-scraping software to harvest all available data from national company registries. OpenCorporates then reformatted and combined the data into a free, online searchable repository of details on an incredible 187,206,651 companies.[96] It bears stressing that the importance of this corporate information is that almost all complex financial crime, especially foreign bribery, grand corruption, and the associated money laundering, relies on companies and other corporate entities (trusts, foundations, partnerships, etc.) to hide the identity of the criminals

93. International Consortium of Investigative Journalists interview 2013.
94. https://offshoreleaks.icij.org/?gclid=Cj0KCQjwyZmEBhCpARIsALIzmnI1-xYYkbxi_a4tDYAzbjjbkh3pXYGSt4uZgegh2Z_xzjjoH512WKEaAqf9EALw_wcB.
95. https://opencorporates.com/info/about/.
96. https://opencorporates.com/.

at work.[97] The joint effect of all this technology-enabled free, searchable information is once again to drastically lower barriers to entry for subsequent NGO financial investigators. A final boon to both state and nonstate investigators in making sense of all this data is software that allows the simple visual rendering of complicated criminal finance schemes.[98] Although these new capacities can be used for advocacy, their technical character reflects the fact that they were designed for investigation.

SOCIAL MEDIA AND DRONES

Another technological trend that has unintentionally benefitted anti-corruption NGOs is the rise of social media, thanks to the tendency of those at the heart of corruption schemes to boast about their ill-gotten gains online.[99] Facebook, Instagram, and similar platforms have provided investigators of all types with invaluable tip-offs.[100]

A relatively inconspicuous form of conspicuous consumption is wristwatches, which may be valued at up to $1 million each. Aleksei Navalny's Anti-Corruption Foundation in Russia has specialized in valuing the wristwatches worn by Russian officials spotted on social media. These watch often cost many multiples of these officials' annual salary, raising pointed questions concerning where they got the money for such accessories. A twist on this tactic saw the Russian Orthodox Church airbrush out of a photo an ostentatiously expensive watch worn by Patriarch Kirill. However, the church forgot to remove the reflection of the watch from the highly polished table the Patriarch was sitting at, a discrepancy gleefully identified by the Anti-Corruption Foundation.[101]

The Anti-Corruption Foundation has also been assiduous in identifying corrupt officials by 'yacht-spotting'. Bellingcat has parsed the Russian NGO's approach in one of its series of online corruption investigation how-to guides.[102] The foundation received a tip that Dmitri Peskov, Putin's press secretary (and wearer of a $600,000 wristwatch, four times greater than his

97. Stolen Asset Recovery Initiative 2011; Findley, Nielson, and Sharman 2014; Financial Action Task Force 2018.

98. Sentry interview 2016.

99. Wright and Hope 2018; International Consortium of Investigative Journalists, https://www.icij.org/tags/luanda-leaks/.

100. Open Society Foundations interview 2015.

101. Schwirtz 2012.

102. Toler 2015.

annual income), was celebrating his honeymoon between Sicily and Sardinia in mid-August 2015 on the super-yacht *Maltese Falcon*. Peskov vehemently denied the claim. The vessel is the second-most expensive yacht ever built, featuring its own submarine, amongst other amenities. The rental price for a week, €385,000, is well beyond Peskov's $140,000 official annual salary.

Just as there are public flight-tracking websites, so too are there public ship-tracking websites, and one of these, VesselFinder, placed the *Falcon* off Sicily at the time in question. Instagram posts from Peskov's fifteen-year-old stepdaughter Aleksandra and nineteen-year-old daughter Elizaveta at the same time showed them both unmistakably onboard the yacht. Aleksandra also posted geo-located photos from Sardinia within the same period. Fellow oligarchs associated with Peskov were located by similar means with their yachts at the same place at the same time, suggesting a party. Publicly accessible webcams from the Sardinian coast again confirmed the presence of the yachts in question.[103]

Of course it could be objected that Peskov is hardly in danger of being prosecuted by the Russian authorities as a result of this NGO investigation, given his close relationship to Putin. However, the point of vulnerability for Peskov, and for kleptocrats in general facing NGO exposure of this kind, is that while they are safe in their own countries (unless and until there is a change of political fortunes), both they and their assets are vulnerable once abroad. The mastermind at the heart of Malaysia's biggest corruption scandal had his $250 million yacht confiscated in Indonesia at the behest of U.S. authorities in February 2018.[104] Targeted U.S. sanctions, and measures like G20 visa travel bans for suspected corrupt officials, can put a considerable crimp in such officials' lifestyles. Furthermore and by way of comparison, even if most police investigations do not lead to convictions, these investigations still constitute enforcement.

Where public officials suspected of corruption have not self-incriminated via social media, drones are another technological advance that facilitate NGO investigations. As one source puts it: 'In anticorruption activists' efforts to get a glimpse behind the gated palaces of the Kremlin elite, perhaps no tool has been as valuable for the opposition as drones fitted with cameras'.[105] The Anti-Corruption Foundation recorded footage of what was alleged to be former president (and previous and later prime minister)

---

103. See Seddon 2015.
104. Lopez 2018.
105. Balmforth 2018.

Medvedev's collection of mansions and villas.[106] Other officials whose luxury real estate was likewise suspected to be bought with ill-gotten gains received the same type of drone visits.

By volume, however, most corruption offences are relatively small-scale, perpetrated by mid- and lower-level government employees rather than their super-yacht-and-mansion-owning superiors. Here too technology has helped anti-corruption enforcement. One example is from Ukraine's public procurement system. In 2016 the government attempted to tame rampant corruption in state procurement by introducing an open online accounting system, ProZorro, that picked up on common indicators of fraud and corruption. Although it was a success, corrupt officials and their private sector accomplices worked out how to avoid these indicators. In response, Transparency International-Ukraine independently developed another complementary software system, DoZorro.[107] The volume of procurement orders, 4,500 a day, meant relying on a decentralized crowd-sourced model of scrutiny via the website and app. The 140,000 users lodged reports which led to 1,200 suppliers being changed and 22 were criminally prosecuted.[108] ProZorro and DoZorro may have been too successful for their own good: in 2020 the Ukrainian government introduced reform to remove the newer, more transparent procurement system.[109]

A study funded by the OSF has suggested the use of four complementary types of technology to detect corruption in Latin American countries' public procurement processes: online procurement according to open data standards; crowd-sourced citizen verification via apps; big data and Artificial Intelligence to search for irregularities in contracts; and Distributed-Ledger Technology (e.g., blockchain) to certify contracts and payments.[110] Unprompted by and independent of governments, such technology does not comprise service delivery contracted by the state, nor do such technical tools represent advocacy; instead, they are enforcement.

One of the most original and widely emulated instances of harnessing technology to combat petty corruption comes from the developing world. In 2010 India's Janaagraha Centre for Citizenship and Democracy launched a crowd-sourced I Paid a Bribe online system.[111] As the name suggests,

106. Anti-Corruption Foundation 2017.
107. Observatory of Public Sector Innovation 2019.
108. Citizen Engage 2018.
109. Transparency International-Ukraine 2020.
110. Arguello and Ziff 2019.
111. ipaidabribe.com.

those pressured to pay bribes to government officials can use their phone to upload details of the transaction to the website, including when, how much, and for what they paid. According to its founder, the aim was to create 'a swarm-like resistance to corruption'.[112] Initially this tool was purely advocacy; the system anonymized the names of both parties to the bribe. Those Indian government departments most often reported were sometimes shamed into reform (over 1.4 million reports have been received). But from 2013 the system provided the option of those reporting to reveal their own name and/or the name of the official demanding payment, lending it an enforcement function. This has led to instances where individual officials have been punished as a result of this evidence.[113] The system has since been widely diffused to over thirty other countries, from Guatemala to Ukraine.[114]

Anti-Corruption NGOs in Context: Competition and Differentiation

So far the chapter has looked at the drivers behind the trend towards greater NGO enforcement of international anti-corruption standards. On the demand side, this is the large and growing enforcement gap caused by the expansion of anti-corruption law, compared with the difficulties in actually reducing transnational corruption. On the supply side, the drivers are legal and technological changes that increase the opportunities for nonstate actors to engage in a range of enforcement strategies, from investigation to prosecution. Also important for NGO strategies are interactions between NGOs and with other actors. As in other policy areas, there is only so much money, media attention, and political access to go around. Although the absolute numbers are much smaller, just as there has been strong growth in international anti-corruption rules, so too there has been a corresponding increase in the number of NGOs in this area (from a baseline of zero in 1990), progressively sharpening competition. Where others see competition as producing sameness,[115] a focus on enforcement instead throws strategic difference into light. Although there is a definite trend towards NGO vigilante enforcement, it is by no means uniform.

The largest anti-corruption NGO, Transparency International, has largely (but not completely) defined itself in opposition to enforcement, even at the

---

112. Asia Foundation 2011.
113. http://www.janaagraha.org/i-paid-a-bribe/.
114. Marin 2012.
115. Cooley and Ron 2002.

softer or more indirect end of investigation and evidence gathering. Why has this dominant group opted for Fabian strategies of advocacy and capacity building, while others have chosen to be anti-corruption vigilantes? This last section of the chapter examines this divergence in NGOs' strategies via the contrast between Transparency International, the dominant insider organization, and Global Witness, the most prominent of the vigilantes.

TRANSPARENCY INTERNATIONAL

By the end of the 1980s, the World Bank (among many others in the development sector) was confronted with an embarrassing problem: after decades of advice and conditional lending, many countries, especially in Africa, had become poorer rather than richer. What had gone wrong? Some began to speak of corruption. One of these was Peter Eigen, the World Bank director for East Africa. Initially the response to breaching the corruption taboo was strongly negative. Eigen recounts that he was told to 'shut up' by his superiors in the bank and that initially his 'efforts to advance the anti-corruption drive were met with hostility and ridicule in government and business circles'.[116]

Yet Eigen was far from the only one arguing for a link between corruption and development failure.[117] From 1991, more backers came on board, including ministers from developing countries, the director of the German aid agency GTZ, senior World Bankers Frank Vogl and Michael Wiehen, and businessmen George Moody-Stuart, Gerald Parfitt, and Fritz Heimann. Together they launched Transparency International in Berlin in 1993.[118] The initial meeting was a high-profile affair, paid for by GTZ, attended by heads of state and former World Bank president Robert McNamara. Jeremy Pope, the first managing director from January 1994, had been director of the Commonwealth Secretariat legal services division.[119] Transparency International was thus constituted from 'a network of like-minded elites round the world'.[120] In its elite, insider, rather clubby nature Larmour (himself a Transparency International member) observed 'a weird institutional isomorphism between the corrupt networks—dependent on face to face contacts, trust, and a shared background—and the anti-corruption networks opposed to them'.[121]

116. Vogl 2012: 61; Eigen 2013: 1291, 1293.
117. Weaver 2008.
118. Vogl 2012: 62.
119. De Sousa 2005: 4.
120. Wang and Rosenau 2001: 39.
121. Larmour 2005: 7.

From its initially small but high-powered cadre of founders, Transparency International quickly developed into a globe-spanning decentralized organization. Established in Berlin as a German foundation, the group adopted a franchise model of national accredited chapters, currently numbering about one hundred.[122] As a result, the organization has a genuinely global presence, in contrast to the notably European cast of most other international anti-corruption NGOs. National chapters have a high degree of autonomy and are generally self-funding, which has often meant working on a tiny budget.[123] Historically, most have not had enough money even for a single full-time staff member.[124] The Transparency International secretariat in Berlin has also had financial ups and downs, seeing its roster shrink from almost two hundred staff to around one hundred in 2017.[125]

The group mainly seeks to achieve influence by persuading businesses and governments to commit to integrity standards designed in accord with Transparency International's recommendations and tools. Perhaps its main strategies have been networking and coalition building with corporations and governments.[126] This is not to say that Transparency's relations with governments have always been amiable. Its most high-profile output is the annual Corruption Perceptions Index (first made public by accident in 1995), a survey-based league table ranking countries from presumptively least to most corrupt.[127] Attracting widespread media attention, those governments ranked towards the bottom of the list, or losing ground from one year to the next, have commonly been vocal critics of the index.[128]

Transparency International's three founding principles were a holistic approach to reducing corruption, a reliance on mobilizing civil society, and 'non-investigation of individual cases of corruption for exposure'[129] because the organization 'is not intent on exposing villains, or casting blame'.[130] In this last respect, Transparency International self-consciously adopted a 'sharply contrasting methodology' from human rights organizations.[131]

---

122. https://www.transparency.org/whoweare/organisation. Many individual chapters have also tended to reproduce Transparency International's elite membership. De Sousa 2005: 13.

123. Larmour 2005: 7.

124. De Sousa 2005: 16.

125. Transparency International interview 2017.

126. De Sousa 2005: 20; Transparency International interview 2011, 2015, 2017, 2020.

127. Bukovansky 2015.

128. The index also has its share of academic critics, e.g., Andersson and Heywood 2009.

129. Eigen 2013: 1294.

130. Eigen 1996: 162; see also Wang and Rosenau 2001: 36; Gutterman 2014: 405.

131. Eigen 1996: 162.

The decision to eschew investigations reflected concerns about libel threats in developed countries, and much more direct threats of physical harm in developing countries, as well as a lack of faith in criminal justice responses to corruption. Transparency International wanted to work with big business and government, not against them. In line with this founding principle, the group has rarely taken on staff with investigative skills.[132]

Transparency's 'no investigation' rule has raised doubts about and some opposition to the organization. Twenty years after the group's founding, Eigen noted that the decision not to investigate, and the reliance on making common cause with business and governments, had been criticized by other 'more confrontational' NGOs.[133] He reflected, 'TI noticed that a total abstention from focusing on individual cases could turn it into a toothless tiger. . . . However, this still did not change our intention to co-operate as much as possible with governments, international organizations, and business'.[134] While some younger members reported being drawn to the more exciting cloak-and-dagger enforcement approaches of Global Witness, more senior members of Transparency International saw this as a price worth paying for close relations with business.[135] One view in the Open Society Foundations suggests that there is a natural division of labour between the major anti-corruption NGOs: national Transparency International chapters privately flag cases in their country that should be investigated, specialists from the Organized Crime and Corruption Reporting Project investigate, and then OSF prepares the cases for legal action, often in conjunction with other local NGOs.[136] Thus there is a blueprint for an NGO anti-corruption enforcement chain.

Despite this general orientation, the national chapter structure of Transparency International means that different chapters have chosen different strategies. After an initial period of diffidence, by 1996–97 Transparency International-Germany had been taken into the fold by big business, attracting the endorsement and support of the country's major multinational corporations.[137] No doubt this friendly reception was helped by the fact that Eigen and other key backers were German and by the early support of the

---

132. Transparency International interview 2015, 2017; Larmour 2005: 6.

133. Eigen 2013: 1296.

134. Ibid.

135. Transparency International interview 2011, 2020; Global Witness interview 2011.

136. Open Society Foundations interview 2017, 2020; Transparency International interview 2020a.

137. Gutterman 2014: 402.

German government. Transparency International-France, by contrast, was generally shunned by both government and business. It had little media profile and was widely seen as a creature of the United States,[138] perhaps even the CIA. Eigen stated in 2001 that the French 'fear that we are more or less a secret brigade for corporate America . . . that we are simply doing the dirty business of the Americans'.[139] Reflecting this distance from the French government, the national chapter closely examined corruption in political financing, a sensitive topic that had been assiduously avoided by the central secretariat and most other national chapters.[140] This outsider status helps explain why TI-France took a very different stance from the 'no investigation' principle in joining Sherpa's effort to prosecute Teodorin Obiang from 2007.

Transparency International-UK formed good relations with many prominent businesses,[141] and it became particularly close with the Department for International Development.[142] It has grown to be one of the largest national chapters, from only three full-time staff to around fifty in 2019.[143] Around 2015 it considered conducting its own investigations but decided against this on the grounds that too many other NGOs were already investigating corruption, especially in Britain, and that Transparency International's core strength lay in its advocacy and research roles.[144] Indicative of this self-perception, the group's director referred to an anti-bribery instruction manual for UK firms as follows: 'In a typical TI fashion, it was guidance written by experts, for experts, and was just what companies needed'.[145]

Transparency International has accepted funding from firms like Deloitte and Touche and Exxon and tends to take governments evincing a commitment to fighting corruption at their word, even when others are sceptical. Corporate sponsorship was an early and important source of funding for Transparency International, with a special business forum open to those paying a £30,000 per annum membership fee.[146] In contrast, Global Witness and other, smaller anti-corruption NGOs are much more likely to see, in

138. Transparency International interview 2020a.
139. Quoted in Gutterman 2014: 412.
140. De Sousa 2005: 26.
141. Barrington 2020.
142. Gutterman 2017: 160. The Department for International Development was replaced by the Foreign, Commonwealth and Development Office in 2020.
143. Transparency International-UK 2019.
144. Transparency International-UK interview 2017.
145. Barrington 2020: 13.
146. Transparency International, Cambridge, interview 2017.

particular, banks and law accountancy, and oil firms as part of the problem rather than the solution.[147]

In this respect, competition for funding may be ameliorated between the different NGOs: Transparency International cultivates donors that are beyond the pale for other anti-corruption groups. It has intimate connections to big business and governments that other groups could not get and may not even want. Its initial decision not to engage in investigations may have locked in this strategy, as other groups arose to exploit this vacant niche. Finally, unlike other anti-corruption groups that grew directly or indirectly out of human rights or environmental activism, Transparency International explicitly defined itself and its strategy against earlier NGOs' models of confronting firms and governments, either in the courtroom or on the street.

GLOBAL WITNESS

Perhaps most NGOs relish an origins story of a few individuals starting with nothing but passion and principles. Global Witness has one too. In November 1993 Simon Taylor, Charmian Gooch, and Patrick Alley formed the group after a series of long talks at the pub, 'sourcing their first computer out of the trash, and relying on friends and family to pay for their international calls' (in the pre-internet era when international calls had to be paid for).[148] Their first financing strategy was soliciting donations outside Bank Underground station in London.[149]

The contrast with Transparency International's beginnings is stark. The three founders met while working at the Environmental Investigation Agency (EIA) in London.[150] The EIA pioneered the use of undercover investigations in whaling and the illicit trade in wildlife. Indicating the importance of inter-NGO learning and skills transfer, Global Witness initially hewed very closely to the precedent set by the EIA, positioning itself at the overlap of environmental, resource, and corruption issues. Alley, Gooch, and Taylor travelled to Cambodia to do undercover work to expose illegal logging by Khmer Rouge guerrillas, posing as timber buyers and using a secret camera.[151] The resulting report, 'Cambodia, Where Money Grows on Trees', was released in 1996. It

---

147. Global Witness interview 2011; Transparency International interview 2020b.
148. Global Witness 2019; Global Witness interview 2020c.
149. Robinsson 2014; Global Witness interview 2020c.
150. Duncan 2014.
151. Gooch talk San Francisco, 15 October 2014, https://www.youtube.com/watch?v =L9Oa74JyUD8; Global Witness interview 2020c.

was followed by Global Witness successfully investigating and popularizing the issue of 'blood diamonds' in West African civil wars. The group was supported by the Open Society Foundations, which were particularly keen on financing investigations.[152]

Global Witness is no longer the three-person upstart it once was. Ten years after its founding, in 2003, there had been a modest expansion to around 20 staff.[153] By 2018, the group had a budget of £10 million and 110 employees, with an office in Washington as well as London.[154] Along with the change in size has come a change in emphasis. There is now more importance placed on building a media profile and somewhat less on in-depth investigations. In the first decade of Global Witness, staff were told to go out and get good material, with very little specific direction. They then would write up the results in the form of a detailed report, with success measured in terms of policy change and prosecutions. Investigators managed their own relations with the media, which were seen as secondary. More recently, however, each team has acquired a dedicated communication person. Reports have got shorter, more in the form of press briefings, with success increasingly proxied by media impact.

These strategic and tactical changes seem to reflect changing competitive pressures. In the early days Global Witness had 'carved out a niche' for itself as the only anti-corruption NGO doing investigative work; there were few other groups working on corruption, and Transparency International had foresworn investigations.[155] Not only are there now many more anti-corruption NGOs, but they are increasingly involved in the same types of enforcement pioneered by Global Witness. Very different groups like Bellingcat, Hermitage Capital, Organized Crime and Corruption Reporting Project, and the ICIJ all moved into investigating corruption a decade or two after Global Witness. At the same time human rights and environmental organizations including TRIAL, Sherpa, Re:Common, the Corner House, the Sentry, Conflict Awareness Project, OSF, and APDHE have taken an interest in directly fighting corruption, while development-oriented bodies like Oxfam, ActionAid, and Christian Aid have also begun work on less confrontational means of addressing this problem. Some of these newer entrants brought a depth of expertise in the harder end of the enforcement spectrum, especially in litigation and prosecution, from earlier experience in the human rights and environmental

152. Global Witness interview 2015, 2020a, 2020b.
153. Global Witness interview 2020a, 2020b, 2020c.
154. Global Witness 2018a; Global Witness 2019.
155. Global Witness interview 2020a.

spheres. Thus even though international anti-corruption enforcement is a newer policy priority with far fewer NGOs active in this area, some of the same trends of inter-NGO differentiation and specialization are evident as have been described in the previous two chapters.

Conclusion

This chapter began with questions and ends with questions. There is a new trend for nonstate anti-corruption actors to try to enforce international standards against cross-border financial crime. On the demand side, this reflects the enforcement gap created by the spread of international law and the deficiencies in making it effective. On the supply side, legal and techno-logical advances have increased the potential for nonstate anti-corruption enforcement. Many of the NGOs availing themselves of these new strate-gies have followed earlier enforcement efforts in international human rights prosecutions and environmental enforcement, Global Witness being the exemplar. At the same time, there is notable variation in NGO strategy, with Transparency International eschewing enforcement, by and large sticking to a consensual, insider strategy of networking and coalition building.

Yet there are important unanswered questions about vigilante anti-corruption enforcement by NGOs that feed directly into the broader con-siderations to be addressed in the final chapter. First, what difference has such enforcement made in policy terms? So far, there have been at least as many failures as successes, and it is difficult to say that the enforcement gap has been appreciably closed. Second, what is the relationship between vigi-lantes and the state? Does a continuing lack of effectiveness reflect govern-ments increasingly shirking their duty to enforce the commitments they have made and passing the buck to NGOs? To what degree are the authorities and NGOs competing or colluding in seeking to hold law-breakers to account? Finally, is the rise of vigilante enforcement against corruption and other global ills morally a good or bad thing? The groups themselves and many supporters say that they are selflessly working to combat some of the most serious transnational threats to human well-being. Yet the idea of 'vigilante justice' raises concerns about unaccountable actors taking the law into their own hands without respect for due process. In comparing the findings of the previous three chapters, we now move on to address each of these points.

Conclusion

Nonstate actors increasingly play the role of vigilante enforcers of international law. Rather than treating governments as inimitable enforcers of international law, we need to re-evaluate, to shift our view to a more pluralistic understanding which recognizes the multiple enforcement roles of other actors in world politics, especially NGOs. So far we have illustrated the rise of autonomous NGO enforcement in three broad domains of international law: human rights, the environment, and anti-corruption. We have explained this trend by several facilitating factors: a growing mismatch between increasing legalization and limited state enforcement; legal and technological innovations empowering nonstate enforcers; and the changing ecologies of NGO populations. In some cases, states have deliberately or inadvertently created conditions for NGOs to step into an autonomous enforcement role, particularly when governments have committed to wide-ranging legal obligations and then failed to supply adequate enforcement, or when unintended consequences of law have opened new doors to nonstate enforcement. In other cases, NGOs have wrested power from states by turning domestic or international enforcement mechanisms against governments in response to sins of omission or commission.

Although it is important to stress that nonstate enforcement of domestic law was the rule rather than the exception until well into the nineteenth century, and that there are at least some precedents of cross-border enforcement prior to the twentieth century, vigilante enforcement of international law is nevertheless a new trend. In a trivial sense this reflects the fact that

much of the international law in question is itself new. Yet beyond the proliferation of law and the parallel growth of transnational NGOs are other
drivers, including learning and strategic emulation by NGOs, both within
and across policy domains. In this sense, the rise of transnational enforcement is cumulative. Importantly, the chief drivers of NGO enforcement are
not 'exogenous' to the actors involved. Instead, transnational actors have
played a central role in promoting and developing the technological and
legal advances which facilitate nonstate enforcement. As domestic and international courts continue to accept cases brought by NGOs, they tend to
create further precedents for transnational litigation. In this sense too, NGO
enforcement may have cumulative effect.

Fertile legal conditions were first available in the domain of human
rights, and this is largely where NGOs developed and honed the litigation
strategies that would later be emulated by NGOs elsewhere. From the 1970s
onwards, human rights NGOs adopted increasingly transnational strategies, as domestic private prosecutions were complemented by petitions
to regional and international courts, the assertion of universal jurisdiction, and, later, collaboration with the International Criminal Court. In the
last decades of the twentieth century, a rapid expansion of international
environmental law together with rapid technological progress enabled a
growing enforcement role for environmental NGOs, further reinforced by
cross-fertilization between environmental and human rights norms. Most
recently, vigilante enforcement in the domains of human rights and environmental law has strongly shaped a similar trend in the anti-corruption
sphere.

While this spill-over is conditioned on legal developments, it also results
from mimicry and learning. As individuals move between NGOs in different policy domains, or break from existing groups to form new outfits, they
bring strategic knowledge and expertise with them. At the same time, the
activities of many NGOs increasingly span what are in many ways arbitrary
distinctions between the three policy areas reviewed in this book, enabling
wider learning and strategic experimentation across different domains of
policy and bodies of international law. As we have seen in the foregoing
chapters, while human rights violations, environmental degradation, and
corruption are often linked in practice, activists also increasingly link such
issues as a matter of strategy, sometimes because a high public profile of
one issue can help to attract greater public and political attention, at other
times because legal opportunities encourage such links as a way to improve
enforcement.

Contrasts between Policy Domains

This book has focused mainly on broad commonalities in NGO enforcement of international laws governing human rights, environmental policy, and corruption. At one level, the same drivers have given rise to the same general outcome: the rise of autonomous NGO enforcement of international law. But the chapters also illustrate notable differences in the way this overall story has played out in each policy area.

One difference is the relative novelty of international anti-corruption law (dating from the second half of the 1990s) and the lower numbers and relative youth of NGOs in this area. While the number of international NGOs dedicated to fighting corruption has increased sharply since the turn of the century, in absolute terms there are still far fewer such groups than those focused on defending human rights or environmental standards. This raises the question whether the ecological pressures for differentiation we have identified also hold in this domain. While a numerically smaller population may have dampened the effects of inter-NGO competition to an extent, it does not mean such effects are absent. Population density and resulting resource scarcity is not a direct function of growing numbers of organizations but rather a question of relative demand versus supply of essential organizational resources (e.g., funding, political access, media attention, demand for technical expertise or for service delivery, etc.). A small population can experience fierce competition if the size of the pie they are competing for is also correspondingly small. The growing strategic differentiation between anti-corruption groups detailed in chapter 4 illustrates these dynamics. As the dominant incumbent, Transparency International has generally stuck to more moderate insider tactics while newer, smaller groups have been more likely to investigate and take legal action.

Yet the relative novelty of anti-corruption NGOs also introduces different dynamics from other areas. There may be 'advantages of backwardness' for anti-corruption NGOs, to the extent that they can learn the lessons of autonomous enforcement from other domains without having to go through the same process of trial and error. In keeping with the recent professionalization of the NGO sector as a distinct career path,[1] many individuals working in anti-corruption groups have come from previous jobs with environmental or human rights NGOs, bringing with them a stock of experience

1. Oxfam interview 2020.

and know-how.[2] This has meant that blueprints for niche profiles and strategies have been more readily available to anti-corruption groups, speeding up processes of strategic differentiation and encouraging pluralization.

A second difference of note is the varying targets of enforcement. Although there are again plenty of exceptions, human rights and anti-corruption NGOs have so far been primarily concerned with holding individuals accountable for breaches of international law. In contrast, environmental groups are more likely to target companies and governments. The reasons for this disparity seem to be more a product of the relevant legal regimes than inherent in the issues at stake. A priori, it is hard to see why governments as such (rather than particular individuals within governments) are any less responsible for campaigns of state repression or systematic corruption than they are for breaches of international environmental law. Indeed, as law has evolved, we see more examples of human rights litigation against transnational corporations and governments. For example, in March 2015, the NGO Sherpa filed a complaint in France against Vinci Construction and the managers of its Qatari subsidiary over allegations of 'forced labour, servitude and concealment' in its construction sites for the football World Cup in Qatar.[3] As discussed in chapter 3, many recent cases of climate litigation seek to hold governments to account for violations of international human rights obligations.

Finally, NGOs in these three areas may differentially cluster around different points of the enforcement spectrum. For example, although groups in all three areas investigate, collect evidence for court cases, and litigate, human rights and anti-corruption enforcement feature few equivalents to environmental groups' use of direct-action strategies such as maritime interdiction, physical blockades, or armed anti-poaching patrols. Again, we see this as a reflection of specific opportunity structures rather than an expression of fundamentally different approaches to, or degrees of, autonomous enforcement. In many cases, direct environmental action is facilitated by concentrated physical infrastructures (say, power plants, oil rigs, or factory ships) which can be isolated and targeted in a way that human rights or corruption offenders mostly cannot. Yet, tactical differences may also reflect different organizational histories and identities. As discussed in chapter 3, direct action has a long history in the environmental movement, whereas

2. Seabrooke and Henriksen 2017.

3. European Center for Constitutional and Human Rights 2018; https://www.business
-humanrights.org/en/latest-news/vinci-lawsuits-re-forced-labour-in-qatar/.

transnational litigation has deeper roots among human rights groups. Still, over time, increasing overlap between legal frameworks and interaction among groups may facilitate growing cross-fertilization, diminishing strategic and tactical differences.

Are there, then, any instances of direct action among human rights and anti-corruption groups? Consider Women on Waves, a small Dutch-based NGO founded in 1999, which operates a ship from which they provide safe abortions in countries where abortion rights are restricted. The group argues that restrictive abortion laws violate fundamental human rights to health, recognized in numerous international treaties,[4] and also cites the Convention on the Elimination of All Forms of Discrimination against Women which states that women have the right to 'decide freely and responsibly on the number and spacing of their children'.[5] To defend these rights, the group operates a floating international abortion clinic. National penal legislation—and thus abortion laws—extends only to a state's territorial waters; outside that twelve-mile radius the law of the country where the ship is registered, in this case Dutch law, applies. Thus, after picking up women in national harbours, Women on Waves sail into international waters where medical abortions can be provided safely and legally. Through its maritime campaigns and its 'tele-medicine' services (which deliver drugs for medical abortions via mail or by using drones and provide licensed medical assistance via mobile video link), the group delivers about a thousand safe medical abortions every month—all in countries where access to abortion is restricted or denied. This direct approach has frequently resulted in clashes with governments or national security forces. In 2004 the group was blocked from entering Portuguese national waters by two warships. In 2012 Moroccan authorities forced a Women on Waves ship to leave Smir Harbour under navy escort.[6]

Women on Waves justifies its actions as upholding international law, but does this fit our definition of autonomous enforcement? On the one hand, this group is clearly independent rather than being contracted or orchestrated by a government or inter-governmental organization. It is taking direct action to deliver abortions rather than engaging in advocacy. Yet unlike the examples of vigilante enforcement in the book so far, Women on Waves is

4. For example, the Universal Declaration of Human Rights, the International Convention on the Elimination of All Forms of Racial Discrimination, the International Covenant on Economic, Social and Cultural Rights.

5. See Skinner 2015.

6. Women on Waves interview 2020.

not seeking to hold a specific individual, firm, or government accountable for violating international law but rather, one might argue, is seeking to remedy the consequences of insufficient implementation of international human rights through domestic legislation in some countries.

What about corruption? In 2017, the Autonomous Nation of Anarchist Libertarians (who style themselves as 'ANAL') occupied an empty £15 million mansion in Belgravia owned by Russian oligarch Andrey Goncharenko, on the logic that the mansion represented the proceeds of criminal behaviour. Much like Obiang's Californian and Parisian mansions, the occupation took place against a background of speculation about the laundering of foreign corruption proceeds in the London luxury property market. In the opinion of the Advisory Service for Squatters (ASS), because the activists had gained access to the mansion through an open window their occupation was technically legal.[7] Indeed, when attackers threw bricks and bottles through the windows of the occupied building ANAL called the police, later thanking law enforcement for their efforts.[8]

Although clearly not an example of enforcement of international law, could ANAL's action provide inspiration for anti-corruption direct action against mansions or yachts bought with looted funds? There is no practical reason why not, but the very improbability of such action by any of the NGOs discussed in the book underlines their commitment to working through legal processes of enforcement. One of the few exceptions to this strict commitment to legalism seems to be the use of stolen leaked data, like the Panama Papers.

Vigilante Enforcement in Other Policy Domains?

Our emphasis on legal opportunity structures raises the question: Is there enforcement beyond human rights, the environment, and corruption? Are there structural conditions that may encourage the spread of enforcement to other policy realms? Here we briefly provide some illustrations and speculate as to which international laws NGOs may try to enforce next. There is nothing inexorable or foreordained about the spread of enforcement beyond human rights, the environment, and anti-corruption, and the examples below are essentially modest and potentially reversible. Yet the

---

7. ASS supports the requisitioning of empty property to house homeless people and for other social uses; see https://www.squatter.org.uk/about-ass/.

8. England 2017; Taylor 2017.

fuzzy boundaries and overlap between issues like human rights and the arms trade, the environment and health, and cross-border corruption and other forms of transnational crime greatly facilitate the diffusion of enforcement through strategic cross-fertilization, as does the continuing diffusion of new enforcement technology. The inter-organizational dynamics discussed at the beginning of this chapter may also provide incentives for new enforcement groups to arise in these areas or for existing groups to branch out into new areas, much as some development, human rights, and environmental NGOs came to take an interest in enforcing anti-corruption law. Even in areas that might be seen as especially inhospitable to NGOs, such as nuclear nonproliferation, arms trade, and international sanctions, we see instances of NGO enforcement. Still, the incidence of vigilante enforcement is highly variable across different domains of global policy and looks likely to remain so in the future.

NGOs have played a role in enforcing national and international law governing arms transfers, working from the close connection between arms regulations and International Humanitarian Law and human rights. In April 2019, Bellingcat and the Global Legal Action Network (GLAN) released the results of their joint investigation into the campaign of airstrikes carried out by a Saudi-UAE led coalition in Yemen since 2015 (heavily aided by the United States, the UK, and other European states).[9] The investigation did not merely seek to call attention to the military action in Yemen but focused on producing verified material viable for court cases.[10] GLAN's director, Gearóid Ó Cuinn, explained, 'We see this partnership with Bellingcat as a powerful way to push the boundaries on legal evidence. We have already been able to contradict the statements and investigations of the Saudi-led Coalition'.[11]

Based on this evidence, in June 2019, the Campaign Against the Arms Trade brought a judicial review claim against the British government's decision to continue arms sales to Saudi Arabia, which it argued was unlawful in light of the clear proof of unlawful attacks by the Saudi-UAE coalition. British law—specifically the Consolidated EU and National Arms Export Licencing Criteria—requires the government to carefully vet recipients' attitude towards relevant principles of international law and bars the government from granting export licences if there is a *risk* that weapons might be

9. The results were posted on yemen.bellingcat.com.

10. Global Legal Action Network 2019a.

11. https://www.bellingcat.com/news/mena/2019/04/22/the-yemen-project-announcement/.

used in the commission of a serious violation of International Humanitarian Law. Nevertheless, rather than doing due diligence, the British government had chosen to rely on the Saudi coalition's own statements regarding its airstrikes to justify the arms exports. On 20 June 2019 the Court of Appeal held that the government's decision-making process was indeed unlawful, ordering that the decisions be retaken.[12] The case was only a partial win for NGOs. After the Court of Appeal's verdict, the government developed a 'revised methodology' to assess the airstrikes which concluded that 'possible violations of IHL . . . were "isolated incidents"' and that 'Saudi Arabia has a genuine intent and the capacity to comply with IHL'.[13]

Bellingcat's role as a 'nonstate intelligence agency' providing evidence on issues from Saudi airstrikes to cross-border flows of dirty money has been discussed already, but there are other groups performing equivalent roles. Such actors have provided intelligence to enforce compliance with the nuclear nonproliferation regime and international sanctions. An illustrative example is the exposure in December 2002 of two previously undisclosed nuclear facilities in Iran by the Institute for Science and International Security, a Washington-based NGO. Using information and coordinates provided by a dissident group called the National Council of Resistance of Iran together with high-resolution satellite images form DigitalGlobe, the Institute was able to locate the sites.[14] The disclosure forced the Bush administration to acknowledge the Iranian nuclear enrichment program—a violation of Iran's commitments under the Nuclear Non-Proliferation Treaty—which it had been aware of but kept secret for over a year.[15]

This example is not unique. Since 1999 the Center for Advanced Defense Studies (C4ADS) has dedicated itself to providing intelligence to combat a range of state and nonstate threats to U.S. national security.[16] Like Bellingcat, much of its work relies on crunching huge volumes of publicly available information to expose illicit actors and ensure that targets can be held accountable. Rather than legal changes, here it is technological shifts that have provided the main fillip. While also working on nuclear nonproliferation, cross-border corruption, and illicit trade in wildlife, sanctions

---

12. Judgement of the Court of Appeal of 20 June 2019 regarding licences for military exports to Saudi Arabia for possible use in the conflict in Yemen.

13. https://questions-statements.parliament.uk/written-statements/detail/2020-07-07/HCWS339.

14. Aday and Livingston 2009.

15. Ibid.

16. https://c4ads.org/.

enforcement has been a key priority for C4ADS. Correlating ship- and plane-tracking websites with trade, financial, and other data, the Center has shone new light on specific Iranian, North Korean, Libyan, and Syrian sanctions violations, often in real time. As well as informing UN sanctions monitoring bodies, these exposés have directly prompted national law enforcement intercepts and arrests.[17] Beyond its own efforts, through freely sharing its databases and the software needed to navigate them, C4ADS further lowers barriers to entry for other would-be NGO enforcers.

In another instance of NGOs assisting sanctions enforcement, in 2020 Global Fishing Watch in collaboration with Outlaw Ocean exposed a fleet of nine hundred Chinese ghost ships fishing for squid in North Korean waters in direct violation of the UN sanctions regime (in place since 2017), which explicitly bans North Korea from earning foreign currency through the provision of fishing licences to foreign vessels.[18]

These are just a few examples of NGO enforcement reaching into an area, international security, which might be thought particularly impenetrable to nonstate enforcers. As international law proliferates, and as previously distinct bodies of international law increasingly overlap, further and wider opportunities may open for transnational enforcement. For example, since the turn of the century, it has become increasingly common for environmental treaties to contain health-related provisions. A recent study found ninety-six international environmental treaties in which the protection or promotion of human health is one of the treaty's objectives and a smaller number of treaties which cite the right to health.[19] Nine international environmental treaties have institutional provisions which explicitly require parties to take into account standards and guidelines set by the World Health Organization (e.g., for quality of drinking water), while four commit parties to investing in health services and capacity building.[20] Such linkages may create new opportunities for leveraging environmental law to hold states and corporations responsible for protection of and investment in human health, or vice versa.

17. C4ADS, Annual Report 2019–20, https://static1.squarespace.com/static/566ef8b4d8af107232d5358a/t/5f07337c2b31722e0c51358a/1594307479873/C4ADS+Annual+Report+2019_2020.pdf.

18. Sang-Hun 2020a.

19. Morin and Blouin 2019.

20. The 1978 Treaty for Amazonian Cooperation; the 2001 Stockholm Convention on persistent organic pollutants; the Framework cooperation agreement between Austria and Venezuela; and the 2013 Minamata Convention on mercury.

As these examples suggest, vigilante enforcement is not confined to the areas of human rights, environment, or anti-corruption, nor is this brief list exhaustive. In practice, it is a short step from investigating cross-border corruption and the illicit trade in wildlife to vigilante efforts to combat other transnational crimes, like human trafficking and online child pornography. Moreover, as examples of vigilante enforcement in areas like human rights, the environment, and anti-corruption continue to grow, there is reason to think that groups in other domains will take notice and seek to copy successful practices. Nevertheless, for now at least, the volume and nature of transnational enforcement vary significantly across different domains, both as a reflection of the enforcement gap, and available technological and legal tools, and as a reflection of inter-organizational learning dynamics and competitive pressures.

Strategic Differentiation among NGOs

The foregoing sections and chapters have shown variation in nonstate enforcement, not only across policy domains but also across different transnational groups. Given the underlying broad trends facilitating nonstate enforcement, why have some groups opted for such strategies, while others, probably the majority, have stuck with more conventional strategies of advocacy and service provision? First, we should note that the fact that legal and political changes have facilitated enforcement does not imply that advocacy or service delivery have somehow become more difficult or less productive strategies for NGOs. Although reliable data are not available, in line with the overall increase in the number of NGOs, it seems a safe bet to venture that, in absolute terms, there are more NGOs engaging in transnational enforcement, advocacy, *and* service delivery than there were a few decades ago. Many of the technological advances that have made it easier for nonstate actors to engage in enforcement have had an equivalent positive effect on service delivery and advocacy.[21]

This still leaves the question of why some groups embrace autonomous enforcement while others shy away. Our starting point is that the growing number of NGOs worldwide creates competitive pressures, which in turn affect choices on strategy. Though as principled actors NGOs are not primarily 'in it for the money', they generally need external funding and support to survive. They also compete for other resources, such as access

21. E.g., Wong and Brown 2013.

to policy-makers and media publicity. At one level, such pressures may work to make NGOs more similar to each other in the strategic profiles and organizational models they adopt as each seeks to adapt to similar environmental incentives and seeks legitimacy by emulating existing organizational models.[22] Yet, beyond a certain point—when competition from a growing peer group becomes increasingly fierce—resource scarcity also encourages strategic differentiation, as organizations look for niches in which they can avoid direct competition with peers.[23] In this way, a growing population is likely to go hand in hand with growing organizational diversity and plurality of strategies and tactics.

We are not the first to detect a growing divergence in the organizational profiles and strategic repertoires of NGOs. Comparative studies have found that a few large international NGOs enjoy an increasingly disproportionate share of the available funding, publicity, and access to national and international policy-makers.[24] These same NGOs also tend to make more attractive partners to private corporations. However, their very success means that such groups are often compelled to pursue moderate, 'inside' strategies in order to avoid alienating mainstream audiences—what Stroup and Wong label the 'authority trap'.[25] Their large size and bureaucratic structures may also make these groups less adept at innovation and risk-taking. Conversely, the much larger population of small NGOs which fly under the public radar are relatively freer to pursue more confrontational tactics, precisely because they are effectively marginalized and have little government or corporate backing to lose. On this basis, some portray confrontational strategies as next-best options for NGOs that are unable to engage in global advocacy.[26]

We offer a different perspective. Our premise is that competition for resources and visibility leads NGOs to seek to differentiate themselves from their peers in order to survive and grow. Rather than a question of ideal versus second-best strategies, differentiation is often a question of 'horses for courses', of exploiting comparative advantages. Many of our interviewees were explicit about the imperative to carve out or inhabit a particular niche and thereby separate their group from the competition. Sometimes this

22. Carroll and Hannan 2000; Cooley and Ron 2002.

23. These dynamics are theorized in organizational ecology models of 'density dependence' and 'resource differentiation'. E.g., Hannan and Freeman 1977; Soule and King 2008; Carroll and Hannan 2000; Baum and Shipilov 2006; Eilstrup-Sangiovanni 2019.

24. Bob 2005; Carpenter 2011; Thrall, Stecula, and Sweet 2014; Stroup and Wong 2017.

25. Stroup and Wong 2017.

26. Grant 2001; Thrall, Stecula, and Sweet 2014; Stroup and Wong 2017.

rivalry is subtle, sometimes less so. For example, Sea Shepherd's website states, 'Unlike many other well-known international conservation groups, Sea Shepherd is a grassroots movement run almost entirely by dedicated, passionate volunteers, not a bureaucratic organization with corporate offices and a well-staffed fundraising department'.[27] Many other environmental groups, such as The Black Fish and the Environmental Justice Foundation, echo this mood, arguing that 'what's needed in the field is not another WWF or another Greenpeace'.[28]

When seeking to differentiate themselves from a growing peer group, individual NGOs' strategic choices are not random but tend to reflect existing organizational endowments and cultures. At a high level of generalization ecological models of 'density dependence' and 'resource differentiation' foresee the partitioning of organizational populations into 'generalists' and 'specialists'.[29] Larger, incumbent organizations that tend to be richer on financial resources and connections to other 'market players' tend to opt for generalist profiles, meaning that they compete to occupy the centre of a market where demand and resources are concentrated and where they can achieve economies of scale, whereas newcomers are more likely to seek out a role at the fringes of a market where they can draw on different resources than generalists do. In the context of NGO strategies, this means that one would expect larger legacy NGOs to be more likely to adopt a generalist profile and to opt for soft strategies which appeal to broad audiences, whereas more radical niche strategies which appeal to smaller audiences are left to newcomers.

Our findings broadly support the notion that greater organizational size and strategic moderation go together, but with important exceptions. There are a small number of dominant NGOs in each sector that take a large share of funding and publicity and benefit from substantial political access: Amnesty International and Human Rights Watch; household names like the World Wildlife Fund, Friends of the Earth, and Greenpeace; and Transparency International. As a crude generalization, these organizations have primarily stuck with advocacy roles or, in the case of Greenpeace, with protest directed at gaining publicity and raising awareness.

Yet because they are large, global organizations, these groups have also to some degree been able to spread their bets, with each engaging in forms

27. https://www.seashepherdglobal.org/who-we-are/our-approach/.
28. Black Fish interview 2015.
29. Soule and King 2008; Carroll 1995; Amburgey and Rao 1996.

of enforcement at some point. For example, both Human Rights Watch and Amnesty International have been party to litigation against governments or government officials (e.g., Human Rights Watch and the Hissène Habré trial). Although it has withdrawn from its radical confrontational stance of the 1970s and 1980s, Greenpeace too has engaged in limited direct-action enforcement and has taken on important cases of strategic litigation since 2000, as has Friends of the Earth. Even Transparency International, in some ways the stereotypical 'insider' among anti-corruption NGOs, has partly retreated from its initial 'no investigation' rule over time. Nonetheless, for each, enforcement has remained a subordinate or secondary strategy to a primary focus on advocacy, centred on awareness-building, public education, and policy and norm-entrepreneurship. Thus when these groups have adopted advanced surveillance technologies to reveal crime, it has been more often in order to raise public awareness and/or shame governments and corporations than with the goal of holding specific transgressors to account through direct intervention.

In contrast, we found that the majority of NGOs that operate primarily as enforcers are relatively small and specialized, operating on modest budgets. Again, there are important exceptions. Global Witness, a leading enforcement organization in the realms of human rights and corruption, also does a great deal of advocacy work. More broadly, most NGOs engage in some form of advocacy through education and information provision.[30] Nevertheless, on average, we found that enforcement strategies tend to be favoured by smaller and younger groups. As we have documented, smaller NGOs which are privately funded often face fewer constraints on strategic innovation and may be able to take up issues or employ strategies that larger groups feel unable to on account of their higher public profiles.

This does not mean that enforcement is a second-best strategy for groups doomed to political irrelevance. Indeed, each chapter features numerous examples of niche groups which individually and collectively have played a vital role in driving the general rise of vigilante enforcement of international law, especially in terms of strengthening the technological underpinnings of this trend, and in doing so have achieved substantial political victories. When NGOs bring successful legal cases against governments or corporations, much like David before Goliath, they sometimes (but far from always) achieve important results with limited financial means. The same can be true of direct confrontational strategies which may drive up operational costs

---

30. Stroup and Wong 2017.

for private corporations. Importantly, influence is achieved without appeal to wider public audiences. Indeed, many of the groups we interviewed for this book explicitly eschew media attention, arguing that it would get in the way of their investigations and undermine the credibility of their evidence.

Once again, it is not a matter of either/or when it comes to enforcement versus advocacy or service delivery, or of one strategy being superior. Transnational NGOs, whether working in coalition or merely in parallel, often bring together different skills and resources in tackling a given policy problem. Often campaigns consist of concerted efforts by multiple groups—including NGOs, corporations, inter-governmental organizations, and universities—whose different strategies play off and reinforce one another. This is not to ignore the challenges of competition between NGOs (prominent amongst them deciding how to share the credit for successful projects or how to defend and nourish a particular image while cooperating with others using different strategies or asserting different priorities). Nevertheless, the majority of our interviewees stressed the necessity and benefits of collaboration. In this sense, the more appropriate metaphor for the NGO population is perhaps less an economic market comprised of competing, inter-changeable firms and more the ecological model flagged earlier, of a mature ecosystem populated by inhabitants evolved to fill different niches in a broadly symbiotic relationship.

Vigilantes and States: Conflict, Control, and Collusion

The empowerment of NGOs we describe is neither uniform nor inexorable. In many places, governments have sought to clip the wings of both advocacy and enforcement groups. Since the mid-1990s, some countries have increasingly tried to constrain NGO activities, banning the funding of domestic NGOs from abroad and limiting the activities of foreign organizations.[31] Many authoritarian regimes have adopted restrictions in subordinating NGOs to the state and even setting up a parallel ecosystem of 'transnational uncivil society'.[32] In Russia, the government passed legislation in 2012 which requires Russian groups that accept foreign funding to register as 'foreign agents'—a term that implies 'spy'. As a result, many environmental groups have ceased operations in recent years, and the head of the prominent group Ekozashchita! (Ecodefence!), Alexandra Koroleva, fled

---

31. Dupuy, Ron, and Prakash 2016; Berny and Rootes 2018.
32. Cooley and Heathershaw 2017.

the country in June 2019 to avoid prosecution under the draconian Law on Foreign Agents.[33] Aleksei Navalny's Anti-Corruption Foundation was labelled a 'foreign agent' in October 2019 before being liquidated by court order in June 2021 on the grounds that it was an 'extremist organization'.[34]

Similar moves are visible in some democratic countries. In the Philippines, President Rodrigo Duterte in 2018 placed six hundred civil society activists on a list of alleged members of the country's Communist Party, labelled a terrorist organization. The list included Victoria Tauli-Corpuz, the UN special Rapporteur on the rights of indigenous people.[35] In October 2018, Pakistan's Interior Ministry ordered eighteen NGOs to shut down, labelling them 'non-combatant foreign enemies'. In France, anti-terrorist legislation was used to prevent French activists from leaving their homes during the 2015 Climate Change Conference in Paris, and dozens of climate activists were put under house arrest by French police for organizing protests during the summit.[36] In 2017, eighty-four members of the U.S. Congress requested that the Justice Department prosecute activists mobilizing against the construction of oil pipelines as terrorists. In the UK, environmental activists have also been subject to widespread anti-terrorism surveillance.[37] As of 2018, more than fifty countries worldwide had enacted restrictions on foreign funding for civil society organizations.[38]

All the same, the trend (for now at least) is still towards greater numbers of NGOs taking an increased role in a wider range of transnational activities, including law enforcement. Even as one door closes, another may open: for example, as earlier chapters show, NGOs are adept at 'jurisdiction-shopping', finding countries and courts willing to hear their cases. To this extent, they are both the beneficiaries and agents of globalization. Furthermore, pluralization and organizational differentiation may make transnational civil society as a whole more resilient by increasing adaptability in turbulent times. Over many decades, NGOs have relied heavily on a standard set of advocacy tools centred on naming and shaming governments into compliance with international norms. However, as Rodríguez-Garavito and Gomez note, the already limited efficacy and legitimacy of such shaming strategies focused

33. Human Rights Watch 2019.
34. Ljubas 2021.
35. Ibid.
36. Neslen 2015; Human Rights Watch 2019.
37. Mateova, Parker, and Dauvergne 2018.
38. Buyse 2018. See also Neslen 2015; Human Rights Watch 2019; Mateova, Parker, and Dauvergne 2018; Ron 2015; Kiyani and Murdie 2020.

on the traditional centres of power have recently been further eroded by the rise of populism.[39] In this context, vigilante enforcement may present a potent tool where other routes of action are blocked—especially insofar as (unlike standard shaming strategies) it does not take some governments as allies and others as targets.

The question of direct or indirect state control over transnational NGO enforcers has been raised at several points in the book already, especially in chapter 1. Even though the instances of investigation, interdiction, and prosecution by NGOs chronicled in earlier chapters have been undertaken independently of governments, they still occur within the legal space and institutions created by states. Because states create the domestic and international laws and wider legal systems within which NGO enforcers operate, the latter's enforcement actions might be seen as being indirectly controlled or 'orchestrated' by states.[40] Yet it is a fundamental mistake to see the creation of the arena in which enforcement plays out as the same thing as controlling the players.

To the extent that they are seeking to enforce existing international laws (rather than advocate for new ones), NGOs are in important ways facilitated and constrained by states. Yet the notion of state control—direct or indirect—simply fails to resonate with much of the evidence, as very often governments themselves are the targets of NGO enforcement actions. For example, it is hard to reconcile the current rash of NGOs suing governments for allegedly inadequate responses to global warming with the notion that these groups are under state control, no matter how indirect. More broadly, since human rights violations and corruption usually involve crimes committed by state officials, the state and NGOs tend to come from structurally opposed positions when it comes to enforcement, frequently placing them on a collision course.[41]

Furthermore, exactly what international law entails is rarely set in stone, instead being worked out in practice by courts and participants (including NGOs) over time.[42] International courts and tribunals have been found to play an important role in shaping the structure and content of international law.[43] Indeed, the evidence in this book illustrates that both NGOs and courts can be very creative and effective in extending the scope and reach of specific international rule sets. This point about the meaning of international

39. Rodríguez-Garavito and Gomez 2018: 12.
40. Tallberg 2015.
41. Michel and Sikkink 2013.
42. Zarbiyev 2012; Hurd 2018; Putnam 2020.
43. Alter 1998; Hurd 2018; Putnam 2020.

law being to some extent up for grabs holds especially when it is applied in domestic courts, as well as in international customary law. In this context, the idea that states are the puppet-masters and NGO enforcers merely their puppets ignores the importance of unintended consequences. For example, the fact that governments in the United States, Spain, and Belgium narrowed the scope of universal jurisdiction over human rights claims in their courts strongly suggests that NGOs creatively used these legislative provisions in ways that government did not anticipate or desire, let alone control.

Perhaps a more interesting and productive way of looking at the relationship between states and NGO enforcers than either permanent conflict or indirect control would be to look at the intermediate possibilities of contestation, collusion, and collaboration. Such a perspective also helps to break down the convenient but misleading shorthand of 'the state'. Different parts of the same state may hold very different attitudes towards NGO enforcers. Relations between state and nonstate law enforcers may range from downright hostility to open cooperation, but informal alliances and surreptitious deals seem to be at least as common as either of these extremes. The police are often reluctant to publicly cede their official monopoly on enforcement, while NGOs are usually keen to assert their independence. Yet in many circumstances both sets of actors are working to uphold the same laws and hold the same violators to account. Our interviews suggest that police and NGOs sometimes exchange confidential material under the table, and vigilante actions that may embarrass some sections of the government may well empower others. Interpol has officially condemned the maritime interdiction efforts by the Sea Shepherd and has shied away from officially conceding the crucial role of evidence submitted by Sea Shepherd to the apprehension of fugitive vessels such as the *Thunder*—yet Interpol officials anonymously acknowledge close collaboration with the group on specific cases. As illustrated in chapter 3, many low-capacity jurisdictions have reached out directly, inviting environmental vigilantes to come and work alongside or in lieu of public police.

These notions of the unbundling of the state, of global governance as a tacit (or sometimes explicit) 'public-private partnership', and of challenges and responses that are transnational rather than purely domestic or purely international are now well-worn themes.[44] But while many before us have

---

44. Amongst many others, Meyer et al. 1997; Avant, Finnemore, and Sell 2010; Neumann and Sending 2010; Halliday and Shaffer 2015; Djelic and Quack 2010, 2018; Kim and Boyle 2012; Farrell and Newman 2015; Putnam 2016; Seabrooke and Henrikson 2017; Bartley 2018.

noted the growth of private authority in global governance,[45] most work on transnationalism and globalization underplays enforcement. To the extent it is considered, enforcement is often understood in such expansive, indirect terms that it hardly qualifies as such: self-regulation, voluntary codes of conduct, best-practice guides, arbitration, mediation, peer pressure, socialization, indirect market signals, and reputational concerns.[46] Soft laws, increasingly seen as the dominant kind, go with soft enforcement.[47] By contrast, enforcement through injunctions, fines, and imprisonment, as well as the preceding investigations—the kind of enforcement we have put in the picture—are rarely considered central. By implication, much globalization literature treats such methods as obsolescent, parochially state-centric relics of a pre-globalized era. Globalization is said to rest on the pluralization of those governing. But new governors such as corporations, expert communities, professional networks, and social movements cannot fine or imprison people. Even states have great difficulty doing so beyond their borders. On this basis, the presumption is generally that global governance by its nature must rest on more refined, enlightened, and indirect means of promoting compliance. Yet in this book we have shown the opposite: while by definition transnational vigilantes operate autonomously from the state, they nevertheless turn classic, hard-edged statist tools of enforcement to their own ends: courts, fines, blockades, police, prosecutors, and prisons. There is no reason why the pluralization of enforcers per se entails softer or more indirect tactics in targeting rule-breakers. To the contrary, our vigilantes appropriate some of the most powerful implements in the state arsenal of coercion in targeting those transgressing international rules.

Evaluating Vigilante Enforcement: Effectiveness and Legitimacy

What does it mean for world politics, and for the state-led international legal system, that nonstate actors are now pervasive in international law enforcement? Looking up from the detailed evidence presented so far, to what extent is this a good or bad thing? In weighing the pros and cons we first consider questions of effectiveness before looking at legitimacy and normative

45. Cutler, Haufler, and Porter 1999; Seabrooke and Henriksen 2017.

46. Simmons 2010; Büthe 2010; Abbott et al. 2015; Halliday and Shaffer 2015; Djelic and Quack 2018.

47. Abbott et al. 2000; Abbott, Green, and Keohane 2016.

concerns. The positives may perhaps come to mind more quickly than the negatives, but as the unease associated with the notion of vigilante justice attests, appraising autonomous NGO enforcement is not a simple matter.

Almost by definition, international law expresses and aims to advance goals that are widely endorsed in the international community. After all, signing on to international treaties is voluntary. Few states will directly take a stance against defending human rights, protecting the environment, or fighting corruption. Nevertheless, non-compliance is pervasive. If a major obstacle to achieving these widely shared aims is a lack of enforcement, as is commonly believed, then this creates a strong presumption in favour of NGO enforcement. Not surprisingly, NGOs themselves portray their enforcement actions in this light, as defending universal principles and advancing public goods, whether it is the rights of the voiceless suffering under oppressive and corrupt governments or the environmental concerns of future generations.[48]

As discussed in chapter 1, NGO enforcement serves to strengthen the rule of law 'from below' in a number of ways.[49] First, when they supply enforcement NGOs help strengthen the rule of law directly. When direct interventions against law-breakers succeed, or when cases brought by NGOs win in court and stand up on appeal, they can have a direct impact on the problems they seek to address. Of course, far from every lawsuit brought against governments or corporations for criminal action, negligence, or tort is successful. Even winning in court does not guarantee success. Though it is widely assumed that judicial rulings shape policy, compliance with international court rulings has been found to be both patchy and slow.[50]

But successful interdictions and legal victories are not only measures of success for NGO enforcers. Whether or not they succeed in halting a specific illegal activity and bringing individual law-breakers to justice, NGO interventions may help to deter future offences. Laws that are not respected and whose violation triggers no sanctions may soon cease to have an effect. On the other hand, demonstrating that violators will be held to account can serve to create a 'compliance pull' by changing the cost calculations of would-be transgressors and by strengthening legal norms. Thus, enforcement actions, whether ultimately successful or not, may create focal points and benchmarks for a wider range of political and private decision making. For example, climate litigation risk, defined by UNEP as 'any risk related

48. Peters 2009: 230.
49. See also Dancy and Michel 2016.
50. Von Staden 2018; Schenoni 2021.

to litigation pertaining to climate change and breach of the underlying legal frameworks on both the business and corporate levels', is increasingly disclosed by many corporations, investors, banks, and insurers and has been found to directly impact investment decisions and share prices.[51]

Second, as we have argued, by highlighting the inadequacy of state enforcement of international law, NGOs may indirectly provoke and pressure governments to increase their own enforcement efforts. There are several examples throughout the book of governments only taking action when upstaged by NGOs' enforcement action—as when Australia, after years of futile diplomatic protests, eventually decided to confront Japan in the International Court of Justice after being put under strong political pressure from repeated Sea Shepherd actions aimed to enforce Australian law in territorial waters claimed by Australia.[52]

Aside from potentially advancing global welfare in the abstract and pressuring governments to improve their enforcement efforts, NGO enforcement carries a range of direct and indirect benefits for states. Perhaps most obviously, it shifts the cost of the most expensive and burdensome aspect of international law away from governments to third parties. NGO enforcement multiplies the resources available to investigating and prosecuting transgressions of international law. NGOs often have privileged access to information about compliance in specific domains, or expertise and technology that equal or even exceed that of their government counterparts,[53] especially in developing countries. They generally have far fewer bureaucratic constraints than either governments or inter-governmental organizations. It is not necessarily a matter of amateur NGO versus professional state enforcers. In contrast to governments or supranational actors, NGOs often have deep local expertise.[54] This enables them to better detect violations of rules, perhaps because they encounter violations directly in their local work. Motivated by principled commitment, often to a single cause, NGOs may also be more willing to devote time and resources to issues than are their government counterparts.[55] Because NGOs are often funded by actors other than governments, especially in the developing world, they can often be more aggressive enforcers of international norms and standards than states, as

51. Setzer and Higham 2021: 18.
52. Eilstrup-Sangiovanni and Phelps Bondaroff 2014.
53. Higgins 2021.
54. Tallberg 2015.
55. Ibid., 6.

they are not subject to the same political pressures. This aspect might be particularly important in investigating corruption and human rights crimes.

This gets to a second benefit of vigilante enforcement: providing a diffuse public good to states. Despite often getting on the wrong side of individual governments, vigilante enforcement may help to strengthen the overall credibility of international commitments. Many international laws presuppose reciprocity as a basis of compliance, for example, disarmament treaties but also many trade and environmental agreements. Explicitly enlisting third parties to enforce agreements can increase actors' confidence that other participants will honour their promises but is likely to be less credible than more decentralized, randomized enforcement such as that supplied by NGOs.[56]

A third benefit of nonstate enforcement lies in clarification and interpretation of law. As noted earlier, laws are often imperfectly determinate whether because it is too costly for states to address all future foreseeable contexts in which the law may apply or because contracting parties decide to gloss over their differences with vague language to reach agreement.[57] Thus, specific laws are often only given precise meaning and effect when tested by courts.[58]

Yet, at the end of the day, looking at the value of nonstate enforcement only through the lens of legal clarification, legal precedent, or 'deterrence' would lead to an inadequate understanding of the complex processes that actors unleash when they engage in enforcement. Just as law itself has normative effects, so too does enforcement. 'Our laws express what we believe in, what we stand for and what we are as a society'. As a result, conflict in relation to laws 'can provide an opportunity for society collectively to identify, articulate, debate, and choose those public values and a conception of identity of society'.[59] In this way, enforcement has an undeniable political function in drawing attention to, testing, and potentially reinforcing international norms.

Lastly, and perhaps most importantly, NGO enforcement can be crucial where governments are unable, rather than simply unwilling, to uphold their international commitments. Although traditionally violations of international human rights law have been seen as a deliberate betrayal by cynical repressive governments, others have argued that even sincere governments

---

56. Green 2013; Green and Colgan 2013.
57. Howse and Teitel 2010; Chayes and Chayes 1993.
58. Howse and Teitel 2010.
59. Preston 2016: 14.

may have genuine difficulty implementing their commitments.[60] From this perspective, whether human rights are actually observed and violations prosecuted is as much dependent on the presence of a functioning state apparatus and criminal justice system as on signing up to international treaties. International fishing operators are widely known to 'fish down the governance index' seeking out weaker jurisdictions where lack of enforcement capacity means criminals can operate with relative impunity with detrimental social and economic impacts on local populations. The countries that suffer when their officials steal assets and spirit them abroad seldom have the expertise to follow the money trail to foreign financial centres. In this context, NGO enforcement can provide a crucial injection of capacity. The same point about NGOs augmenting capacity may apply to under-funded and over-stretched inter-governmental organizations, with the International Criminal Court's dependence on NGO 'intermediaries' being a prominent example.

Lake describes the extensive role of international NGOs in substituting for the state in enforcing human rights in the Congo, specifically in responding to sexual violence.[61] Rather than supplementing the public criminal justice system, foreign NGOs and inter-governmental organizations come close to completely substituting for it. Lake sets out the problem in stark terms: for a country of 80 million people the size of Western Europe with massive human rights abuses, the annual government budget for the entire court system is a little over $1 million.[62] Courts lack basic facilities like electricity, and judges often cannot even find out what the laws are, let alone apply them. Despite these massive obstacles, when it comes to prosecuting rape, the Congolese justice system works surprisingly well, often directly based on the provisions of the Rome Statute that set up the International Criminal Court.[63] This relative success is largely due to foreign nonstate actors like the Open Society Justice Initiative and the American Bar Association that have stepped into the void where the state should be.[64] NGOs have even been responsible for keeping prisons in working order.[65]

60. Chayes and Chayes 1993; Cole and Ramirez 2013; Cole 2015.
61. Lake 2014, 2018; see also Khan and Wormington 2011; Zongwe 2012; Lake, Muthaka, and Walker 2016.
62. Lake 2014: 517.
63. Lake 2018: 3.
64. Lake 2014: 521–24.
65. Baylis 2009: 140.

To pose a recurring question of this book: do such activities really count as autonomous enforcement, or are these simply an example of a particularly wide-ranging service delivery role for NGOs? With the usual caveat that clear-cut analytical distinctions often get blurred in practice, given the near-total absence of the Congolese government, it seems hard to say that these foreign NGOs are effectively agents of the state, implementing the will of the authorities in the faraway capital of Kinshasa. Given that foreign NGOs have also largely drafted the relevant Congolese law,[66] action to combat sexual violence seems far more to do with outsiders' priorities rather than those of the government, or perhaps even the local population.[67]

There are also potential drawbacks to NGO enforcement, in terms of both effectiveness and legitimacy. As we noted in chapter 1, by doing states' job for them in enforcing international law, NGO enforcers may actively reduce pressure on governments to address growing enforcement short-falls.[68] Governments may free-ride on NGOs' efforts, passing the buck and shirking their duty. Under this scenario, an increase in nonstate enforcement may lead to a decrease in state enforcement, offering no improvement on the status quo.

A different risk is that vigilante enforcers may be too successful for their own good. If NGOs increasingly succeed in holding states accountable for international commitments by challenging them in domestic or international courts, this may have the perverse effect of discouraging states from accepting binding international obligations and to be increasingly careful about publicly admitting to policy failures or committing to concrete policy targets (witness the growing success of NGOs in holding governments legally to account for failing to meet their stated targets on CO_2 emission reductions under the non-binding Paris Agreement). This possibility was discussed by NGO participants at a closed workshop on avenues for climate litigation in March 2020: 'If we start trying to hold states accountable by challenging them on their self-selected NDCs [national climate plans highlighting emissions targets], can this have the perverse effect of encouraging states to say less in international forums? Will states take into account the litigation coming their way and frame their state practice and *opinion juris* accordingly? How do we manage for this strategically?'[69]

---

66. Zongwe 2012: 45.
67. Autesserre 2010, 2014.
68. Ayling 2013.
69. Anonymous.

The prospect of vigorous enforcement of international law by actors not accountable to any government may make governments less likely to sign up to relevant international treaties and conventions in the first place. As another participant warned in respect to the possibility of seeking an advisory opinion from the International Court of Justice on climate change, 'We have to be careful. Party states to the Paris Agreement have been very reluctant to allow third-party attribution or interpretation. If courts were to come in and resolve some of the ambiguities in that treaty that could be politically damaging by removing "fudge"'. In short, robust NGO enforcement might prompt states to pull back from international treaties.

Whether or not such an effect would be a bad thing is itself debatable. Presumably international law is not strengthened by governments signing up to treaties with no intention of fulfilling the promises involved. On the other hand, it is argued that states need reassurance that treaty enforcement will be flexible enough to cope with unforeseen circumstances (perhaps suspending environmental regulations during deep recessions)[70] or that even initially insincere commitments later evolve into principled acceptance.[71] Vigilante enforcement by single-issue zealots may jeopardize such flexibility. Returning to the importance of unintended consequences and the re-interpretation of international law, governments may worry about signing up to one set of rules, only to be held accountable to another.

At the boundary of effectiveness and legitimacy is a concern over consistency. Nonstate providers have a major advantage over public law enforcers with respect to the tasks they perform—they can pick and choose their missions, whereas at least in theory public police must provide the full range of police services.[72] Patchy or selective enforcement by NGOs, perhaps only taking on the most media-worthy or the easiest cases, may undermine state capacity to apply a coherent regulatory scheme. NGOs filing claims risks flooding domestic courts with foreign human rights, corruption, or environmental suits thanks to world-ranging 'litigation tourism'. Some lawyers rage against private litigation by NGOs on these grounds.[73]

In practice the objection to NGOs' selective enforcement seems to rest on the rather naive presumption that police agencies pursue all breaches of the law. Some state law enforcement agencies are explicitly enjoined to be selective in investigating crimes (e.g., the FBI), and some state prosecutors

70. Downs and Rocke 1995.
71. Risse, Ropp, and Sikkink 1999.
72. Bayley and Shearing 2001.
73. Peters 2009.

are similarly instructed to be selective in only taking cases that are winnable and 'in the public interest' (e.g., the British Crown Prosecution Service). More importantly, police agencies may be just as sensitive to media coverage as NGOs in choosing what to investigate and what to ignore.

Reaching a definitive judgement regarding the overall effectiveness of NGO enforcement is virtually impossible given that we don't know what the world would be like without it. Providing such an evaluation is not our aim. Still, although there may be individual instances of states passing the buck to NGO enforcers, evidence from earlier chapters strongly suggests that the most probable alternative to NGO enforcement is not more or more consistent state-led enforcement but no enforcement at all. This is most clearly the case where NGOs are taking direct action against governments, particularly in environmental matters. Even in cases where NGO enforcement has served as a substitute for state action, for example, private human rights prosecutions in Latin America, it is rarely plausible to argue that this has diminished or inhibited public efforts. Indeed, the reverse seems to be true, with early NGO efforts having had a multiplier effect in spurring greater state action.[74] At other times, vigilantism simply represents an urgent or last-ditch effort to preserve vulnerable ecosystems or to protect the rights of vulnerable populations in the face of persistent state inaction.

What of the backlash against NGO enforcement? The goal of this book has been to draw attention to an important but widely overlooked trend of growing NGO enforcement and to explain its sources. As such the backlash against NGOs noted above (or against international rule of law more generally) is largely beyond our remit. Although it is real, it is hard to say that this backlash has so far reduced either the overall number or the general impact of NGOs working transnationally. The contextual factors that have favoured NGOs' enforcement efforts can certainly be reversed, just as globalization more generally can be reversed. Technology can enable violating international law as much as it can empower those defending the law. While there is an overall trend towards expanding NGOs' access to courts, some countries have acted to deny NGOs standing. Yet for now, despite individual challenges and retreats, the overall impression from our examination of NGO enforcement of human rights, environmental, and anti-corruption law is that such enforcement is increasing rather than declining. There are more NGOs adopting enforcement strategies against a broader set of targets, and they have a wider range of effective legal options and technologies to do so.

74. Mallinder 2009; Dancy and Michel 2016.

It is important not to overstate either the current effects or future promise of nonstate enforcement. Despite NGOs' best efforts, the enforcement
gap remains, even if it is smaller than it would be otherwise. Having argued
that autonomous transnational enforcement of international law is new
and highly significant, it is also important not to over-sell NGO action as a
magic bullet, 'the solution' to the fundamental problem of the anarchical
international system. Thanks to vigilante groups, there is more transnational
enforcement, and international law is relatively more effective than it otherwise would be. But a large majority of those guilty of human rights and corruption crimes are still not held to account, and violations of international
environmental commitments continue to be widespread.

The Legitimacy of Vigilante Enforcement

Moving on from concerns about effects and effectiveness, is transnational
vigilante enforcement legitimate? After all, perhaps the greatest concern
regarding actors taking law enforcement into their own hands is not whether
or not it delivers results but that it runs directly against important principles
of the rule of law and due process.

While NGOs play a growing role in law enforcement, they remain outside
formal law enforcement structures. A major concern is therefore whether
due process is followed to prevent innocent people being falsely accused
and punished. NGOs are likely to be motivated to engage in enforcement
for different reasons than are formal enforcement officials. They may have
ideological or personal motives which might undermine their impartiality.[75]
Though many NGOs have a high degree of expertise and professionalism,
some do not, and so nonstate enforcement may result in empowering unaccountable amateurs and enthusiasts who may engage in questionable, reck-
less, or even outright illegal practices.[76]

A second concern is lack of representativeness or accountability to
national electorates or global publics. Enforcement through the courts shifts
decision-making and legitimating power from elected officials to legal professionals.[77] More broadly, nonstate enforcement may weaken executive
and legislative oversight of policy implementation, thereby reducing democratic legitimacy and accountability.[78]

75. Brenner 2007.
76. Ulfstein 2009; Environmental Justice Foundation interview 2020.
77. Howse and Teitel 2010.
78. Bayley and Shearing 2001; Ayling 2013.

In the context of enforcing state-enacted laws, the objection that NGOs enforcers are unrepresentative or 'undemocratic' is questionable. As Price argues, 'The criticism that civil society activists are unrepresentative deflects hard questions away from the legitimacy of existing political institutions ... when it is the very unresponsiveness of such institutions that creates the conditions for transnational civil society activism in the first place'.[79] This observation appears particularly true in the context of states failing to enforce legal obligations which they have formally accepted.

Still, the basic justification of the (supposed) state monopoly on enforcement is that the state is uniquely empowered in moral and legal terms to advance the public interest, whereas private parties pursue private interests. Aside from being mandated to act for a particular goal, the public good, state law enforcers are also strictly regulated to pursue this goal in a certain manner, adhering to due process in arrests and criminal prosecutions, for example. Given that vigilante justice is sometimes seen as a contradiction in terms, what defence can be offered in terms of legitimacy for transnational enforcement by NGOs?

Scholars often distinguish between procedural and substantive legitimacy. Procedural legitimacy is taken to flow from proper procedure.[80] Thus, if a treaty prescribes that only governments have authority to enforce, then only state-sanctioned enforcement shall be deemed legitimate. Substantive legitimacy is more concerned with the contents of rules and institutions. Hence, insofar as NGOs duly enforce laws which are passed and ratified by states in cases where states lack the means or will to do so, this may be deemed legitimate. It is a commonplace that contracts are enforced by private parties via the courts. Why not accept that legitimacy in regard to international enforcement arises from the legitimacy of international laws— not from who enforces them? This is especially so when, as noted earlier, the international laws in question enjoy near-universal acceptance. On these grounds transnational enforcement could be interpreted and welcomed as a trend towards greater inclusiveness and empowerment of a wider range of global actors.

In terms of the rule of law and due process, it is important to emphasize that NGOs are not above the law. Ultimately, like companies, NGOs are creatures of law and are only distinguished from collections of individuals by formal registration and recognition that ultimately comes from the

---

79. Price 2003: 591.
80. Klabbers 2016: 39.

state. Whether or not they are engaged in enforcement, NGOs enjoy none of the immunities granted to the police.[81] NGOs can be and are occasionally prosecuted and sued for their transgressions. The shortcomings of NGO enforcement, which are real, need to be compared not against some ideal standard but against the practical alternative of state enforcement, warts and all. 'NGO brutality' is not a common problem, whereas police brutality is. The same goes for corruption. For our purposes, vigilante enforcement does not mean that anything goes. If NGOs accept bribes to target specific companies or individuals in order to help their competitors, this counts as corruption. If activists assassinate corrupt officials or human rights abusers, this counts as terrorism, not the enforcement of international law, in line with the definition laid out in the introduction.

More than this, as discussed extensively in the body of the book, NGOs have often become more rather than less legalistic as they have taken on an enforcement role. Strategic litigation and the 'Pinochet effect' have meant that NGOs are increasingly operating through courts, using the laws as they exist to promote their objectives. Even when NGOs are not in court themselves, the more indirect side of enforcement commonly centres on prompting and supporting police action via preliminary investigations and evidence gathering. Vigilante NGOs are more likely to be in tacit alliance with law enforcement agencies than protest and advocacy groups are. The most spectacular examples of direct NGO enforcement, like Sea Shepherd hurling smoke flares at Japanese whaling ships, may indeed be outright illegal, but this is an unrepresentative example of what most NGO enforcers actually do, with few if any parallels in the human rights or anti-corruption sphere. It is not even representative of most of Sea Shepherd's activities.

International enforcement increasingly looks like the sort of pluralized order we are familiar with in other domains of global politics. This development has generally gone unnoticed, in part because of the circular assumption that only states can enforce, in part because scholars have failed to distinguish between delegated and autonomous enforcement. Whereas in the 'traditional' world order, legitimate authority rested with states and states alone, enforcement is now supplied by a variety of actors and institutions. For-profit contracted private security companies are one example. Enforcement authority may also be exercised by inter-governmental organizations, but these are likely to be pursuing tasks and exercising powers delegated by states. The same cannot be said for the NGOs we have focused on. They are

81. Bayley and Shearing 2001.

both spontaneously reinforcing, substituting for, and in some cases competing with, states for political and legal authority. They do not merely wish to be involved in monitoring international law, as the traditional role of NGOs was often conceived; rather, they increasingly take the law into their own hands.

This has important implications for global politics. World politics in the twenty-first century is increasingly a hybrid system in which the enforcement of international rules is both delegated but also independently practiced by nonstate actors. From the perspective of states, inter-governmental organizations, and NGOs alike, this hybrid approach raises the possibility of achieving more effective and efficient enforcement of international laws. In the absence of a unitary world state with a police force to match, a combination of public and private enforcement may be the only way to maintain the operability of an ever more ambitious body of international law. In supplying law enforcement, NGOs make a plausible claim to be supplying a public good, since a lack of enforcement ultimately risks making international law irrelevant.

NONGOVERNMENTAL ORGANIZATIONS
(FEATURED IN THE BOOK)

ActionAid
Advisory Service for Squatters
Albanian Institute of Science
American Academy for the Advancement of Science
American Bar Association
Amnesty International
Anti-Corruption Foundation
Asociación Pro Derechos Humanos de España (APDHE)
Association for Nature Conservation Tapiola
Asylum Access
Autonomous Nation of Anarchist Libertarians (ANAL)
Bangladesh Environmental Lawyers Association
Bellingcat
The Black Fish
The Blue Seals
Bosque Antiguo
Both ENDS
Bruno Manser-Fonds
Bureau of the Ramsar Convention on Wetlands
Campaign Against the Arms Trade
Center for Constitutional Rights
Center for Human Rights Science
Center for International Environmental Law
Center for Justice and Accountability
Center for Justice and International Law
Center for Public Integrity
Centro de Estudios Legales y Sociales (CELS)
Chadian Association for the Protection and Defence for Human Rights
Christian Aid
Civitas Maxima
ClientEarth
Climate Action Network Europe

Coalition for the International Criminal Court
Cobra Collective
Codpeace and the Society for the Retention of Our Sealing Industry
Comité Catholique contre la Faim et pour le Développement
Commission for International Justice and Accountability (CIJA)
Committee for Human Rights in North Korea
Conflict Awareness Project
Conservation Drones
Conservation International
The Corner House
Earth League International
Earthjustice
Earthlife
EarthRights International
Eco Activists for Governance and Law Enforcement (EAGLE)
Ecodefense!/Ekozaschita!
EG Justice
EnoughProject
Environmental Investigation Agency
Environmental Justice Foundation
Environmental Law Association
eyeWitness to Atrocities (eyeWitness)
Fédération des Congolais de la Diaspora
Federation Internationale des Ligues des Droits de l'Homme (FIDH)
France Nature Environment
Free Trade Unions of Burma
Friends of the Earth
Global Legal Action Network (GLAN)
Global Witness
Grandmothers of the Plaza de Mayo/Asociación Civil Abuelas de Plaza de Mayo
Greenpeace
Helsinki Watch
Human Rights Data Analysis Group
Human Rights Watch
Imazon
International Animal Rescue
International Anti-Poaching Foundation
International Bar Association London
International Commission of Jurists
International Consortium of Investigative Journalists (ICIJ)
International Labor Rights Fund
International Partnership for Human Rights

International Rights Advocates
International Union for Conservation of Nature
Janaagraha Centre for Citizenship and Democracy
Kenya Wildlife Service
Klimaatzaak
Lawyers' Environmental Action Team
Liberian Global Justice and Research Project
MacArthur Foundation
Milieudefensie
Natural Resources Defense Council
Oak Foundation
Oceana
Open Society Foundations (OSF)
Open Society Justice Initiative
OpenCorporates
Organized Crime and Corruption Reporting Project
Oxfam
Paso Pacífico
Paul G. Allen Family Foundation
Physicians for Human Rights
Plan B
Planet Indonesia
Poder Ciudadano
Portuguese Youth
Re:Common
Rotary International
Royal Society for the Protection of Birds
Sea Shepherd Conservation Society (SSCS)
Secretariat of the Convention on International Trade in Endangered Species
Senior Women for Climate Protection, Switzerland
The Sentry
ShadowView
Shell Petroleum Development Company
Sherpa
SITU
SkyTruth
SoarOcean
South African Law Centre
Southern African Litigation Centre
Spatial Monitoring and Reporting Tool Partnership
Survie
Swedish Society for Nature Conservation

Syrian Archive
TRACE
TRAFFIC
Transitional Justice Research Collaborative
Transparency International (TI)
Transparency International-France
Transparency International-Germany
Transparency International-UK
Transparency International-Ukraine
TRIAL International
Truth Hounds
UNCAC Civil Society Coalition
Urgenda
Vulcan
Wikileaks
Wildlife Justice Commission
Wildlife Protection Solutions
WITNESS
WOLA
Women on Waves
Women on Web
World Justice Project
World Organization for the Protection of the Environment
World Resource Institute
World Vision
World Wildlife Fund (WWF)
Zero Corruption Coalition of Nigeria
Zoological Society London

INTERVIEWS

Amnesty International, former, by phone, 22 April 2020.

Bellingcat, via Skype, Eliot Higgins, 9 September 2020.

Bern Declaration, Lausanne, 16 October 2015.

The Black Fish, Wietse van de Verf, founder and director, London, 16 June 2015.

Bruno Manser-Fonds, Basel, 15 October 2015.

Civitas Maxima, London, 20 September 2019.

Conservation Drones, Serge Wich, via Zoom, 18 September 2020.

Corner House, former, 2020.

Corruption Watch, former, via Skype, 1 May 2020.

EAGLE, Ofir Drohi, founder and director, via WhatsApp, 3 September 2020.

Earth League International, via Zoom, 9 September 2020.

Environmental Justice Foundation, Stephen Trent, Founder and Director, via phone, 30 April 2020.

eyeWitness to Atrocities, via Skype, 10 September 2020.

Global Witness, former, Exeter, 18 September 2015.

Global Witness, former, London, 11 March 2020a.

Global Witness, former, via Skype, 5 May 2020b.

Global Witness, London, 7 September 2011.

Global Witness, via Skype, 7 May 2020c.

International Consortium of Investigative Journalists, Washington, DC, 11 April 2013.

Open Society Foundations, New York, 13 February 2015.

Open Society Foundations, New York, 7 April 2017.

Open Society Foundations, via Skype, 8 May 2020.

Oxfam, former, by phone, 24 September 2020.

Sea Ranger Service, Wietse van de Verf, founder and director, via phone, 11 October 2019.

Sea Shepherd Conservation Society, Omar Todd, via Skype, 30 September 2019.

The Sentry, Brisbane, Australia, 27 October 2016.

The Sentry, via email.

Sherpa, Paris, 28 April 2017.

SkyTruth, John Amos, president and founder, via Skype, 18 September 2020.

TRACE, Wildlife Forensics Network, Rob Ogden, via Skype, 21 September 2020.

Transparency International, Berlin, 13 September 2015.

Transparency International, Berlin, 30 June 2017.

Transparency International, Berlin, 5 September 2011.

Transparency International, Cambridge, 28 November 2017.

Transparency International, former, by phone, 22 April 2020b.

Transparency International, former, by Skype, 30 April 2020a.

Transparency International-UK, London, 30 June 2017.

U.S. Department of Justice, Washington, DC, 9 December 2014.

U.S. Senate Permanent Subcommittee on Investigations, Washington, DC, 11 December 2014.

WildLeaks/Earth League International, Andrea Costa, founder, via Skype, 9 September 2020.

Wildlife Justice Foundation, Saskia Cornelissen, Director of Finance and Operations, via e-mail, September 2020.

Women on Waves, outreach coordinator, Asia, via Zoom, 8 September 2020.

Women on Waves, outreach coordinator, Europe and Middle East, via Zoom, 8 September 2020.

BIBLIOGRAPHY

Abbott, Kenneth W., Philipp Genschel, Duncan Snidal, and Bernhard Zangl. 2015. Orchestration: Global Governance through Intermediaries. In International Organizations as Orchestrators, ed. Kenneth W. Abbott, Philipp Genschel, Duncan Snidal, and Bernhard Zangl. Cambridge: Cambridge University Press. 3–36.

Abbott, Kenneth W., Jessica F. Green, and Robert O. Keohane. 2016. Organizational Ecology and Institutional Change in Global Governance. International Organization 70 (2): 247–77.

Abbott, Kenneth W., Robert O. Keohane, Duncan Snidal, Andrew Moravcsik, and Anne-Marie Slaughter. 2000. The Concept of Legalization. International Organization 54 (3): 401–19.

Abbott, Kenneth W., and Duncan Snidal. 1998. Why States Act through Formal International Organizations. Journal of Conflict Resolution 42 (1): 3–32.

———. 2002. Values and Interests: International Legalization in the Fight against Corruption. Journal of Legal Studies 31 (1): 141–78.

———. 2010. International Regulation without International Government: Improving IO Performance through Orchestration. Review of International Organizations 5 (3): 315–44.

Abrahamsen, Rita, and Michael C. Williams. 2011. Security beyond the State: Private Security and International Politics. Cambridge: Cambridge University Press.

Aceves, William J. 2007. The Anatomy of Torture: A Documentary History of Filartiga v. Pena-Irala. New York: Transnational Publishers.

Adams, Guy. 2012. Teodoro Nguema Obiang: Coming to America (to launder his millions?). Independent, 16 June. https://www.independent.co.uk/news/world/americas/teodoro-nguema -obiang-coming-to-america-to-launder-his-millions-7855043.html.

Aday, Sean, and Steven Livingston. 2009. NGOs as Intelligence Agencies: The Empowerment of Transnational Advocacy Networks and the Media by Commercial Remote Sensing in the Case of Iran. Geoforum 40 (3): 514–22.

Akella, A. S., and J. B. Cannon. 2004. Strengthening the Weakest Links: Strategies for Improving the Enforcement of Environmental Laws Globally. Center for Conservation and Government, Conservation International, Washington, DC.

Alexander, Kern. 1997. The Mareva Injunction and Anton Piller Order: The Nuclear Weapons of English Commercial Litigation. Florida Journal of International Law 11 (3): 487–516.

Alford, Roger. P. 2000. The Proliferation of International Courts and Tribunals: International Adjudication in Ascendance. American Society International Law Proceedings 94: 160. https://scholarship.law.nd.edu/law_faculty_scholarship/9.

Alter, Karen J. 1998. Who Are the 'Masters of the Treaty'? European Governments and the European Court of Justice. International Organization 52 (1): 121–47.

———. 2006. Private Litigants and the New International Courts. Comparative Political Studies 39 (1): 22–49.

———. 2011a. The Global Spread of European Style International Courts. Faculty Working Papers 7. https://scholarlycommons.law.northwestern.edu/facultyworkingpapers/7.

———. 2011b. The Evolving International Judiciary. Annual Review of Law and Social Science 7 (1): 387–415.

———. 2014. The New Terrain of International Law: Courts, Politics, Rights. Princeton: Princeton University Press.

Alter, Karen J., L. R. Helfer, and O. Saldias. 2012. Transplanting the European Court of Justice: The Experience of the Andean Tribunal of Justice. American Journal of Comparative Law 60 (3): 629–64.

Alter, Karen J., and Sophie Meunier. 2009. The Politics of International Regime Complexity. Perspectives on Politics 7 (1): 13–24.

Alter, Karen J., and Kal Raustiala. 2018. The Rise of International Regime Complexity. Annual Review of Law and Social Science 14 (1): 329–49.

Amburgey, Terry L., and Hayagreeva Rao. 1996. Organizational Ecology: Past, Present, and Future Directions. Academy of Management Journal 39 (5): 1265–86.

American Academy for the Advancement of Science. 2006. Geospatial Technologies and Human Rights. https://www.aaas.org/programs/scientific-responsibility-human-rights-law/geospatial-technologies-and-human-rights-%E2%80%93-ethiopian-occupation.

Amnesty International. 2007. The Scope of Universal Civil Jurisdiction. https://www.amnesty.org/en/documents/ior53/008/2007/en/.

Andersson, Staffan, and Paul M. Heywood. 2009. The Politics of Perception: Use and Abuse of Transparency International's Approach to Measuring Corruption. Political Studies 57 (4): 746–67.

Andonova, Liliana B. 2010. Public-Private Partnerships for the Earth: Politics and Patterns of Hybrid Authority in the Multilateral System. Global Environmental Politics 10 (2): 25–53.

Andonova, Liliana B., and Ronald B. Mitchell. 2010. The Rescaling of Global Environmental Politics. Annual Review of Environment and Resources 35 (1): 255–82.

Andreas, Peter. 2011. Illicit Globalization: Myths, Misconceptions, and Historical Lessons. Political Studies Quarterly 126 (3): 403–25.

Anti-Corruption Foundation. 2017. Alexei Navalny's Anti-Corruption Foundation Presents a New Large-Scale Investigation. 2 March. https://fbk.info/english/english/post/304/.

Archer, Simon. 2020. The Trafigura Actions as Problems of Transnational Law. In Global Private International Law, ed. Horatia Muir Watt, Lucia Bíziková, Agatha Brandão de Oliveira, and Diego P. Fernandez Arroyo. Cheltenham: Edward Elgar: 102–17.

Arguello, Maria Fernanda Perez, and Tamar Ziff. 2019. Hacking Corruption: Tech Tools to Fight Graft in the Americas. Atlantic Council. https://www.atlanticcouncil.org/in-depth-research-reports/report/hacking-corruption-tech-tools-to-fight-graft-in-the-americas/.

Asia Foundation. 2011. Q&A with Founder of 'I Paid a Bribe', India's Anti-Corruption Online Movement. 21 September. https://asiafoundation.org/2011/09/21/qa-with-founder-of-i-paid-a-bribe-indias-anti-corruption-online-movement/.

Asylum Access. 2018. Asylum Access Legal Team Wins Groundbreaking African Court Ruling. 10 April. www.asylumaccess.org/asylum-access-legal-team-wins-groundbreaking-african-court-case-setting-new-precedent-citizenship-rights-deportation-proceedings-tanzania/.

Austin, Kathi Lynn. 2013. The Pillage of Eastern Congo Gold: A Case for the Prosecution of Corporate War Crimes. Conflict Awareness Project Briefing Interim Report. https://7a3bfeaf-c467-456a-bcad-6c8225c5f2af.filesusr.com/ugd/161db9_1eb06a308fb84727a9609a6a8753242c.pdf.

Autesserre, Séverine. 2010. The Trouble with the Congo: Local Violence and the Failure of International Peacebuilding. New York: Cambridge University Press.

———. 2014. Peaceland: Conflict Resolution and the Everyday Politics of International Intervention. New York: Cambridge University Press.

Avant, Deborah D. 2005. The Market for Force: The Consequences of Privatizing Security. Cambridge: Cambridge University Press.

Avant, Deborah D., Martha Finnemore, and Susan K. Sell, eds. 2010. Who Governs the Globe? Cambridge: Cambridge University Press.

Ayling, Julie. 2013. Harnessing Third Parties for Transnational Environmental Crime Prevention. Transnational Environmental Law 2:339–62.

Ayres, Ian, and John Braithwaite. 1991. Responsive Regulation: Transcending the Deregulation Debate. Oxford: Oxford University Press.

Bahoo, Salman, Ilan Alon, and Andrea Paltrinieri. 2020. Corruption in International Business Research: A Review and Research Agenda. International Business Review 29 (4): 1–24.

Baker, John C., and Ray A. Williamson. 2006. Satellite Imagery Activism: Sharpening the Focus on Tropical Deforestation. Singapore Journal of Tropical Geography 27 (1): 4–14.

Balmforth, Tom. 2018. Navalny Needs a Bigger Drone. Radio Free Europe (Radio Liberty), 26 January. https://www.rferl.org/a/russia-navalny-drone-restrictions-medvedev-estate -corruption/29000853.html.

Banda, Maria L. 2018. Inter-American Court of Human Rights' Advisory Opinion on the Environment and Human Rights. American Society of International Law 22 (6). 10 May. https://www .asil.org/insights/volume/22/issue/6/inter-american-court-human-rights-advisory-opinion -environment-and-human.

Barnett, Michael, and Raymond Duvall, eds. 2005. Power in Global Governance. Cambridge: Cambridge University Press.

Barnett, Michael, Kal Raustiala, and John Pevehouse, eds. 2020. The Evolution of Global Governance: Hierarchies, Markets, and Networks. Cambridge: Cambridge University Press.

Barrington, Robert. 2020. The Bribery Act 2010: Key Moments in the Campaign. University of Sussex. http://sro.sussex.ac.uk/id/eprint/98754/.

Barry, Donald. 2005. Icy Battleground: Canada, the International Fund for Animal Welfare, and the Seal Hunt. St. John's: Breakwater Books.

Bartley, Tim. 2018. Rules without Rights: Land, Labor, and Private Authority in the Global Economy. Oxford: Oxford University Press.

Baum, Joel A. C., and Andrew V. Shipilov. 2006. Ecological Approaches to Organizations. In Sage Handbook for Organization Studies, ed. Stewart. R. Clegg, Cynthia Hardy, Thomas B. Lawrence, and Walter R. Nord. London: Sage. 55–110.

Bayley, David H., and Clifford D. Shearing. 2001. The New Structure of Policing: Description, Conceptualization, and Research Agenda Series: Research Report. U.S. Department of Justice Office of Justice Programs, National Institute of Justice.

Baylis, Elena. 2009. Outsourcing Investigations. UCLA Journal of Law and International Affairs 14 (1): 121–48.

Bean, Elise J. 2018. Financial Exposure: Carl Levin's Senate Investigations into Finance and Tax Abuse. New York: Palgrave Macmillan.

Bekou, Olympia. 2015. Doing Justice for the Liberian Victims of Mass Atrocity: NGOs in Aid of Universal Jurisdiction. Journal of International Criminal Justice 13 (2): 219–27.

Bellingcat. 2019. 'A Birdie Is Flying Towards You': Identifying the Separatists Linked to the Downing of MH17. https://www.bellingcat.com/app/uploads/2019/06/a-birdie-is-flying-towards -you.pdf.

Benvenisti, Eyal, and George W. Downs. 2007. The Empire's New Clothes: Political Economy and the Fragmentation of International Law. Stanford Law Review 60 (2): 595–632.

Berny, Nathalie, and Christopher Rootes. 2018. Environmental NGOs at a Crossroads? Environmental Politics 27 (6): 947–72.

Berube, C. 2021. Sea Shepherd: The Evolution of an Eco-vigilante to Legitimized Maritime Capacity Builder. United States Naval Academy. https://digital-commons.usnwc.edu/ciwag-case -studies/18/.

Betsill, Michele. 2014. Transnational Actors in International Environmental Politics. In Advances in International Environmental Politics, ed. Michele Betsill, Kathryn Hochstetler, and Dimitris Stevis. London: Palgrave Macmillan. 185–210.

Betsill, Michele M., and Elisabeth Corell. 2001. NGO Influence in International Environmental Negotiations: A Framework for Analysis. Global Environmental Politics 1 (4): 65–85.

———. 2008. NGO Diplomacy: The Influence of Nongovernmental Organizations in International Environmental Negotiations. Cambridge, MA: MIT Press.

Betts, Wendy. 2017. Untapped Potential for Statistical Evidence to Buttress Witness Testimony in International Atrocity Crime Trials. International Criminal Justice Today, 17 April. https://www.international-criminal-justice-today.org/arguendo/untapped-potential-for-statistical-evidence-to-buttress-witness-testimony-in-international-atrocity-crime-trials/.

Biersteker, Thomas J., and Rodney B. Hall, eds. 2002. The Emergence of Private Authority in Global Governance. New York: Cambridge University Press.

Binderkrantz, Anne. 2005. Interest Group Strategies: Navigating between Privileged Access and Strategies of Pressure. Political Studies 53 (4): 694–715.

Binderkrantz, Anne Skorkjær, Peter Munk Christiansen, and Helene Helboe Pedersen. 2015. Interest Group Access to the Bureaucracy, Parliament, and the Media. Governance 28 (1): 95–112.

Bioneers. 2015. Ka Hsaw Wa and Katie Redford: Earth Rights. 13 March. YouTube video, 34:40. https://www.youtube.com/watch?v=Y2vKxtcLfA8.

Bladen, Sarah. 2018. Close Encounters of the Fishy Kind. Global Fishing Watch, 8 June. https://globalfishingwatch.org/news-views/close-encounters-of-the-fishy-kind/.

Bloodgood, Elisabeth. 2011. The Yearbook of International Organizations and Quantitative Non-State Actor Research. The Ashgate Research Companion to Non-State Actors. New York: Routledge.

Bloodgood, Elisabeth, and Emily Clough. 2017. Transnational Advocacy Networks: A Complex Adaptive Systems Simulation Model of the Boomerang Effect. Social Science Computer Review 35 (3): 319–35.

Bob, Clifford. 2005. The Marketing of Rebellion: Insurgents, Media, and International Activism. New York: Cambridge University Press.

Boisson de Chazournes, Laurence. 2004. Review of The Competing Jurisdictions of International Courts and Tribunals by Yuval Shany. American Journal of International Law 98 (3): 622–25.

Borger, J. 2015a. Syria's Truth Smugglers. Guardian, 13 May. www.theguardian.com/world/2015/may/12/syria-truth-smugglers-bashar-al-assad-war-crimes.

———. 2015b. Smuggled Syrian Documents Enough to Indict Bashar al-Assad, Say Investigators. Guardian, 13 May. www.theguardian.com/world/2015/may/12/smuggled-syrian-documents-indict-assad-investigators.

Both ENDS. 2019. Annual Report 2018. https://www.bothends.org/uploaded_files/document/Both_ENDS_Annual_Report_2018.pdf.

———. n.d. Dossier: The Climate Lawsuit against Shell. https://www.bothends.org/en/Our-work/The-Climate-case-against-Shell-?template=print.

Bouwer, Kim. 2020. Lessons from a Distorted Metaphor: The Holy Grail of Climate Litigation. Transnational Environmental Law 9 (2): 347–78.

Bouwer, Kim, and Joanna Setzer. 2020. New Trends in International Climate and Environmental Advocacy. Paper presented at Workshop on New Trends in Climate Litigation: What Works? Bologna, 15 May.

Boyle, Alan. 2012. Human Rights and the Environment: Where Next? European Journal of International Law 23 (3): 613–42.

———. 2018. Climate Change, the Paris Agreement and Human Rights. International and Comparative Law Quarterly 67: 759–77.

Bradley, Curtis A., and Judith G. Kelley. 2008. The Concept of International Delegation. Law and Contemporary Problems 71 (1): 1–36.

Breitmeier, Helmut, and Volker Rittberger. 1997. Environmental NGOs in an Emerging Global Civil Society. Prepared for the United Nations University Symposium 'The United Nations and the Global Environment in the 21st Century: From Common Challenges to Shared Responsibilities', UN Headquarters, New York, 14–15 November.

———. 2000. Environmental NGOs in an Emerging Global Civil Society. In The Global Environment in the 21st Century: Prospects for International Cooperation, ed. Pamela Chasek. Tokyo: United Nations University Press. 130–63.

Brenner, Susan. 2007. Private-Public Sector Cooperation in Combating Cybercrime: In Search of a Model. Journal of International Commercial Law and Technology 2 (2): 58–67.

British Broadcasting Corporation. 2018. Cameroon Atrocity: Finding the Soldiers Who Killed This Woman. 23 September. https://www.bbc.com/news/av/world-africa-45599973.

Brody, Reed. 2015. Bringing a Dictator to Justice: The Case of Hissène Habré. Journal of International Criminal Justice 13 (2): 209–17.

———. 2017. Victims Bring a Dictator to Justice: The Case of Hissène Habré. Berlin: Brot für die Welt.

Browder, Bill. 2015. Red Notice: How I Became Putin's No. 1 Enemy. London: Penguin.

Brower, Charles W. 2005. Calling All NGOs: A Discussion of the Continuing Vitality of the Alien Tort Statute as a Tool in the Fight for International Human Rights in the Wake of Sosa v. Alvarez-Machian. Whittier Law Review 26 (3): 929–52.

Brun, Marie-Amélie. 2019. France Is Latest Country Facing the Courts on Climate Inaction. News Channel of the European Environmental Bureau, 10 January. https://meta.eeb.org/2019/01/10/france-is-latest-country-facing-the-courts-on-climate-inaction/.

Brunnée, Jutta, and Stephen J. Toope. 2010. Legitimacy and Legality in International Law: An Interactional Account. Cambridge: Cambridge University Press.

Bukovansky, Mlada. 2015. Corruption Rankings: Constructing and Contesting the Global Anti-Corruption Agenda. In Ranking the World: Grading States as a Tool of Global Governance, ed. Alexander Cooley and Jack Snyder. Cambridge: Cambridge University Press. 60–85.

Burbank, Stephen, Sean Farhang, and Herbert Kritzer. 2013. Private Enforcement. Lewis and Clark Law Review 17 (3): 637–722.

Burgers, L. 2020. Should Judges Make Climate Change Law? Transnational Environmental Law 9 (1): 1–21.

Burgis-Kasthala, Michelle. 2019. International Justice and Accountability and the Renewal of International Criminal Justice. European Journal of International Law 30 (4): 1165–85.

Burgorgue-Larsen, Laurence, and Amaya Ubeda de Torres. 2011. The Inter-American Court of Human Rights: Case Law and Commentary. Oxford: Oxford University Press.

Burnand, Frédéric. 2018. Fight against Impunity for Mass Crimes Becomes More Universal. Justiceinfo.net, Fondation Hirondelle, 20 March. https://www.justiceinfo.net/en/tribunals/national-tribunals/36767-fight-against-impunity-for-mass-crimes-becomes-more-universal.html.

Burns, Kyle 2016. Constitutions and the Environment: Comparative Approaches to Environmental Protection and the Struggle to Translate Rights into Enforcement. Georgetown Environmental Law Review 1–14.

Bush, Sarah S., and Jennifer Hadden. 2019. Density and Decline in the Founding of International NGOs in the United States. International Studies Quarterly 63 (4): 1133–46.

Büthe, Tim. 2010. Private Regulation in the Global Economy: A (P)Review. Business and Politics 12 (3): 1–23.

Buxbaum, Hannah L. 2019. Extraterritoriality in the Public and Private Enforcement of US Regulatory Law. Indiana University, Legal Studies Research Papers 408.

Buyse, Antonie. 2009. Women on Waves. ECHR Blog. 4 February. http://echrblog.blogspot.com /2009/02/women-on-waves.html.

———. 2018. Squeezing Civic Space: Restrictions of Civil Society Organizations International Journal of Human Rights 22 (8): 966–88.

Cardeñosa, Diego, Jessica Quinlan, Kwok Ho Shea, and Demian D. Chapman. 2018. Multiplex Real-Time PCR Assay to Detect Illegal Trade of CITES-Listed Shark Species. Sci Rep 8, 16313.

Cardona, Luz Angela, Horacio Ortiz, and Daniel Vázquez. 2018. Corruption and Human Rights: Possible Relations. Human Rights Quarterly 40 (2): 317–41.

Carpenter, R. Charli. 2007. Studying Issue (Non)-Adoption in Transnational Networks. International Organization 61 (3): 643–67.

———. 2011. Vetting the Advocacy Agenda: Networks, Centrality and the Paradox of Weapons Norms. International Organization 65 (1): 69–102.

Carranza, Ruben. 2008. Pain and Plunder: Should Transitional Justice Engage with Corruption and Economic Crimes? International Journal of Transitional Justice 2: 310–30.

Carrington, Damian. 2016. High Court Rules UK Government Plans to Tackle Air Pollution Are Illegal. Guardian, 2 November. https://www.theguardian.com/environment/2016/nov/02 /high-court-rules-uk-government-plans-to-tackle-air-pollution-are-illegal.

Carroll, Glenn R. 1985. Concentration and Specialization: Dynamics of Niche Width in Populations of Organizations. American Journal of Sociology 90 (6): 1262–83.

Carroll, Glenn R., and Michael T. Hannan. 2000. The Demography of Corporations and Industries. Princeton: Princeton University Press.

Cashore, Benjamin, Graeme Auld, and Deanna Newsom. 2004. Governing through Markets: Forest Certification and the Emergence of Non-State Authority. New Haven: Yale University Press.

Center for Constitutional Rights. 2019. Filártiga v. Peña-Irala. https://ccrjustice.org/home/what -we-do/our-cases/fil-rtiga-v-pe-irala.

Centro de Estudios Legales y Sociales (CELS). 2011. Making Justice: Further Discussions on the Prosecution of Crimes against Humanity in Argentina. Trans. Paula Arturo. https://www.cels .org.ar/web/wp-content/uploads/2011/10/makingjustice.pdf.

Chayes, Abram, and Antonia Handler Chayes. 1993. On Compliance. International Organization 47 (2): 175–205.

Cheliotis, Leonidas K., and Sappho Xenakis. 2016. Punishment and Political Systems: State Punitiveness in Post-Dictatorial Greece. Punishment and Society 18 (3): 268–300.

Citizen Engage. 2018. Ukraine: Empowering Citizen Watchdogs. 27 December. https://www .ogpstories.org/impact_story/ukraine-empowering-citizen-watchdogs/.

Clancy, Deirdre. 2015. 'They Told Us We Would Be Part of History': Reflections on the Civil Society Intermediary Experience in the Great Lakes Region. In Contested Justice: The Politics and Practice of International Criminal Court Interventions, ed. Christian De Vos, Sara Kendall, and Carsten Stahn. Cambridge: Cambridge University Press. 219–48.

Clark, Ann Marie, and Kathryn Sikkink. 2013. Information Effects and Human Rights Data: Is the Good News about Increased Human Rights Information Bad News for Human Rights Measures? Human Rights Quarterly 35 (3): 539–68.

Claude, Richard Pierre. 1983. The Case of Joelita Filartiga and the Clinic of Hope. Human Rights Quarterly 5 (3): 275–301.

ClientEarth. 2017. Ten Years of ClientEarth 2007–2017. https://www.documents.clientearth .org/wp-content/uploads/library/2018-04-23-ten-years-of-clientearth-2007-to-2017-ce -en.pdf.

———. 2019. News: Finnish Wolves: Milestone Ruling for EU Wildlife Protection. 10 October. https://www.clientearth.org/finnish-wolves-milestone-ruling-for-eu-wildlife-protection/.

Climate Case Ireland. 2018. 2018: The Year of Climate Litigation: Courts Are the New Frontline in the Fight against Climate Change. 7 May. https://www.climatecaseireland.ie/2018-the-year -of-climate-litigation-courts-are-the-new-frontline-in-the-fight-against-climate-change/.

Climate Change Litigation Databases. 2016. Union of Swiss Senior Women for Climate Protection v. Swiss Federal Council and Others. http://climatecasechart.com/non-us-case/union -of-swiss-senior-women-for-climate-protection-v-swiss-federal-parliament/?cn-reloaded=1.

Cmiel, Kenneth. 2004. The Recent History of Human Rights. American Historical Review 109 (1): 117–35.

Coalition for the ICC. http://www.coalitionfortheicc.org/.

Cogan, Jacob K. 2006. Noncompliance and the International Rule of Law. Yale Journal of International Law 31 (1): 189–210.

Coish, Calvin. 1979. Season of the Seal: The International Storm over Canada's Seal Hunt. St. John's: Breakwater.

Cole, Wade M. 2015. Mind the Gap: State Capacity and the Implementation of Human Rights Treaties. International Organization 69 (2): 405–41.

Cole, Wade M., and Francisco O. Ramirez. 2013. Conditional Decoupling: Assessing the Impact of National Human Rights Institutions, 1981–2004. American Sociological Review 78 (4): 702–25.

Colin, Barry M., K. Chad Clay, and Michael E. Flynn. 2013. Avoiding the Spotlight: Human Rights Shaming and Foreign Direct Investment. International Studies Quarterly 57 (3): 532–44.

Collingsworth, Terry. 2002. The Key Human Rights Challenge: Developing Enforcement Mechanisms. Harvard Human Rights Journal 15: 183–204.

Cooley, Alexander, and John Heathershaw. 2017. Dictators without Borders: Power and Money in Central Asia. New Haven: Yale University Press.

Cooley, Alexander, and James Ron. 2002. The NGO Scramble. International Security 27 (1): 5–39.

Corner House. 2014. Press Release: Secrecy Order Lifted on Legal Challenge to Corrupt Nigerian Oil Deal. 7 November. http://www.thecornerhouse.org.uk/sites/thecornerhouse.org.uk/files /Press%20Release%207%20Nov%202014_1.pdf.

Council of Europe. 2012. Manual on Human Rights and the Environment. https://www.echr.coe .int/Documents/Pub_coe_Environment_2012_ENG.pdf.

Cutler, Claire A. 2002. Private International Regimes and Interfirm Cooperation. In The Emergence of Private Authority in Global Governance, ed. Tomas J. Biersteker and Rodney B. Hall. Cambridge: Cambridge University Press. 23–42.

Cutler, Claire A., Virginia Haufler, and Tony Porter, eds. 1999. Private Authority and International Affairs. Albany: State University of New York Press.

Dai, Xinyuan. 2002. Information Systems in Treaty Design. World Politics 54 (4): 405–36.

———. 2013. The Compliance Gap and the Efficacy of International Human Rights Institutions. In The Persistent Power of Human Rights: From Commitment to Compliance, ed. Thomas Risse, Stephen Ropp, and Kathryn Sikkink. New York: Cambridge University Press. 85–102.

Danaher, Michael. 1981. Torture as a Tort in Violation of International Law: Filartiga v. Peña-Irala. Stanford Law Review 33 (2): 353–69.

Dancy, Geoff, and Veronica Michel. 2016. Human Rights Enforcement from Below: Private Actors and Prosecutorial Momentum in Latin America and Europe. International Studies Quarterly 60 (1): 173–86.

Dancy, Geoff, and Florencia Montal. 2017. Unintended Complementarity: Why International Criminal Court Investigations May Increase Domestic Human Rights Prosecutions. American Journal of International Law 111 (3): 689–723.

Darby, Andrew. 2007. Harpoon: Into the Heart of Whaling. Sydney: Allen & Unwin.

Davis, Edward. 2011. Transnational Civil Asset Recovery of the Proceeds of Crime and Corruption: A Practical Approach. In Non-State Actors and Asset Recovery, ed. Daniel Thelesklaf and Pedro Gomes Pereira. Bern: Peter Lang. 63–93.

Davis, Kevin E. 2019. Between Impunity and Imperialism: The Regulation of Transnational Bribery. Oxford: Oxford University Press.

Davis, Tina. 2020. Episode 12: Terry Collingsworth Interviewed by Dr. Tina Davis. Slavefree Today Podcast (podcast). 13 April. https://poddtoppen.se/podcast/1481592968/slavefree-today-podcast/episode-12-terry-collingsworth-interviewed-by-dr-tina-davis.

Day, David. 1987. The Whale War. New York: Routledge.

de Moerloose, Benedict. 2016. Challenging the Pillage Process: Argor-Heraeus and Gold from Ituri. Open Society Foundations. https://www.justiceinitiative.org/uploads/55e114ad-42d3-425a-8127-4cd62967ad8a/legal-remedies-10-demoerloose%20-20161107.pdf.

de Silva, Nicole. 2017. The International Criminal Court's Use of NGOs in Regulating International Crimes. Annals of the American Academy of Political and Social Sciences 670: 170–88.

de Sousa, Luis. 2005. TI in Search of a Constituency: The Franchising of the Global Anti-corruption Movement. Asia-Pacific School of Economics and Government, Canberra.

Deitelhoff, Nicole. 2009. The Discursive Process of Legalization: Charting Islands of Persuasion in the ICC Case. International Organization 63 (1): 33–65.

DeMars, William E. 2005. NGOs and Transnational Networks: Wildcards in World Politics. London: Pluto.

DiMaggio, P., and W. Powell. 1983. The Iron Cage Revisited: Institutional Isomorphism and Collective Rationality in Organizational Fields. American Sociological Review 48 (2): 147–60.

Djelic, Marie-Laure, and Sigrid Quack, eds. 2010. Transnational Communities: Shaping Global Economic Governance. Cambridge: Cambridge University Press.

———. 2018. Globalization and Business Regulation. Annual Review of Sociology 44 (1): 123–43.

Dowie, Mark. 1996. Losing Ground: American Environmentalism at the Close of the Twentieth Century. Cambridge, MA: MIT Press.

Downs, George W., and David M. Rocke. 1995. Optimal Imperfection? Domestic Uncertainty and International Institutions. Princeton: Princeton University Press.

Drezner, Daniel W. 2009. The Power and Peril of International Regime Complexity. Perspectives on Politics 7 (1): 65–70.

Duncan, Natricia. 2014. Interview: I Want to End Anonymous Companies. Guardian, 11 April. https://www.theguardian.com/global-development-professionals-network/2014/apr/11/charmian-gooch-global-witness-transparency.

Dupuy, Kendra E., James Ron, and Aseem Prakash. 2015. Who Survived? The Effects of Ethiopia's Regulatory Crackdown on NGOs. Review of International Political Economy 22 (2): 419–56.

———. 2016. Hands Off My Regime! The Backlash against Foreign Funding to Local NGOs. World Development 84: 299–311.

Dupuy, Pierre-Marie, and Luisa Vierucci, eds. 2008. NGOs in International Law: Efficiency in Flexibility? Cheltenham: Edward Elgar.

Earthjustice. 2005. Petition to the Inter American Commission on Human Rights Seeking Relief from Violations Resulting from Global Warming Caused by Acts and Omissions of the United States. https://earthjustice.org/sites/default/files/library/legal_docs/petition-to-the-inter-american-commission-on-human-rights-on-behalf-of-the-inuit-circumpolar-conference.pdf.

EarthRights International. 1996. Total Denial: A Report on the Yadana Pipeline Project in Burma. https://earthrights.org/publication/total-denial/.

———. 2003. Doe v. Unocal: The First Case of Its Kind: Holding a U.S. Company Responsible for Rape, Murder, and Forced Labor in Myanmar. https://earthrights.org/case/doe-v-unocal/#documentsff69-1a905f26-f4b6.

Efrat, Asif, and Abraham L. Newman. 2020. Intolerant Justice: Ethnocentrism and Transnational Litigation Frameworks. Review of International Organization 15 (1): 271–99.

Eigen, Peter. 1996. Combatting Corruption around the World. Journal of Democracy 7 (1): 158–68.

———. 2013. International Corruption: Organized Civil Society for Better Global Governance. Social Research 80 (4): 1287–1308.

Eilstrup-Sangiovanni, Mette. 2019. Competition and Strategic Differentiation among Transnational Advocacy Groups. Interest Groups & Advocacy 8: 376–406.

Eilstrup-Sangiovanni, Mette, and Teale N. Phelps Bondaroff. 2014. From Advocacy to Confrontation: Direct Enforcement by Environmental NGOs. International Studies Quarterly 58 (2): 348–61.

Eilstrup-Sangiovanni, Mette, and J. C. Sharman. 2021. Enforcers beyond Borders: Transnational NGOs and the Enforcement of International Law. Perspectives on Politics 19 (1): 131–47.

Engel Rasmussen, Sune. 2014. Meet the Australian Ex-Commando Saving Zimbabwe's Rhinos: On the Front Line of Zimbabwe's Fight against Poaching. Time, 22 February. https://perma .cc/3WC2-6T9V.

Engels, Chris. 2016. Written Testimony before the Commission on Security and Cooperation in Europe. 22 September. www.csce.gov/sites/helsinkicommission.house.gov/ les/1_Chris%20 Engels_Testimony.pdf.

England, Charlotte. 2017. Anarchist Squatters Take Over £15m London Mansion Owned by Russian Billionaire. Independent, 29 January. https://www.independent.co.uk/news/uk/home -news/anarchist-squatters-ps15-million-london-mansion-russian-billionaire-oligarch-andrey -goncharenko-eaton-square-anal-homeless-shelter-a7549136.html.

Epstein, Yaffa, and Jan Darpö. 2013. The Wild Has No Words: Environmental NGOs Empowered to Speak for Protected Species as Swedish Courts Apply EU and International Environmental Law. Journal of European Environmental & Planning Law 10 (3): 250–61.

European Center for Constitutional and Human Rights. 2016. Universal Jurisdiction in Germany? The Congo War Crimes Trial: First Case under the Code of Crimes against International Law. Berlin. https://www.ecchr.eu/fileadmin/Juristische_Dokumente/Report_Executive _Summary_FDLR_EN.pdf.

———. 2018. Accountability for Forced Labor in a Globalized Economy: Lessons and Challenges in Litigation, with Examples from Qatar. https://www.ecchr.eu/fileadmin/Publikationen /ECCHR_QATAR.pdf.

European Commission. 2019. Report on European Union Implementation of the Aarhus Convention in the Area of Access to Justice in Environmental Matters. Commission Staff Working Document. https://ec.europa.eu/environment/aarhus/pdf/Commission_report_2019.pdf.

European Court of Human Rights (ECHR). 2020. Factsheet: Environment and the ECHR. https:// www.echr.coe.int/Documents/FS_Environment_ENG.pdf.

Europol. 2015. Report on Environmental Crime in Europe. June. https://www.europol.europa.eu /publications-documents/report-environmental-crime-in-europe.

———. 2020. https://www.europol.europa.eu/crime-areas-and-trends/crime-areas/environmental -crime.

EyeWitness Project. 2016. EyeWitness to Atrocities Director Speaks to the Shaakshi Project. 12 May. Video, 7:38. https://www.youtube.com/watch?v=ktK2yjJZn2I.

EyeWitness to Atrocities. 2017. Fighting Misinformation and Supporting Human Rights Advocacy in Ukraine. https://www.eyewitness.global/Fighting-misinformation-and-supporting-human -rights-advocacy-in-Ukraine.

———. n.d. Bringing Historical Crimes to a Domestic Court in the Democratic Republic of Congo (DRC). https://www.eyewitness.global/Bringing-historical-crimes-to-a-domestic-court-in -the-DRC.

Fältbiologerna, PUSH Sverige, et al. 2016. Summons Application for the Stockholm District Court—Unofficial Translation. 15 September. http://blogs2.law.columbia.edu/climate -change-litigation/wp-content/uploads/sites/16/non-us-case-documents/2016/20160915 _3649_summons.pdf.

Farrell, Henry, and Abraham Newman. 2015. The New Politics of Interdependence: Cross-national Layering in Transatlantic Regulatory Disputes. Comparative Political Studies 48 (4): 497–526.

Faull, Lionel, Ted Jeory, and Jamie Doward. 2017. The Oil Deal, the Disgraced Former Minister, and $800m Paid via a UK Bank. Guardian, 5 March. https://www.theguardian.com/business /2017/mar/05/the-oil-deal-the-disgraced-minister-and-800m-paid-via-a-uk-bank.

Fenner-Zinkernagel, Gretta, Charles Monteith, and Pedro Gomes Pereira, eds. 2013. Emerging Trends in Asset Recovery. Bern: Peter Lang.

Financial Action Task Force (FATF)/Egmont Group. 2018. Concealment of Beneficial Ownership. Paris. https://www.fatf-gafi.org/publications/methodsandtrends/documents/concealment -beneficial-ownership.html.

Findley, Michael G., Daniel L. Nielson, and J. C. Sharman. 2014. Global Shell Games: Experiments in Transnational Relations, Crime and Terrorism. Cambridge: Cambridge University Press.

Fine, Janice. 2017. Enforcing Labor Standards in Partnership with Civil Society: Can Co-Enforcement Succeed Where the State Alone Has Failed? Politics and Society 45 (3): 359–88.

Finnemore, Martha. 2000. Are Legal Norms Distinctive? Journal of International Law and Politics 32 (3): 699–705.

Finnemore, Martha, and Kathryn Sikkink. 1998. International Norm Dynamics and Political Change. International Organization 52 (4): 887–917.

Florini, Ann, ed. 2000. The Third Force: The Rise of Transnational Civil Society. Tokyo and Washington: Japan Centre for International Change and Carnegie Endowment for International Peace.

Forensic Architecture. 2012. The Left-to-Die Boat. 11 April. https://forensic-architecture.org /investigation/the-left-to-die-boat.

Forensic Oceanography. 2012. Report on the 'Left-to-Die Boat'. Centre for Research Architecture, Goldsmiths, University of London. https://www.fidh.org/IMG/pdf/fo-report.pdf.

Forstater, Maya. 2018. Illicit Financial Flows, Trade Misinvoicing, and Multinational Tax Avoidance: The Same or Different? Center for Global Development. https://www.cgdev.org /publication/illicit-financial-flows-trade-misinvoicing-and-multinational-tax-avoidance.

France Nature Environment. 2017. Capercaillie: State Condemned for Six Years of Illegal Hunting. 7 November. https://www.fne.asso.fr/actualites/grand-t%C3%A9tras%C2%A0 -l%E2%80%99%C3%A9tat-condamn%C3%A9-pour-six-ann%C3%A9es-de-chasse -ill%C3%A9gale.

Franck, Thomas M. 1990. The Power of Legitimacy among Nations. Oxford: Oxford University Press.

———. 2006. The Power of Legitimacy and the Legitimacy of Power: International Law in an Age of Power Disequilibrium. American Journal of International Law 100 (1): 88–106.

Friends of the Earth. 2017. Government Should Have Stopped Sand-Dredging at 'Wildlife Jewel' Lough Neagh. 28 June. https://friendsoftheearth.uk/who-we-are/government-should-have -stopped-sanddredging-wildlife-jewel-lough-neagh.

———. 2019. Total in Court for Human Rights Violations in Uganda: Historic Hearing in France under the Duty of Vigilance Law. 16 December. https://www.foei.org/features/total-court -human-rights-uganda-france-duty-vigilance.

Gagné-Acoolon, Sandrine. 2020. France: What to Do with Funds Seized from Corrupt Foreigners? Organized Crime and Corruption Reporting Project, 18 February. https://www.occrp.org/en /daily/11636-france-what-to-do-with-funds-seized-from-corrupt-foreigners.

Gallagher, Janice. 2017. The Last Mile Problem: Activists, Advocates, and the Struggle for Justice in Domestic Courts. Comparative Political Studies 50 (12): 1666–98.

Gent, Stephen E., Mark J. C. Crescenzi, Elizabeth J. Menninga, and Lindsay Reid. 2015. The Reputation Trap of NGO Accountability. International Theory 7 (3): 426–63.

Global Fishing Watch. Does Global Fishing Watch Track Illegal Activity? Has Global Fishing Watch Ever Identified Illegal Fishing Activity? https://globalfishingwatch.org/faqs/can -citizen-watchdogs-use-gfw-to-monitor-fishing-activity/.

Global Legal Action Network. 2019a. Bellingcat and GLAN Initiate Investigation into Yemen Airstrikes. 22 April. https://www.glanlaw.org/single-post/2019/04/22/Bellingcat-and-GLAN -initiate-investigation-into-Yemen-airstrikes.

———. 2019b. Launch of the 'Yemen Project' Website; Open Source Investigations into Saudi-Led Yemen Airstrike Campaign. 30 April. https://www.glanlaw.org/single-post/2019/04/29 /Launch-of-The-Yemen-Project-website-Open-source-investigations-into-Saudi-led-airstrike -campaign-in-Yemen.

Global Witness. 2003. Press Release: Does US Bank Harbour Equatorial Guinea's Oil Millions in Secret Accounts? US Department of Justice Must Investigate. 20 January. https://www .globalwitness.org/en/archive/does-us-bank-harbour-equatorial-guineas-oil-millions-secret -accounts-us-department-justice/.

———. 2006. African Minister Buys Multi-Million Dollar California Mansion. 8 November. https:// www.globalwitness.org/en/archive/african-minister-buys-multi-million-dollar-california -mansion/.

———. 2009. The Secret Life of a Shopaholic: How an African Dictator's Playboy Son Went on a Multi-Million Dollar Shopping Spree in the US. 17 November. https://www.globalwitness.org /en/campaigns/corruption-and-money-laundering/banks/secret-life-shopaholic/.

———. 2017. Shell Knew: Emails Show Executives at UK's Biggest Company Knew It Was Party to a Vast Bribery Scheme. 10 April. https://www.globalwitness.org/en/campaigns/oil-gas -and-mining/shell-knew/.

———. 2018a. Annual Report and Financial Statements. 31 December. https://www.globalwitness .org/en/about-us/global-witness-annual-reports/.

———. 2018b. Shell and Eni Go to Trial: A New Chapter Opens. 5 March. https://www .globalwitness.org/en/blog/shell-and-eni-go-trial-new-chapter-opens/.

———. 2019. 25 Years of Creating Change. https://www.globalwitness.org/en/about-us/25-years -creating-change/.

Gommers, Mirjam. 2015. Conservation Tools: How Drones Can Save Rainforests. Conservation International, 13 May. https://www.conservation.org/blog/conservation-tools-how-drones -can-save-rainforests.

Gonzalez-Ocantos, Ezequiel. 2014. Persuade Them or Oust Them: Crafting Judicial Change and Transitional Justice in Argentina. Comparative Politics 46 (4): 479–98.

Gonzalez-Ocantos, Ezequiel, and Wayne Sandholtz. 2021. International Human Rights Courts and Sources of Resilience: The Case of the Inter-American System. https://ssrn.com/abstract =3816892.

Goodman, Martin, and James Connelly. 2018. The Public Interest Environmental Law Group: From USA to Europe. Environmental Politics 27 (6): 1014–32.

Grant, Wyn. 2001. Pressure Politics: From 'Insider' Politics to Direct Action? Parliamentary Affairs. https://www.researchgate.net/profile/Wyn_Grant/publication/31014133_Pressure _Politics_From_'Insider'_Politics_to_Direct_Action/links/568cffb008ae197e426b6ab5 /Pressure-Politics-From-Insider-Politics-to-Direct-Action.pdf.

Grantham Research Institute on Climate Change and the Environment. 2020. Climate Change Laws of the World. https://climate-laws.org/.

———. 2021. EarthLife Africa Johannesburg v. Minister of Environmental Affairs & Others. https://climate-laws.org/cclow/geographies/south-africa/litigation_cases/earthlife-africa -johannesburg-v-minister-of-environmental-affairs-others.

Green, Jessica. 2014. Rethinking Private Authority: Agents and Entrepreneurs in Global Environmental Governance. Princeton: Princeton University Press.

Green, Jessica F., and Jeff Colgan. 2013. Protecting Sovereignty, Protecting the Planet: State Delegation to International Organizations and Private Actors in Environmental Politics. Governance 26 (3): 473–97.

Green, Matthew. 2016. The Black Fish: Undercover with the Vigilantes Fighting Organised Crime at Sea. Guardian, 24 February. https://www.theguardian.com/environment/2016/feb/24 /black-fish-undercover-with-vigilantes-fighting-organised-crime-at-sea.

Grossman, David A. 2003. Warming Up to a Not-So-Radical Idea: Tort-Based Climate Change Litigation. Columbia Journal of Environmental Law 28 (1): 1–61.

Guilbert, Kiran Grant, and Magdalena Mis. 2018. Exclusive: North Korean Worker Seeks Dutch Shipbuilder's Prosecution over Labor Abuses. Reuters, 8 November. https://www.reuters .com/article/us-netherlands-lawsuit-trafficking-exclu/exclusive-north-korean-worker-seeks -dutch-shipbuilders-prosecution-over-labor-abuses-idUSKCN1ND1BR.

Guilluame, Gilbert. 2001. President of the International Court of Justice, Speech to the General Assembly of the United Nations. 30 October. http://www.icj-cij.org/files/press-releases/5 /2995.pdf.

Gutterman, Ellen. 2014. The Legitimacy of Transnational NGOs: Lessons from the Experience of Transparency International in Germany and France. Review of International Studies 40 (2): 391–418.

———. 2017. Poverty, Corruption, Trade or Terrorism? Strategic Framing in the Politics of UK Anti-Bribery Compliance. British Journal of Politics and International Relations 19 (1): 152–71.

Gwynn, Mariá Antonia. 2018. Legal Developments in the Enforcement of International Environmental Commitments. Global Economic Governance Working Paper No. 138. University of Oxford.

Haag, Matthew. 2018. North Korea Is Ordered to Pay Otto Warmbier's Family over $501 Million in Damages. New York Times, 24 December. https://www.nytimes.com/2018/12/24/us/otto -warmbier-north-korea.html?searchResultPosition=1.

Haddad, Heidi N. 2012. Judicial Institution Builders: NGOs and International Human Rights Courts. Journal of Human Rights 11 (1): 126–49.

Haddad, Heidi Nichols. 2018. The Hidden Hands of Justice: NGOs, Human Rights and International Courts. Cambridge: Cambridge University Press.

Hadden, Jennifer. 2015. Networks in Contention: The Divisive Politics of Climate Change. New York: Cambridge University Press.

Hafner-Burton, Emilie M. 2008. Sticks and Stones: Naming and Shaming the Human Rights Enforcement Problem. International Organization 62 (3): 689–716.

———. 2013. Making Human Rights a Reality. Princeton: Princeton University Press.

Hafner-Burton, Emilie, and Kiyoteru Tsutsui. 2007. Justice Lost! The Failure of International Human Rights Law to Matter Where Needed Most. Journal of Peace Research 44 (4): 407–25.

Halberstam, Malvinia. 2003. Belgium's Universal Jurisdiction Law: Vindication of Universal Justice or Pursuit of Politics? Cardozo Law Journal 25: 247–66.

Hale, Thomas. 2015. The Rule of Law in the Global Economy: Explaining Intergovernmental Backing for Private Commercial Tribunals. European Journal of International Relations 21 (3): 483–512.

———. 2020. Transnational Actors and Transnational Governance in Environmental Politics. Annual Review of Political Science 23 (1): 203–20.

Hale, Thomas, and Charles Roger. 2014. Orchestration and Transnational Climate Governance. Review of International Organization 9 (1): 59–82.

Halliday, Terrence C., and Gregory Schaffer, eds. 2015. Transnational Legal Orders. Cambridge: Cambridge University Press.

Han, Yuna. 2017. Rebirth of Universal Jurisdiction? 31 August. https://iow.eui.eu/2017/08/31/rebirth-universal-jurisdiction/.

Hannan, Michael T., and John Freeman. 1977. The Population Ecology of Organizations. American Journal of Sociology 82 (5): 929–64.

Harrison, James. 2014. Significant International Environmental Law Cases: 2012–14. Journal of Environmental Law 26 (3): 519–40.

Harvey, Fiona. 2018. Air Pollution: UK Government Loses Third Court Case as Plans Ruled 'Unlawful'. Guardian, 21 February. https://www.theguardian.com/environment/2018/feb/21/high-court-rules-uk-air-pollution-plans-unlawful.

Haslam, Emily. 2011. Subjects and Objects: International Criminal Law and the Institutionalization of Civil Society. International Journal of Transitional Justice 5 (2): 221–40.

Haslam, Emily, and Rod Edmunds. 2012. Managing a New 'Partnership': 'Professionalization', Intermediaries and the International Criminal Court. Criminal Law Forum 24: 49–85.

Hathaway, Oona A. 2007. Why Do Countries Commit to Human Rights Treaties? Journal of Conflict Resolution 51 (4): 588–621.

Hawkins, Darren G., David A. Lake, Daniel L. Nielson, and Michael J. Tierney. 2006. Delegation under Anarchy: States, International Organizations, and Principal-Agent Theory. Cambridge: Cambridge University Press.

Heinze, Alexander. 2019. Private International Criminal Investigations. Zeitschrift für Internationale Strafrechtsdogmatik 169–81. http://www.zis-online.com/dat/artikel/2019_2_1274.pdf.

Herscher, Andrew. 2014. Surveillant Witnessing: Satellite Imagery and the Visual Politics of Human Rights. Public Culture 26 (3): 469–500.

Heyns, Christoph, and Magnus Killander. 2013. Universality and the Growth of Regional Systems. In Oxford Handbook of International Human Rights Law, ed. Dinah Shelton. Oxford: Oxford University Press. 670–99.

Higgins, Eliot. 2021. We Are Bellingcat: An Intelligence Agency for the People. London: Bloomsbury.

Hillebrecht, Courtney. 2019. Advocacy and Accountability in the Age of Backlash: NGOs and Regional Courts. In Contesting Human Rights, ed. Alison Brysk and Michael Stohl. Cheltenham: Edward Elgar. 160–79.

Hoek, Andrew. 2010. Sea Shepherd Conservation Society v. Japanese Whalers, the Showdown: Who Is the Real Villain? Stanford Journal of Animal Law and Policy 3:159–93.

Hoffman, Andrew. 2009. Shades of Green. Stanford Social Innovation Review (Spring): 40–49.

Holzmeyer, Cheryl. 2009. Human Rights in an Era of Neoliberal Globalization: The Alien Torts Claims Act and Grassroots Mobilization in Doe v. Unocal. Law and Society Review 43 (2): 271–304.

Hopgood, Stephen. 2006. Keepers of the Flame: Understanding Amnesty International. Ithaca: Cornell University Press.

Howse, Robert, and Ruti Teitel. 2010. Beyond Compliance: Rethinking Why International Law Really Matters. Global Policy 1 (2): 127–36.

Hsu, Shi-Ling. 2008. A Realistic Evaluation of Climate Change Litigation through the Lens of a Hypothetical Lawsuit. University of Colorado Law Review 79 (3): 701–66. https://heinonline.org/HOL/P?h=hein.journals/ucollr79&i=707.

Hubbard, Ben. 2020. Germany Takes Rare Step in Putting Syrian Officers on Trial in Torture Case. New York Times, 23 April. https://www.nytimes.com/2020/04/23/world/middleeast/syria-germany-war-crimes-trial.html.

———. 2021. German Court Convicts Former Syrian Official of Crimes Against Humanity. New York Times, 24 February. https://www.nytimes.com/2021/02/24/world/middleeast/germany-court-syria-war-crimes.html.

Huelss, Hendrik. 2017. After Decision-Making: The Operationalization of Norms in International Relations. International Theory 9 (3): 381–409.

Human Rights Data Analysis Group. 2010. State Violence in Chad: A Statistical Analysis of Prison Mortality in Chad's DDS Prisons and Command Responsibility of Hissène Habré, 1982–1990. https://hrdag.org/content/chad/State-Violence-in-Chad.pdf.

Human Rights Watch. 1993. Prosecute Now! Helsinki Watch Releases Eight Cases for War Crimes Tribunal on Former Yugoslavia. 1 August. https://www.hrw.org/reports/1993/yugoslavia/.

———. 2011. 'Turning Pebbles': Evading Accountability for Post-Election Violence in Kenya. https://www.hrw.org/report/2011/12/09/turning-pebbles/evading-accountability-post-election-violence-kenya.

———. 2013. The Plain of the Dead. https://www.hrw.org/sites/default/files/reports/chad1213summary_english.pdf.

———. 2014. The Long Arm of Justice. https://www.hrw.org/sites/default/files/reports/IJ0914_ForUpload.pdf.

———. 2019. Targeted. https://www.hrw.org/news/2019/11/28/targeted-counterterrorism-measures-take-aim-environmental-activists.

———. n.d. The Pinochet Case: A Wake-up Call to Tyrants and Victims Alike. https://www.hrw.org/legacy/campaigns/chile98/precedent.htm#The%20Prosecution%20of%20Hissein%20Habre.

Humby, T.-L. 2018. The Thabametsi Case: Case No. 65662/16 Earthlife Africa Johannesburg v. Minister of Environmental Affairs. Journal of Environmental Law 30 (1): 145–55. https://doi.org/10.1093/jel/eqy007.

Hune, Tim. 2015. 110-Day Ocean Hunt Ends with Sea Shepherd Rescuing Alleged Poachers. CNN, 8 April. http://edition.cnn.com/2015/04/07/africa/sea-shepherd-rescue-fishing-ship/index.html.

Hurd, Ian. 2018. How to Do Things with International Law. Princeton: Princeton University Press.

Inter-American Court of Human Rights. 2017. Opinión Consultiva OC-23/17 de 15 de Noviembre de 2017 Solicitada por la República de Colombia. https://www.corteidh.or.cr/docs/opiniones/seriea_23_esp.pdf.

International Anti-Poaching Foundation. Akashinga ('The Brave Ones') Nature Protected by Women. https://www.iapf.org/news/akashinga.

International Bar Association London. 2020. Model Statute for Proceedings Challenging Government Failure to Act on Climate Change. An International Bar Association Climate Change Justice and Human Rights Task Force Report. February. https://www.ibanet.org/MediaHandler?id=47ae6064-9a61-42f6-ac9e-4f7e1b5b4e7b.

International Criminal Court (ICC). 2017. Financial Investigations and Recovery of Assets. The Hague. https://www.icc-cpi.int/iccdocs/other/Freezing_Assets_Eng_Web.pdf.

International Environmental Agreements Database. 2020. https://iea.uoregon.edu.

International Union for Conservation of Nature. 2008. http://www2.ecolex.org/server2neu.php/libcat/docs/LI/MON-081994.pdf.

Interpol. 2015. Interpol-Supported Illegal Fishing Investigations Lead to Prosecution. https://www.interpol.int/ar/1/1/2015/INTERPOL-supported-illegal-fishing-investigations-lead-to-prosecution.

———. 2019. Interpol Makes Public Appeal to Help Track Environmental Fugitives. https://www.interpol.int/en/News-and-Events/News/2019/INTERPOL-makes-public-appeal-to-help-track-environmental-fugitives.

Jakobi, Anja. 2013. Common Goods and Evils: The Formation of Global Crime Governance. Oxford: Oxford University Press.

Janes. 2020. Podcast: An Interview with Bellingcat Founder Eliot Higgins. 11 February. YouTube video, 52:48. https://www.youtube.com/watch?v=TxZSOMXio6g&t=1421s.

Jeyaretnam, Philip, and Wen Jin Lau. 2016. The Granting of Mareva Injunctions in Foreign Court Proceedings. Singapore Academy of Law Journal 28:503–26.

Kahler, Miles. 2020. The Arc of Complex Governance: From Organization to Coalition. American Political Science Association Working Paper. https://preprints.apsanet.org/engage/apsa/article-details/5f57d47340d6e400121eed21.

Kaleck, Wolfgang. 2009. From Pinochet to Rumsfeld: Universal Jurisdiction in Europe, 1998–2008. Michigan Journal of International Law 30 (3): 927–80.

Keck, Margaret, and Kathryn Sikkink. 1998. Activists beyond Borders: Advocacy Networks in International Politics. Ithaca: Cornell University Press.

Keohane, Robert O., and Joseph S. Nye. 1977. Power and Interdependence: World Politics in Transition. Boston: Little, Brown.

Kerr, Joanna. 2014. Greenpeace Apology to Inuit for Impacts of Seal Campaign. 24 June. https://www.greenpeace.org/canada/en/story/5473/greenpeace-apology-to-inuit-for-impacts-of-seal-campaign/.

Khagram, Sanjeev, James V. Riker, and Kathryn Sikkink. 2002. From Santiago to Seattle: Transnational Advocacy Groups Restructuring World Politics. In Restructuring World Politics: Transnational Social Movements, Networks, and Norms, ed. Sanjeev Khagram, James V. Riker, and Kathryn Sikkink. Minneapolis: University of Minnesota Press. 3–23.

Khan, Tessa, and Jim Wormington. 2011. Mobile Courts in the DRC: Lessons from Development for International Criminal Justice. Oxford Transitional Justice Research Working Paper.

Khatchadourian, Raffi. 2007. Neptune's Navy. New Yorker, 5 November. https://www.newyorker.com/magazine/2007/11/05/neptunes-navy.

Kim, Hunjoon, and Kathryn Sikkink. 2010. Explaining the Deterrence Effect of Human Rights Prosecutions for Transitional Countries. International Studies Quarterly 54 (4): 939–63.

Kim, Minzee, and Elizabeth Heger Boyle. 2012. Neoliberalism, Transnational Education Norms, and Education Spending in the Developing World, 1983–2004. Law & Social Inquiry 37 (2): 367–94.

Kiyani, Gashia, and Amalia Murdie. 2020. Unintended Restrictions: Women's Rights INGOs and Women's Civil Society Restrictions. Human Rights Review 21: 349–72. https://doi.org/10.1007/s12142-020-00597-8.

Klabbers, Jan. 2016. Theorizing International Organizations. In The Oxford Handbook of the Theory of International Law, ed. Anne Orford and Florian Hoffmann. Oxford: Oxford University Press.

Koenig, Alexa. 2017. Harnessing Social Media as Evidence of Grave International Crimes. Human Rights Center, 23 October. https://medium.com/humanrightscenter/harnessing-social-media-as-evidence-of-grave-international-crimes-d7f3e86240d.

Kottasová, Ivana. 2019. Climate Groups Threaten Lawsuit to Force Shell to Ditch Oil. CNN, 12 February. https://edition.cnn.com/2019/02/12/business/climate-change-shell-oil/index.html.

Krahmann, Elke. 2010. States, Citizens and the Privatization of Security. Cambridge: Cambridge University Press.

Krause, Keith. 2014. Transnational Civil Society Activism and International Security Politics: From Landmines to Global Zero. Global Policy 5 (2): 229–34.

Kurlantzick, Joshua. 2004. Taking Multinationals to Court: How the Alien Torts Act Promotes Human Rights. World Policy Journal 21 (1): 60–67.

La Croix, Kevin. 2018. Is Litigation Financing 'The New Black'? Insight Consensus Influence, 29 August. https://www.lmalloyds.com/LMA/Claims/FIPI_Database/database_content/Is_Litigation_Financing_The_New_Black.aspx.

Lake, David. 2010. Rightful Rules: Authority, Order, and the Foundations of Global Governance. International Studies Quarterly 54 (3): 587–613.

Lake, Milli. 2014. Organizing Hypocrisy: Providing Legal Accountability for Human Rights Violations in Areas of Limited Statehood. International Studies Quarterly 58 (3): 515–26.

———. 2018. Strong NGOs and Weak States: Pursuing Gender Justice in the Democratic Republic of the Congo and South Africa. Cambridge: Cambridge University Press.

Lake, Milli, Ilot Muthaka, and Gabriella Walker. 2016. Gendering Justice in Humanitarian Spaces: Opportunity and (Dis)empowerment through Gender-Based Legal Development Outreach in the Eastern Democratic Republic of Congo. Law and Society Review 50 (3): 539–74.

Langer, Máximo. 2011. The Diplomacy of Universal Jurisdiction: The Political Branches and the Transnational Prosecution of International Crimes. American Journal of International Law 105 (1): 1–49.

———. 2015. Universal Jurisdiction Is Not Disappearing: The Shift from 'Global Enforcer' to 'No Safe Haven' Universal Jurisdiction. Journal of International Criminal Justice 13 (2): 245–56.

Langer, Máximo, and Mackenzie Eason. 2019. The Quiet Expansion of Universal Jurisdiction. European Journal of International Law 30 (3): 779–817.

Larmour, Peter. 2005. Civilising Techniques: Transparency International and the Spread of Anti-Corruption. Asia-Pacific School of Economics and Government, Canberra.

Layus, Rosario Figari. 2018. The Reparative Effect of Human Rights Trials: Lessons from Argentina. London: Routledge.

Lester, Lord, and Ben Jaffey. 2005. ECGD's Anti-Corruption and Anti-Bribery Provisions: 'A Legal Opinion'. Corner House, 16 May. http://www.thecornerhouse.org.uk/resource/ecgds-anti-corruption-and-anti-bribery-provisions.

Liss, Carolin. 2011. Oceans of Crime: Maritime Piracy and Transnational Security in Southeast Asia and Bangladesh. Singapore: Institute of Southeast Asian Studies.

Ljubas, Zdravko. 2021. Moscow Court Marks Navalny's Anti-Graft Group 'Extremist'. https://www.occrp.org/en/daily/14620-moscow-court-marks-navalny-s-anti-graft-group-extremist.

Lohne, Kjersti. 2017. Global Civil Society, the ICC, and Legitimacy in International Criminal Justice. In The Legitimacy of International Criminal Tribunals, ed. Nobuo Hayashi and Cecelia Bailliet. Cambridge: Cambridge University Press. 449–72.

Lopez, Leslie. 2018. Indonesia to Hand Over Jho Low's Luxury Yacht, Allegedly Bought with IMDB Funds, to Malaysia. Straits Times, 4 August. https://www.straitstimes.com/asia/se-asia/indonesia-to-hand-over-luxury-yacht-allegedly-bought-with-1mdb-funds-to-malaysia.

Lupu, Yonatan. 2013. Best Evidence: The Role of Information in Domestic Judicial Enforcement of International Human Rights Agreements. International Organization 67 (3): 469–503.

Mackenzie, Ruth, Cesare P. R. Romano, Yuval Shany, and Philippe Sands. 2010. The Manual on International Courts and Tribunals. 2nd ed. Oxford: Oxford University Press.

Mallinder, Louise. 2009. The Ongoing Quest for Truth and Justice: Enacting and Annulling Argentina's Amnesty Laws. Working Paper 5, Institute of Criminology and Criminal Justice, Queens University Belfast.

Manes, Luca. 2018. Nigerian Bribes, the Long J'accuse of the NGO Anti-corruption against ENI. Shell and Eni on Trial. 19 October. https://shellandenitrial.org/2018/10/19/nigerian-bribes-the-long-jaccuse-of-the-ngo-anti-corruption-against-eni/.

Marin, Melina. 2012. How Hacktivism Fights Corruption. New Internationalist, 15 October. https://newint.org/blog/2012/10/15/hackers-against-corruption.

Marshall, Andrew. 2013. What's Yours Is Mine: New Actors and New Approaches to Asset Recovery in Global Corruption Cases. Center for Global Development Paper. 18 April.

Martinez, Jenny S. 2008. Anti-Slavery Courts and the Dawn of International Human Rights Law. Yale Law Journal 117 (4): 550–641.

Mateova, Miriam, Stefan Parker, and Peter Dauvergne. 2018. The Politics of Repressing Environmentalists as Agents of Foreign Influence. Australian Journal of International Affairs 72
(2): 145–62.

Mather, James. 2017. Asset Recovery after the Criminal Finances Bill, 2016–17. Serle Court.

Mattli, Walter, and Tim Büthe. 2005. Accountability in Accounting? The Politics of Private Rule-
Making in the Public Interest. Governance 18 (3): 399–429.

Mayer, Lloyd Hitoshi. 2011. NGO Standing and Influence in Regional Human Rights Courts and
Commissions. Brooklyn Journal of International Law 36 (3): 911–46.

McCormick, John. 2010. The Role of Environmental NGOs in International Regimes. In The
Global Environment: Institutions, Law and Policy, ed. Regina Axelrod and Stacey Vandeveer.
Washington, DC: CQ Press. 92–110.

McCoy, Jennifer L., and Heather Heckel. 2001. The Emergence of a Global Anti-Corruption Norm.
International Politics 38 (1): 65–90.

McCubbins, Matthew D., and Thomas Schwartz. 1984. Congressional Oversight Overlooked:
Police Patrols versus Fire Alarms. American Journal of Political Science 28 (1): 165–79.

Meyer, John W., John Boli, George M. Thomas, and Francisco O. Ramirez. 1997. World Society
and the Nation-State. American Journal of Sociology 103 (1): 144–81.

Michel, Veronica. 2018. Prosecutorial Accountability and Victims' Rights in Latin America. Cambridge: Cambridge University Press.

Michel, Veronica, and Kathryn Sikkink. 2013. Human Rights Prosecutions and the Participation
Rights of Victims in Latin America. Law and Society Review 47 (4): 873–907.

Micus, Annelen. 2015. The Inter-American Human Rights System as a Safeguard for Justice in
National Transitions: From Amnesty Laws to Accountability in Argentina, Chile and Peru.
Leiden: Brill.

Miller, F., J. Cracknell, and H. Williams, 2017. What the Green Groups Said: Insights from the UK
Environment Sector. London: Environmental Funders Network. https://www.greenfunders
.org/wp-content/uploads/2017/07/What-the-Green-Groups-Said-final.pdf.

Miller, Matthew E. 2010. The Right Issue, the Wrong Branch: Arguments against Adjudicating
Climate Change Nuisance Claims. Michigan Law Review 109 (2): 257–89.

Milman, Oliver. 2015. Captain Deliberately Sank Illegal Fishing Vessel, Claim Sea Shepherd Res-
cuers. Guardian, 7 April. https://www.theguardian.com/environment/2015/apr/07/captain
-deliberately-sank-illegal-fishing-vessel-claim-sea-shepherd-rescuers.

Milne, Richard. 2018. Hermitage Capital Files Criminal Complaint against Danske Bank. Financial
Times, 12 July. https://www.ft.com/content/f5df1236-85e5-11e8-96dd-fa565ec55929.

Mission 2020. Climate Change Claims before International Courts and Tribunals. Workshop co-
hosted by Mission 2020 and Oxford School of Law St. Peter's College, Dorfman Centre, 2 March.

Mitchell, George E., and Hans Peter Schmitz. 2014. Principled Instrumentalism: A Theory of
Transnational NGO Behaviour. Review of International Studies 40 (3): 487–504.

Mitchell, Ronald. 2017. International Environmental Agreements Database. https://iea.uoregon
.edu/sites/iea1.uoregon.edu/files/MEAs-1857-2016.jpg.

Mitchell, Ronald B., Liliana B. Andonova, Mark Axelrod, Jörg Balsiger, Thomas Bernauer, Jes-
sica F. Green, James Hollway, Rakhyun E. Kim, and Jean-Frédéric Morin. 2020. Research
Note: What We Know (and Could Know) about International Environmental Agreements.
Global Environmental Politics 20 (1). https://doi.org/10.1162/glep_a_00544.

Morin, Jean-Frédéric, and Chantal Blouin. 2019. How Environmental Treaties Contribute to
Global Health Governance. Globalization and Health 15 (47). https://doi.org/10.1186/s12992
-019-0493-7.

Moyn, Samuel. 2018. Not Enough: Human Rights in an Unequal World. Cambridge, MA: Harvard
University Press.

Mue, Njonjo, and Judy Gitau. 2015. The Justice Vanguard: The Role of Civil Society in Seeking Accountability for Kenya's Post-Election Violence. In Contested Justice: The Politics and Practice of International Criminal Court Interventions, ed. Christian De Vos. Cambridge: Cambridge University Press. 198–218.

Muegge, Daniel, and James Perry. 2014. The Flaws of Fragmented Financial Standard Setting: Why Substantive Economic Debates Matter for the Architecture of Global Governance. Politics and Society 42 (2): 194–222.

Murdie, Amanda. 2014. The Ties That Bind: A Network Analysis of Human Rights NGOs. British Journal of Political Science 44 (1): 1–27.

Murdie, Amanda, and David Davis. 2012a. Shaming and Blaming: Using Events Data to Assess the Impact of Human Rights INGOs. International Studies Quarterly 56 (1): 1–16.

———. 2012b. Looking in the Mirror: Comparing INGO Networks across Issue Areas. Review of International Organizations 7 (2): 177–202.

Najam, Adil, Mihaela Papa, and Nadaa Taiyab. 2006. Global Environmental Governance: A Reform Agenda. International Institute for Sustainable Development.

Neier, Aryeh. 2012. The International Human Rights Movement: A History. Princeton: Princeton University Press.

Neslen, Arthur. 2015. Paris Climate Activists Put under House Arrest Using Emergency Laws. Guardian, 27 November. https://www.theguardian.com/environment/2015/nov/27/paris-climate-activists-put-under-house-arrest-using-emergency-laws.

———. 2018. Poland Violated EU Laws by Logging in Białowieża Forest, Court Rules. Guardian, 17 April. https://www.theguardian.com/world/2018/apr/17/poland-violated-eu-laws-by-logging-in-biaowieza-forest-says-ecj.

Neumann, Iver, and Ole Jacob Sending. 2010. Governing the Global Polity: Practice, Mentality, Rationality. Ann Arbor: University of Michigan Press.

Neumeyer, Eric. 2005. Do Human Rights Treaties Improve Respect for Human Rights? Journal of Conflict Resolution 49 (6): 925–53.

Nielsen, Richard, and Beth A. Simmons. 2015. Rewards for Ratification: Pay-offs for Participating in the Human Rights Regime? International Studies Quarterly 59 (2): 197–208.

Nurse, Angus. 2013. Privatising the Green Police: The Role of NGOs in Wildlife Law Enforcement. Crime, Law and Social Change 59 (3): 305–18.

Obermaier, Frederik, and Bastian Obermayer. 2017. The Panama Papers: Breaking the Story of How the Rich and Powerful Hide Their Money. New York: Oneworld Publications.

Observatory of Public Sector Innovation. 2019. Dozorro. 12 April. https://oecd-opsi.org/innovations/dozorro/.

O'Donnell, Margarita K. 2009. New Dirty War Judgements in Argentina: National Courts and Domestic Prosecutions of International Human Rights Violations. New York University Law Review 84 (1): 333–74.

Oliver, Kenneth. 2011. 'Excellent' I Cried. 'Elementary!' Said He: Mutual Legal Assistance and the Present Challenges Faced by the Legal Community in the Never-Ending Quest for the Recovery of Stolen Assets. In Non-State Actors and Asset Recovery, ed. Daniel Thelesklaf and Pedro Gomes Pereira. Bern: Peter Lang. 160–82.

O'Neill, Sadhbh. 2020. Climate Litigation, Politics and Policy Change: Lessons from Urgenda and Climate Case Ireland. University of Dublin. Unpublished discussion note for Workshop on New Trends in Environmental Advocacy, Johns Hopkins University (SAIS), Bologna, 15 May.

Open Society Justice Initiative. 2021. Justice Initiative Welcomes First-Ever Conviction of Syrian Official for Crimes Against Humanity. 24 February. https://www.justiceinitiative.org/newsroom/justice-initiative-welcomes-first-ever-conviction-of-syrian-official-for-crimes-against-humanity.

———. n.d. APDHE v. Obiang Family. https://www.justiceinitiative.org/litigation/apdhe-v-obiang-family.

Organization for Economic Cooperation and Development (OECD). 2018. Fighting the Crime of Foreign Bribery: The Anti-Bribery Convention and the OECD Working Group on Bribery. Paris. https://www.oecd.org/corruption/Fighting-the-crime-of-foreign-bribery.pdf.

———. 2019. Enforcement of the Anti-Bribery Convention: Investigations, Proceedings, and Sanctions. Paris. https://www.oecd.org/daf/anti-bribery/OECD-Anti-Bribery-Convention-Enforcement-Data-2020.pdf.

Pace, William R. 1999. The Relationship between the International Criminal Court and Non-Governmental Organizations. In The International Criminal Court: The Making of the Rome Statute, ed. Roy S. Lee. The Hague: Kluwer Law. 189–201.

Padilla, David J. 1993. The Inter-American Commission on Human Rights of the Organization of American States: A Case Study. American University International Law Review 9 (1): 95–115.

Parks, Lisa. 2009. Digging into Google Earth: An Analysis of 'Crisis in Darfur'. Geoforum 40 (4): 535–45.

Paso Pacifico. n.d. [last accessed 26 August 2021]. InvestEGGator Sea Turtle Eggs. https://pasopacifico.org/project/investeggator-sea-turtle-eggs/.

Patrick, Aaron. 2019. Brian Preston: The Activist Judge Shaking the Climate Change World. https://www.afr.com/politics/brian-preston-the-activist-judge-shaking-the-climate-change-world-20190214-h1b982.

Pattberg, Philipp. 2005. The Institutionalization of Private Governance: How Business and Non-Profit Organizations Agree on Transnational Rules. Governance 18 (4): 589–610.

Pauwelyn, Joost, Ramses A. Wessel, and Jan Wouters. 2014. When Structures Become Shackles: Stagnation and Dynamics in International Lawmaking. European Journal of International Law 25 (3): 733–63.

Peel, Jacqueline, and Hari M. Osofsky. 2018. Rights Turn in Climate Change Litigation? Transnational Environmental Law 7 (1): 37–67.

Perdriel-Vaissiere, Maud. 2011. How to Turn Article 51 into Reality. In Non-State Actors and Asset Recovery, ed. Daniel Thelesklaf and Pedro Gomes Pereira. Bern: Peter Lang. 17–37.

———. 2017. France's Biens Mal Acquis Affair: Lessons from a Decade of Legal Struggle. Open Society Foundations. https://www.justiceinitiative.org/publications/france-s-biens-mal-acquis-affair-lessons-decade-legal-struggle.

Pérez-Liñán, Aníbal, Luis Schenoni, and Kelly Morrison. 2021. Time and Compliance with International Rulings: The Case of the Inter-American Court of Human Rights. Unpublished paper.

Peters, Anne. 2009. Membership in the Global Constitutional Community. In The Constitution-alization of International Law, ed. Jan Klabbers, Anne Peters, and Geir Ulfstein. Oxford: Oxford University Press. 153–262.

Peterson, Timothy M., Amanda Murdie, and Victor Asal. 2018. Human Rights, NGO Shaming and the Exports of Abusive States 48 (3): 767–86.

Phelps Bondaroff, Teale. 2011. Sailing with the Sea Shepherds. https://www.researchgate.net/publication/266370071.

Physicians for Human Rights. n.d. PHR's Mobile App MediCapt Puts Cutting Edge Technology in the Service of Preventing Sexual Violence. https://phr.org/issues/sexual-violence/medicapt-innovation-2/.

Pimm, S. L., C. N. Jenkins, R. Abell, T. M. Brooks, J. L. Gittleman, L. N. Joppa, P. H. Raven, C. M. Roberts, and J. O. Sexton. 2014. The Biodiversity of Species and Their Rates of Extinction, Distribution, and Protection. Science 30 (6187): 344.

Polizzi, Marc, and Amanda Murdie. 2019. NGOs and Human Rights. In Handbook of NGOs and International Relations, ed. Thomas Davies. Abingdon: Routledge. 253–69.

Ponselet, Gaelle. 2020. Liberia War Crimes: Belgian Investigators Drag Feet on Martina John-son. Justiceinfo.net, Fondation Hirondelle, 2 April. https://www.justiceinfo.net/en/tribunals/national-tribunals/44069-liberia-war-crimes-belgian-investigators-drag-feet-on-martina-johnson.html.

Popoola, Ebunoluwa O. 2017. Moving the Battlefields: Foreign Jurisdictions and Environmental Justice in Nigeria. https://items.ssrc.org/just-environments/moving-the-battlefields-foreign-jurisdictions-and-environmental-justice-in-nigeria/.

Posner, Eric. 2014. The Twilight of Human Rights Law. Oxford: Oxford University Press.

Preston, Brian J. 2016. Characteristics of Successful Environmental Courts and Tribunals. Journal of Environmental Law 26 (3): 365–93.

Price, Richard. 1998. Reversing the Gun Sights: Transnational Civil Society Targets Land Mines. International Organization 52 (3): 613–44.

———. 2003. Transnational Civil Society and Advocacy in World Politics. World Politics 55 (3): 579–606.

Pring, George, and Kitty Pring. 2016. Environmental Courts and Tribunals: A Guide for Policy Makers. United Nations Environment Programme.

Putnam, Tonya. 2016. Courts without Borders: Law, Politics and US Extraterritoriality. Cambridge: Cambridge University Press.

———. 2020. Mingling and Strategic Augmentation of International Legal Obligations. International Organization 74 (1): 31–64.

Quintanilla, Marcus S., and Christopher A. Whytock. 2012. The New Multipolarity in Transnational Litigation: Foreign Courts, Foreign Judgements, and Foreign Law. Southwestern Journal of International Law 18:31–51.

Raustiala, Kal. 1997. States, NGOs and International Environmental Institutions. International Studies Quarterly 41 (4): 719–40.

Raymond, Mark, and Laura DeNardis. 2015. Multistakeholderism: Anatomy of an Inchoate Global Institution. International Theory 7 (3): 572–616.

Reuter, Peter. 2012. Introduction and Overview: The Dynamics of Illicit Flows. In Draining Development? Controlling Flows of Illicit Funds in Developing Countries, ed. Peter Reuter. Washington, DC: World Bank. 1–18.

Reuters Staff. 2019. Campaign Groups Accuse Total of Breaching French Corporate Duty Law in Uganda. Reuters, 25 June. https://www.reuters.com/article/us-total-uganda-ngos/campaign-groups-accuse-total-of-breaching-french-corporate-duty-law-in-uganda-idUSKCN1TQ1OQ.

Risse, Thomas, Stephen C. Ropp, and Kathryn Sikkink, eds. 1999. The Power of Human Rights: International Norms and Domestic Change. New York: Cambridge University Press.

Risse, Thomas, and Kathryn Sikkink. 2013. Conclusions. In The Persistent Power of Human Rights: From Commitment to Compliance, ed. Thomas Risse, Stephen C. Ropp, and Kathryn Sikkink. New York: Cambridge University Press. 275–95.

Risse-Kappen, Thomas, ed. 1995. Bringing Transnational Relations Back In: Non-State Actors, Domestic Structures and International Institutions. Cambridge: Cambridge University Press.

Roberts, Anthea. 2011. Comparative International Law? The Role of National Courts in Creating and Enforcing International Law. International & Comparative Law Quarterly 60 (1): 57–92.

Robinsson, Edward. 2014. Corruption Fighter Gooch Tackles Abusive Shell Companies. Bloomberg Markets Magazine, 12 September. https://www.bloomberg.com/news/articles/2014-09-11/corruption-fighter-gooch-tackles-abusive-shell-companies.

Rodman, Kenneth A. 2006. Compromising Justice: Why the Bush Administration and the NGOs Are Both Wrong about the ICC. Ethics and International Affairs 20 (1): 25–53.

Rodríguez-Garavito, César, and Krizna Gomez. 2018. Responding to the Populist Challenge: A New Playbook for the Human Rights Field. In Rising to the Populist Challenge: A New

Playbook for Human Rights Actors, ed. César Rodríguez-Garavito and Krizna Gomez. Bogotá, Columbia: Dejusticia. 11–56.

Roehrig, Terence. 2002. The Prosecution of Former Military Leaders in Newly Democratic Nations: The Cases of Argentina, Greece, and South Korea. New York: McFarland & Co.

Roht-Arriaza, Naomi. 2005. The Pinochet Effect: Transnational Justice in an Age of Human Rights. Philadelphia: University of Pennsylvania Press.

Roht-Arriaza, Naomi, and Santiago Martinez. 2019. Grand Corruption and the International Criminal Court in the Venezuela Situation. Journal of International Criminal Justice 17 (5): 1057–82.

Ron, James, Howard Ramos, and Kathleen Rodgers. 2005. Transnational Information Politics: NGO Human Rights Reporting, 1986–2000. International Studies Quarterly 49 (3): 557–88.

Rose, Emma. 2020. The UK's Enforcement Gap. https://www.unchecked.uk/wp-content/uploads/2020/11/The-UKs-Enforcement-Gap-2020.pdf.

Rosenau, James N., and Ernst-Otto Czempiel, eds. 1992. Governance without Government: Order and Change in World Politics. Cambridge: Cambridge University Press.

Rothe, Delf, and David Shim. 2018. Remote Sensing on the Ground: On the Global Politics of Satellite-Based Activism. Review of International Studies 44 (3): 414–37.

Ryngaert, Cedric. 2013. Jurisdiction: Towards a Reasonableness Test. In Global Justice, State Duties: The Extraterritorial Scope of Economic, Social, and Cultural Rights in International Law, ed. Malcolm Langford. New York: Cambridge University Press. 192–211.

Sabin Center for Climate Change Law. 2021. http://climatecasechart.com/non-us-climate-change-litigation/.

Sahara Reporters. 2017. Nigeria to Pay over $50m to Swiss Government and Lawyers as Cost of Recovering $321m Abacha Loot. 13 December. http://saharareporters.com/2017/12/13/nigeria-pay-over-50m-swiss-government-and-lawyers-cost-recovering-321m-abacha-loot.

Saiger, Anna-Julia. 2020. Domestic Courts and the Paris Agreement's Climate Goals: The Need for a Comparative Approach. Transnational Environmental Law 9 (1): 37–54.

Salaun, Tangi, and John Irish. 2020. French Court Finds Bashar al-Assad's Uncle Guilty of Property Fraud. Reuters, 17 June. https://uk.reuters.com/article/uk-france-assad-court/french-court-finds-bashar-al-assads-uncle-guilty-of-property-fraud-idUKKBN23O2PT.

Sanderman, J., T. Hengl, G. Fiske, K. Solvik, M. F. Adame, L. Benson, J. J. Bukoski, P. Carnell, M. Cifuentes-Jara, D. Donato, C. Duncan, E. M. Eid, P. zu Ermgassen, C.J.E. Lewis, P. I. Macreadie, L. Glass, S. Gress, S. L. Jardine, T. G. Jones, and E. Landis. 2018. A Global Map of Mangrove Forest Soil Carbon at 30\hspace0.167emm Spatial Resolution. Environmental Research Letters 13 (5), 055002. https://doi. org/10.1088/1748-9326/aabe1c.

Sang-Hun, Choe. 2020a. Defying UN Ban, Chinese Ships Pay North Korea to Fish in Its Waters. New York Times, 22 July. https://www.nytimes.com/2020/07/22/world/asia/north-korea-squid-sanctions-china.html

———. 2020b. For P.O.W., Landmark Verdict against North Korea Is Long-Overdue Justice. New York Times, 7 August. https://www.nytimes.com/2020/08/07/world/asia/north-korea-pow-verdict-kim.html.

Sanz, Muria Garcia, and Manuel Sese. 2013. Political Corruption and Human Rights in Equatorial Guinea. In Emerging Trends in Asset Recovery, ed. Gretta Fenner-Zinkernagel, Charles Monteith, and Pedro Gomes Pereira. Bern: Peter Lang. 295–302.

Schwartz, Mattathias. 2018. At War: Who Killed the Kiev Protesters? A 3-D Model Holds the Clues. New York Times Magazine, 30 May. https://www.nytimes.com/2018/05/30/magazine/ukraine-protest-video.html.

Schwirtz, Michael. 2012. $30,000 Watch Vanishes Up Church Leader's Sleeve. New York Times, 5 April. https://www.nytimes.com/2012/04/06/world/europe/in-russia-a-watch-vanishes-up-orthodox-leaders-sleeve.html.

Schwirtz, Michael, and Ellen Barry. 2018. Armchair Investigators at Front of British Inquiry into Spy Poisoning. New York Times, 9 October. https://www.nytimes.com/2018/10/09/world/europe/bellingcat-skripal-poisoning.html.

Sea Shepherd Conservation Society. 2010. Sea Shepherd News: Sea Shepherd to Focus on Responsible Intervention against Bluefin Tuna Poachers. https://www.seashepherd.org.uk/news-and-commentary/news/archive/sea-shepherd-to-focus-on-responsible-intervention-against-bluefin-tuna-poachers.html.

Sea Shepherd Conservation Society UK. n.d. Message to Greenpeace from Captain Paul Watson of Sea Shepherd Conservation Society. https://www.seashepherd.org.uk/news-and-commentary/commentary/message-to-greenpeace-from-captain-paul-watson-of-sea-shepherd-conservation-society.html.

Seabrooke, Leonard, and Lasse Folke Henriksen, eds. 2017. Professional Networks in Transnational Governance. New York: Cambridge University Press.

Seddon, Max. 2015. A Russian Activist Caught Putin's Spokesman on a $425,000-a-Week Yacht. Buzzfeed News, 18 August. https://www.buzzfeednews.com/article/maxseddon/a-russian-activist-caught-putins-spokesman-on-a-425000-yacht#.ygLqRMooK.

Seelinger, Kim Thuy. 2017. Rape and the President: The Remarkable (Partial) Acquittal of Hissène Habré. World Policy Journal 34 (2): 16–22.

Sell, Susan K., and Aseem Prakash. 2004. Using Ideas Strategically: The Contest between Business and NGO Networks in Intellectual Property Rights. International Studies Quarterly 48 (1): 143–75.

Setzer, Joana. 2018. First Ever EU-Wide Climate Court Case Asks for More Ambition in Cutting Emissions. Grantham Research Institute on Climate Change and the Environment, London School of Economics. 30 May. https://www.lse.ac.uk/GranthamInstitute/news/first-ever-eu-climate-court-invokes-human-rights/.

Setzer, Joana, and Lisa Benjamin. 2020. Climate Change Litigation in the Global South. American Journal of International Law, AJIL Unbound, vol. 114: 56–60.

Setzer, Joana, and Rebecca Byrnes. 2020. Global Trends in Climate Change Litigation: 2020 Snapshot. Policy Report. Graham Research Institute on Climate Change and the Environment, London School of Economics. July. https://www.lse.ac.uk/granthaminstitute/wp-content/uploads/2020/07/Global-trends-in-climate-change-litigation_2020-snapshot.pdf.

Setzer, Joanna, and Catherine Higham. 2021. Global Trends in Climate Change Litigation: 2021 Snapshot. https://www.lse.ac.uk/granthaminstitute/wp-content/uploads/2021/07/Global-trends-in-climate-change-litigation_2021-snapshot.pdf.

Setzer, Joana, and Michal Nachmany. 2018. National Governance: The State's Role in Steering Polycentric Action. In Governing Climate Change, ed. Andrew Jordan, Dave Huitema, Harro van Asselt, and Johanna Forster. Cambridge: Cambridge University Press. 47–62.

Sharman, J. C. 2017. The Despot's Guide to Wealth Management: On the International Campaign against Grand Corruption. Ithaca: Cornell University Press.

Shelley, Louise I. 2014. Dirty Entanglements: Corruption, Crime, and Terrorism. Cambridge: Cambridge University Press.

———. 2018. Dark Commerce: How a New Illicit Economy Is Threatening Our Future. Princeton: Princeton University Press.

Sherpa. 2016. Riffat al-Assad, Uncle of Syrian President Bashar al-Assad, Will Stand Trial in France for Money Laundering Allegedly Using Funds to the Detriment of the Syrian People. 6 December. https://www.asso-sherpa.org/10606-2.

Shirk, Mark. 2021. Making War on the World: How Transnational Violence Shapes World Order. New York: Columbia University Press.

Sikkink, Kathryn. 2002. Transnational Advocacy Networks and the Social Construction of Legal Rule. In Global Prescriptions: The Production, Exportation and Importation of a New Legal

Orthodoxy, ed. Yves Dezalay and Bryant G. Garths. Ann Arbor: University of Michigan Press, 37–64.

———. 2008. From Pariah State to Global Protagonist: Argentina and the Struggle for International Human Rights. Latin American Politics and Society 50 (1): 1–29.

———. 2011. The Justice Cascade: How Human Rights Prosecutions Are Changing World Politics. New York: W. W. Norton.

Silverstein, Ken. 2003. Oil Boom Enriches African Ruler. Los Angeles Times, 20 January. https://www.latimes.com/archives/la-xpm-2003-jan-20-na-riggs20-story.html.

Simmons, Beth A. 2009. Mobilizing for Human Rights: International Law in Domestic Politics. Cambridge: Cambridge University Press.

———. 2010. Treaty Compliance and Violation. Annual Review of Political Science 13 (1): 273–96.

———. 2014. The Future of the Human Rights Movement. International Affairs 28 (2): 183–96.

Simmons, Beth A., Paulette Lloyd, and Brandon M. Stewart. 2018. The Global Diffusion of Law: Transnational Crime and the Case of Human Trafficking. International Organization 72 (2): 249–81.

Singer, Peter. 2003. Corporate Warriors: The Rise of the Privatized Military Industry. Ithaca: Cornell University Press.

SITU Research. 2012a. Forensic Oceanography Report. https://situ.nyc/research/projects/forensic-oceanography-report.

———. 2012b. Syria: Torture Centers Revealed. https://situ.nyc/research/projects/syria-torture-centers-revealed.

———. 2018. Euromaidan Event Reconstruction. https://situ.nyc/research/projects/euromaidan-event-reconstruction.

Skinner, Althea. 2015. Women on Waves: Navigating National and International Laws and Values. Humanity in Action. http://www.humanityinaction.org/knowledgebase/152womenonwavesnavigatingnationalandinternationallawsandvalues.

Smith, Jackie, Ron Pagnucco, and George A. Lopez. 1998. Globalizing Human Rights: The Work of Transnational Human Rights NGOs in the 1990s. Human Rights Quarterly 20 (2): 379–412.

Soley, Ximena. 2019. Symposium on the American Convention on Human Rights and Its New Interlocutors: The Crucial Role of Human Rights NGOs in the Inter-American System. American Journal of International Law Unbound 113: 355–59.

Soule, Sarah A., and Brayden G. King. 2008. Competition and Resource Partitioning in Three Social Movement Industries. American Journal of Sociology 113 (6): 1568–1610.

Southern Africa Litigation Centre. https://www.southernafricalitigationcentre.org/cases/precedent-cases/.

Steinberg, Gerald M., and Anne Herzberg. 2018. NGO Fact-Finding for IHL Enforcement: In Search of a New Model. Israel Law Review 51 (2): 261–99.

Steinitz, Maya. 2019. Book Introduction: The Case for an International Court of Civil Justice. 3 April. https://papers.ssrn.com/sol3/papers.cfm?abstract_id=3361928.

Stephenson, Matthew C. 2016. Standing Doctrine and Anti-Corruption Litigation: A Survey. Open Society Foundations. https://www.justiceinitiative.org/uploads/4759d161-17c9-4264-b5cc-215030ba7223/legal-remedies-2-20160202_0.pdf.

Stinson, Liz. 2016. The Hague Convicts a Tomb-Destroying Extremist with Smart Design. Wired, 25 August. https://www.wired.com/2016/08/hague-convicts-tomb-destroying-terrorist-smart-design/.

Stolen Asset Recovery (StAR) Initiative. 2011. The Puppet Masters: How the Corrupt Use Legal Structures to Hide Their Stolen Assets and What to Do about It. Washington, DC. https://openknowledge.worldbank.org/handle/10986/2363.

———. 2014a. Few and Far: The Hard Facts on Asset Recovery. Washington, DC. https://documents
.worldbank.org/en/publication/documents-reports/documentdetail/379871468146375164
/few-and-far-the-hard-facts-on-stolen-asset-recovery.

———. 2014b. Public Wrongs, Private Actions: Civil Lawsuits to Recover Stolen Assets. https://
www.worldbank.org/en/topic/financialsector/publication/public-wrongs-private-actions
-civil-lawsuits-to-recover-stolen-assets-study.

———. 2019. Going for Broke: Insolvency Tools to Support Cross-Border Asset Recovery in
Corruption Cases. Washington, DC. https://openknowledge.worldbank.org/handle/10986
/32596.

Stone, Joe. 2018. North Korean Labourer Sues European Company for 'Profiting from His Slav-
ery'. Independent, 7 November. https://www.independent.co.uk/news/world/europe/north
-korea-worker-eu-lawsuit-sues-company-slavery-shipbuilder-poland-a8622376.html.

Strick, Benjamin. 2018. Geolocation of Infrastructure Destruction in Cameroon: A Case Study of
Kumbo and Kumfutu. Bellingcat, 21 November. https://www.bellingcat.com/resources/case
-studies/2018/11/21/geolocation-infrastructure-destruction-cameroon-case-study-kumbo
-kumfutu/.

Stroup, Sarah S., and Wendy Wong. 2016. The Agency and Authority of International NGOs.
Perspectives on Politics 14 (1): 138–44.

———. 2017. The Authority Trap: Strategic Choices of International NGOs. Ithaca: Cornell University Press.

Struett, Michael. 2008. The Politics of Constructing the International Criminal Court: NGOs,
Discourse and Agency. New York: Palgrave.

Sturtz, L. 2001. Southern Bluefin Tuna Case: Australia and New Zealand v. Japan. Ecology Law
Quarterly 28 (2): 455–85.

Su, Anna. 2019. The Rise and Fall of Universal Civil Jurisdiction. Human Rights Quarterly 41 (4):
849–72.

Susskind, Lawrence E., and Saleem H. Ali. 2014. Environmental Diplomacy: Negotiating More
Effective Global Agreements. Oxford: Oxford University Press.

Swissinfo. 2019. They Took His Supercars, but Dictator's Son Still Flaunts Riches. Bloomberg, 24
October. https://www.swissinfo.ch/eng/bloomberg/they-took-his-supercars--but-dictator-s
-son-still-flaunts-riches/45321732.

Tallberg, Jonas. 2015. Orchestrating Enforcement: International Organizations Mobilizing
Compliance Communities. In International Organizations as Orchestrators, ed. Kenneth W.
Abbott, Philipp Genschel, Duncan Snidal, and Bernhard Zangl. Cambridge: Cambridge Uni-
versity Press. 166–88.

Tallberg, Jonas, Lisa M. Dellmuth, Hans Agne, and Andreas Duit. 2018. NGO Influence in International Organizations: Information, Access and Exchange. British Journal of Political Science
48 (1): 213–38.

Tarrow, Sidney, and Donatella della Porta. 2005. Transnational Protest and Global Activism:
People, Passions, and Power. Lanham, MD: Rowman and Littlefield.

Taub, Ben. 2016. The Assad Files: Capturing the Top-Secret Documents That Tie the Syrian
Regime to Mass Torture and Killings. New Yorker, 18 April. www.newyorker.com/magazine
/2016/04/18/bashar-al-assads-war-crimes-exposed.

Taylor, Diane. 2017. Bricks Are Thrown through Windows of Central London Squat. Guardian, 29 January. https://www.theguardian.com/uk-news/2017/jan/29/bricks-bottles-hurled
-windows-central-london-squat-belgravia-eaton-square.

Telegraph. 2009. Paul Watson: Sea Shepherd Eco-warrior Fighting to Stop Whaling and Seal
Hunts. 17 April. https://www.telegraph.co.uk/news/earth/5166346/Paul-Watson-Sea
-Shepherd-eco-warrior-fighting-to-stop-whaling-and-seal-hunts.html.

Thrall, A. Trevor, Dominik Stecula, and Diana Sweet. 2014. May We Have Your Attention Please? Human-Rights NGOs and the Problem of Global Communication. International Journal of Press/Politics 19 (2): 135–59.

Times of Malta. 2010. Greenpeace Campaign to Halt Bluefin Tuna Fishing. 15 May. http://www .timesofmalta.com/articles/view/20100515/local/greenpeace-campaign-to-halt-bluefin-tuna -fishing.307411.

Toler, Aric. 2015. Yachtspotting: OSINT Methods in Navalny's Corruption Investigation. 19 August. www.bellingcat.com/resources/case-studies/2015/08/19/yachtspotting/.

Transparency International. 2018. Exporting Corruption Progress Report. Berlin. https://www .transparency.org/en/exporting-corruption.

Transparency International-UK. 2019. Reflections on a Decade in the Fight against Corruption and the Coming Challenges. 15 February. https://www.transparency.org.uk/reflections-decade -fight-against-corruption-and-coming-challenges.

Transparency International-UK and Bellingcat. 2017. Offshore in the UK: Analysing the Use of Scottish Limited Partnerships. https://www.transparency.org.uk/publications/offshore-in -the-uk.

Transparency International-Ukraine. 2020. We Urge the Government to Stop Rollback of Procure-ment Reform. 22 June. https://ti-ukraine.org/en/news/we-urge-cabinet-to-stop-rollback-of -procurement-reform/.

TRIAL International. 2017. Revelations about TRIAL International's Investigation. 25 September. https://trialinternational.org/latest-post/in-switzerland-proceedings-for-war-crimes-against -rifaat-al-assad.

———. 2019. Jamil Hassan. 22 March. https://trialinternational.org/latest-post/jamil-hassan/.

Turner, Julian. 2019. Shell and Eni's OPL 245 Deal: A Catalogue of Scandal. Offshore Technol-ogy, 22 May. https://www.offshore-technology.com/features/shell-and-enis-opl-245-deal-a -catalogue-of-scandal/.

Ulfstein, Geir. 2009. The International Judiciary. In The Constitutionalization of International Law, ed. Jan Klabbers, Anne Peters, and Geir Ulfstein. Oxford: Oxford University Press. 126–52.

Ullrich, Leila. 2016. Beyond the 'Local-Global' Divide: Local Intermediaries, Victims and the Justice Contestations of the International Criminal Court. Journal of International Criminal Justice 14 (3): 543–68.

United Nations. Global Issues: Human Rights. https://www.un.org/en/sections/issues-depth /human-rights/.

United Nations Convention Against Corruption (UNCAC). 2004. https://www.unodc.org/unodc /en/corruption/uncac.html.

United Nations Environment Programme (UNEP). 2016. The Rise of Environmental Crime: A Growing Threat to Natural Resources, Peace, Development and Security, a UNEP-Interpol Rapid Response Assessment. https://wedocs.unep.org/handle/20.500.11822/7662.

———. 2019. https://www.unenvironment.org/resources/assessment/environmental-rule-law -first-global-report.

United Nations Human Rights Council. 2014. Report of the Detailed Findings of the Commission of Inquiry on Human Rights in the Democratic People's Republic of Korea. https://documents -dds-ny.un.org/doc/UNDOC/GEN/G14/108/71/PDF/G1410871.pdf?OpenElement.

United Nations Office on Drugs and Crime. 2010. https://www.unodc.org/res/cld/bibliography /the-globalization-of-crime-a-transnational-organized-crime-threat-assessment_html /TOCTA_Report_2010_low_res.pdf.

———. 2011. Estimating Illicit Financial Flows Resulting from Drug Trafficking and Other Trans-national Organized Crimes. Vienna. https://www.unodc.org/documents/data-and-analysis /Studies/Illicit_financial_flows_2011_web.pdf.

United States Senate Permanent Subcommittee on Investigations. 2004. Money Laundering and Foreign Corruption: Enforcement and Effectiveness of the Patriot Act: A Case Study of Riggs Bank. Washington, DC.

———. 2010. Keeping Foreign Corruption out of the United States: Four Case Histories. Washington, DC.

Urbina, Ian. 2015. A Renegade Trawler, Hunted for 10,000 Miles by Vigilantes. New York Times, 28 July. https://www.nytimes.com/2015/07/28/world/a-renegade-trawler-hunted-for-10000-miles-by-vigilantes.html?mcubz=3.

———. 2019. The Outlaw Ocean. New York: Knopf.

Vaish, Esha, and Gederts Gelzis. 2019. Bill Browder Files Swedbank Money Laundering Complaint in Latvia. Reuters, 17 April. https://www.reuters.com/article/europe-moneylaundering-swedbank-browder/bill-browder-files-swedbank-money-laundering-complaint-in-latvia-idUSL3N21Z1TD.

Valero, Juan L. State of the World's Fisheries. Annual Review of Environment and Resources 28 (2003): 359–99.

Van der Wilt, Harmen. 2015. 'Sadder but Wiser'? NGOs and Universal Jurisdiction for International Crimes. Journal of International Criminal Justice 13: 237–43.

Van Schaack, Beth. 2019. Domestic Courts Step Up: Justice for Syria One Case at a Time. Just Security, 25 March. https://www.justsecurity.org/63289/domestic-courts-step-up-justice-for-syria-one-case-at-a-time/.

Vance, Andrea. 2020. Chinese Vessels off Galapagos 'Cloaking' in New Zealand. Stuff, 6 August. https://www.stuff.co.nz/environment/122339295/chinese-vessels-off-galapagos-cloaking-in-new-zealand.

Vetter, David. 2020. This French Lawsuit Is Making Oil Companies Nervous. Forbes, 30 January. https://www.forbes.com/sites/davidrvetter/2020/01/30/this-french-lawsuit-is-making-oil-companies-nervous/#70a1adcd2fc6.

Vidal, John. 2010. Sea Shepherd Activists Free Hundreds of Threatened Bluefin Tuna off Libya. Guardian, 18 June. http://www.guardian.co.uk/environment/2010/jun/18/sea-shepherd-release-bluefin-tuna-libya.

Vogl, Frank. 2012. Waging War on Corruption: Inside the Movement Fighting the Abuse of Power. Lanham, MD: Rowman and Littlefield.

Von Staden, Andreas. 2018. Strategies of Compliance with the European Court of Human Rights. Philadelphia: University of Pennsylvania Press.

Vreeland, James Raymond. 2008. Political Institutions and Human Rights: Why Dictatorships Enter into the United Nations Convention against Torture. International Organization 62 (1): 65–101.

Wang, Dan J., and Sarah A. Soule. 2012. Social Movement Organizational Collaboration: Networks of Learning and the Diffusion of Protest Tactics, 1960–1995. American Journal of Sociology 117 (6): 1674–1722.

Wang, Hongying, and James N. Rosenau. 2001. Transparency International and Corruption as an Issue of Global Governance. Global Governance 7 (1): 25–49.

Weaver, Catherine. 2008. Hypocrisy Trap: The World Bank and the Poverty of Reform. Princeton: Princeton University Press.

Weber, Max. 1968. Economy and Society. Ed. Guenther Roth and Claus Wittich. New York: Bedminster.

Wenzel, George. 1991. Animal Rights, Human Rights: Ecology, Economy and Ideology in the Canadian Arctic. Toronto: University of Toronto Press.

Westerwinter, Oliver. 2021. Transnational Public Private Governance Initiatives in World Politics. Introducing a New Dataset. Review of International Organizations 16 (4): 137–74.

White, Rob. 2013. Eco-crime and the Enforcement of Environmental Laws. Australian Environment Review 28 (5): 587–91.

Williams, Greg. 2019. Inside Bill Browder's Blood Money Battle with Vladimir Putin. Wired, 10 January. https://www.wired.co.uk/article/bill-browder-russia-red-notice

Witjes, Nina, and Philipp Olbrich. 2017. A Fragile Transparency: Satellite Imagery Analysis, Non-State Actors, and Visual Representation of Security. Science and Public Policy 44 (4): 524–34.

Wolf, Mark L. 2018. The World Needs an International Anti-Corruption Court. Daedalus 147 (3): 144–56.

Wong, Wendy H., and Peter A. Brown. 2013. E-Bandits in Global Activism: Wikileaks, Anonymous and the Politics of No One. Perspectives on Politics 11 (4): 1015–33.

World Justice Project. 2020. Rule of Law Index. https://worldjusticeproject.org/our-work/wjp-rule-law-index.

Wright, Tom, and Bradley Hope. 2018. Billion Dollar Whale: The Man Who Fooled Wall Street, Hollywood, and the World. New York: Hachette.

Yanacopulos, Helen. 2005. The Strategies That Bind: NGO Coalitions and Their Influence. Global Networks 5: 93–110.

Yang, Tseming. 2006. International Treaty Enforcement as a Public Good: Institutional Deterrent Sanctions in International Environmental Agreements. Michigan Journal of International Law 27 (4): 1131–84.

Zarbiyev, Faud. 2012. Judicial Activism in International Law: A Conceptual Framework for Analysis. Journal of International Dispute Settlement 3 (2): 247–78.

Zelko, Frank. 2013. Make It a Green Peace! The Rise of Countercultural Environmentalism. Oxford: Oxford University Press.

Zongwe, Dunia Prince. 2012. The New Sexual Violence Legislation in the Congo: Dressing Indelible Scars on Human Dignity. African Studies Review 55 (2): 37–57.

Zoological Society London. n.d. [last accessed 26 August 2021(a)]. Conservation Technology: Detecting Illegal Fishing Vessels. https://www.zsl.org/conservation/conservation-initiatives/conservation-technology/detecting-illegal-fishing-vessels.

Zoological Society London. n.d. [last accessed 26 August 2021(b)]. Conservation Technology: Instant Detect. https://www.zsl.org/conservation/how-we-work/conservation-technology/instant-detect.

Zürn, Michael. 2014. The Politicization of World Politics and Its Effects: Eight Propositions. European Political Science Review 6 (1): 47–71.

A NOTE ON THE TYPE

This book has been composed in Adobe Text and Gotham.
Adobe Text, designed by Robert Slimbach for Adobe,
bridges the gap between fifteenth- and sixteenth-century
calligraphic and eighteenth-century Modern styles.
Gotham, inspired by New York street signs, was designed
by Tobias Frere-Jones for Hoefler & Co.

CPSIA information can be obtained
at www.ICGtesting.com
Printed in the USA
JSHW031914020222
22479JS00005B/5